CODE-BREAKER READING PROGRAM

AGES 6 - adult

A Game Approach to Teaching Reading

A graphic supplemental reading Program

* **Some of these activities may be played by younger children who show interest and demonstrate readiness to read.**

By Raymond Feucht

Sherlock Combs Press
Spokane, WA 99208 (USA)

Published by Lulu.com

OUTLINE

HOW TO USE THIS BOOK

This book is designed for the benefit of the tutor, the teacher or the home-schooling parent. Its purpose is to provide a method for instructing a child on a one-to-one basis. Two or three children could possibly be taught at the same time as well with this method with attention given equally to each child so that they will all become successful at these tasks. At first, much hands-on instruction and guidance will be required until the student becomes more and more proficient. Some children catch on to the game concepts more quickly than others. This material should not be considered an overall or extensive or complete source of reading information. The program should be used only as a supplementary resource; that is, used to enhance other instruction, as reinforcement, to assist a child who is receiving teaching through other reading programs or methods. A unique approach to teaching reading, this game -like format was developed to challenge the learner while reinforcing their reading skills. At times, teaching reading may seem a most difficult task, but hopefully, this approach will lend variety and excitement to your reading instruction.

PRE-READING SKILLS

An old proverb states, " What is learned with pleasure is learned full measure." With that notion in mind, this program was developed with a game-like design. Its purpose is to serve as supplementary help to standard reading programs.

For a child to be ready to learn to read, before these materials are used, other early acquired skills are required. Various types of learning must take place. Among the preliminary skills necessary are good hand-eye coordination, keen gross motor and fine motor development, a certain ability to stay focused for some length of time (possessing a good attention span which also leads to being able to follow oral directions), ability to hear correctly and pronounce words somewhat correctly, and an understanding of an adequate vocabulary for his/her age level.

Since children learn best during play activities where there is little pressure to perform according to a set of pre-determined standards, toys and games are desirable ways for them to learn. Some of these are listed under the developmental headings below.

HAND-EYE COORDINATION SKILLS

Fine Motor Skills

printed mazes, sticker books, paper dolls, crayons and colored pencils and coloring books, dot-to-dot books, easy card games such as: "GO FISH" or "OLD MAID" or "WAR", "Perfection" game (better for older children), jig saw puzzles (simple wooden ones at first), toy toolbench, plastic fishing games requiring a pole and string, simple origami, string games and simple weaving, tangrams, B-B mazes (plastic slot games in which you must shake the B-B into the slot or hole), stacking and dexterity games

Gross Motor Skills

bicycles, tricycles, slides, swings, running games, ball games, ring toss, bean bag games, jump rope, and various construction games including Tinker Toys, Lincoln Logs, Erector Set and locking blocks, tag games, relay races

ORDER and SEQUENCE GAMES

jig saw puzzles, card games, trains, "Candyland" game or "Chutes and Ladders", electronic "Simon", the group participation oral "Simon Says" game, Red Light—Green Light and other outdoor games , Grandma Went to Boston, matching games such as "Memory", stacked tower of rings (an upright peg upon which are placed a size-sequence of various rings)

SHAPES (helps when learning to recognize letters by their shapes)

jig saw puzzles, "Perfection" game,Tupperware shapes ball, tangrams, construction-type games

LISTENING GAMES

Simon Says, I Spy, Red light — Green light, " Grandma went to Boston.

VISUAL DISCRIMINATION GAMES

jig saw puzzles, I Spy, " What's wrong with this picture?", hidden objects and matching games as found in children's magazines.

READING PROGRAM PROCEDURE

 Use commercially produced FLASH CARDS to assist the child in recognition and assimilation of the upper and lower case alphabet. Use only 10 or 12 cards of the alphabet to begin. Ask him to identify the letter, its sound, and a word that begins with it. As the child becomes proficient at this task, use more letters. Hand him the card when he gets it correct. The goal is for the child to get them all. Also, you may then lay out the letters face up as well as the pictures and have the child match them.

A good oral game to teach alliteration is "Grandma went to Boston" game.

There are two ways this game may be played. First, choose a letter, such as: "B". The first player says, " Grandma went to Boston and took a **basket**." The next player says, "Grandma went to Boston and took a **basket** and a **bunny**." Each player must repeat what all previous players have said plus adding any word in alliteration, and when it comes around again, he must include his own word in the list where he added it and then add another at the end of the list of words. The first player to miss a word loses or is "out", and the game continues until only one player remains.
Version two must proceed down the alphabet starting with the letter "A". Example, "Grandma went to Boston and took an **apple**...then a **box**...then a **catalog**...etc." You may agree to skip "X" or allow it within or at the end of the word.

A great game to teach both alliteration and rhyme endings is the "I'm thinking of a Word" game.
In this game, the adult says to the child, "I'm thinking of a word that starts with the letter "p" and it sounds like **hair**." The answer is "pair". or "I'm thinking of a word that starts with 'sh' and rhymes with 'hip'." = **ship.** You may need to give the child the sound the letter makes at first until he learns the letter sounds.

This is a good time to read aloud alliteration books like " Berenstain's B Book". Alliteration is the use of words in sentences that begin with the same letter, such as the P in: " Peter Piper picked a peck of pickled peppers." Also, reading Dr. Seuss and other such books to reinforce rhyme are very beneficial.

 Once the child demonstrates proficiency with the alphabet, it is time to introduce blends and consonant clusters FLASH CARDS. Again require him to demonstrate understanding by stating a word which begins with the given blend or consonant cluster. For example, a child might say "**black**' or "**blue**" for the blend "**bl**". ("Grandma went to Boston" works well with blends.) Use commercially produced flash cards. Lay out the blend cards and pictures that begin with the clusters, and have the child match them. Hand the child the cluster card when he gets it correct. The goal is for the child to get them all.

 When a child has gained proficiency in both single letters and blends or consonant clusters, it may be time to begin playing the rhyme ending games (These are difficult and you may wish to wait.) and rebus games (in this book).

While the child is playing the games and is having some success with these, he/she may be introduced to the actual reading stories near the back of this book. At this point in the process, you may alternate between the games and reading regular books. Eventually, the child will become proficient with the formulae used in the reading stories, and transitioning will begin to take place between the formulaic words and actual words. Finally, the child will begin to apply the phonics skills he/she has been learning to other books as he/she is on the way to becoming a proficient reader.

NOTES TO PARENT OR TEACHER

The design of this unique system introduces reading tasks that enhance the skills of non-readers. Pictographic hints, such as rebuses, letters and symbols, permit the young child to sound out words in such a way as to compare them with the actual word form. For example, the following rebus-like formula when decoded means " I can see a hippopotamus.".

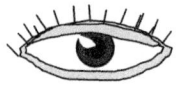  C A  O M S

There are certain graphic clues that naturally help a person decode words. One of these clues is called configuration. As my eyes focus, my brain automatically determines the length and shape of the word, such as the following shape and length:

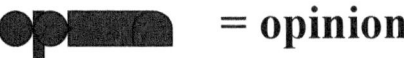 = opinion

The above word's shape could possibly represent the word **opinion.**

Another helpful clue to aid decoding is that words can often be decoded from merely observing their consonants or only a few of the letters. For example: What might this word and phrase be?

        lphnt or **Slplss n Sttl**

Of course, when the missing letters are added, they represent "**elephant**" and "**Sleepless in Seattle**". Also, the capital letters offer a clue.

Decoding words are aided by seeing them in context also, such as: "The _____ were milked morning and evening."
COWS

VARIOUS RULES and DEFINITIONS

Blend — 2 or 3 consonants which sound each letter separately. For example, SPL as in the word "splash" each has its letter pronounced individually.

Digraph — 2 consonants which together represent an entirely different sound than either makes individually. Examples: gh, ch, sh, th, wh.

Contractions consist of **verbs** and the adverb **not** that uses an apostrophe when a letter is absent. Example, didn't for did not; won't for will not, etc.

VOWEL PAIRS — **"When 2 vowels go walking, the first one does the talking." As in the word "boat", the second vowel is silent. Exceptions to this rule involve ie and ei pairs. The rule says, " i before e except after c, except when sounded like 'ay' as in neighbor and weigh". There are also some exceptions to this rule.**

Soft c and g. Sometimes when the letters c and g are followed by the letter e or i, the soft sound results, as in the words cent, or circus or genie and ginger.
Letters that are not pronounced are called silent letters; examples —the "K" of "kn" as in know, the "g" of "gn" as gnome, "e" as the final letter as in kite, "p" as in psychology, etc.

In this book, " r" — is used to represent an "er", "ur", or "ir" sound.

There are diphthong combinations — oi, oy, ow (as in cow), ou (as in pound).

zh — represents the sound made for "s" in words like vision and corrosion.

Silent "gh" is found in words such as: in through or thought or eight or straight.

There are variations of "ou" sounds such as: south, soup, touch. Also, separate sounds of oo as in foot or food or hood.

SOME BASIC TEACHING HELPS

The following grammar forms, such as the word **the,** appear very often in print and may have to be taught separately as sight words. The symbol ⊜ (for **sight word**) will be used to designate such words. Such common words or word endings appear below.

Demonstrative Pronouns are **this, that, these** and **those.**

Personal Pronouns are **I, you,she,he, it, we, us, they, them, my, mine, your, yours, his,her, hers, our, ours, their and theirs.**

Being Verbs are "**is, am, are, was, were, be, been**"

Tense Endings are **ed, ing** as in " painted"and "painting".

Comparative endings are **er, est** as in "faster" and "fastest".

Common Prepositions are **about, above, across, after, against, among around, at, away, away from, before, behind, below, beneath, beside, between, beyond, by, down, during, for, from, in, in back of, inside, in the middle of, into, near, of, off, off of, on, onto, out, out of, over, since, through and throughout.**

Interrogative Pronouns (they ask a question.) are **why, who, whom, when, where, what, which and how.**

The letters **c, s** and **t** often have the "sh" sound within words such as: ocean, mission and nation.

The letter **s** sometimes has the sound of **z** as in the word **poison** or **prison.**

The letter combination **ough** has various sounds in words such as $\overline{o}$ as in the word **dough, off** as in the word **cough, uff** as in the word **tough, oo** as in the word **through, aw** as in the word **thought** and **ow** as in the word **bough.**

LEARNING TO READ

Step 1. A child learns to pronounce the letters of the alphabet—sometimes, in song.

Step 2. A child learns to match the visual letter to its name. For example, A is pronounced "ay".

Step 3   He learns the sounds the letters make when they appear in words. This is where the hard work of learning to read begins. He may learn to recognize a word by its form, such as **CAT**, or learn through a process referred to as phonics—rules of pronouncing words according to their various letter arrangements and letter sounds.

This reading program attempts to teach reading through a rebus or symbol formula.

Step 4. The child will learn to differentiate between upper and lower case letters. **Upper Case** is the form generally referred to as capitals — A, B, C, etc. Capitals appear in text approximately 2-3% of the time. They are found at the beginning of sentences as well as designating proper nouns such as Robert, Boston or Idaho. In the rebus formula, the reader will pronounce the **Upper Case** letter's name. Ten upper and lower case letters share the same shape — Cc,Kk,Oo,Pp,Ss,Uu,Vv,Ww,Xx and Zz. You may wish to teach the other 16 as irregular or as differing between upper and lower case.

The **Lower Case** letters, are generally referred to as the small letters; when used in the rebus formula will make its own specially designated sound. Sometimes, these letters may be pronounced more than one way.

FOUR LOWER CASE LETTERS that are often confused and difficult to differentiate because of their reversed or opposite forms are **b,d, p** and **q.** Three of the four vary in shape between upper and lower case.They consist of a circle and a line. A helpful memory aid may be to present them as follows:

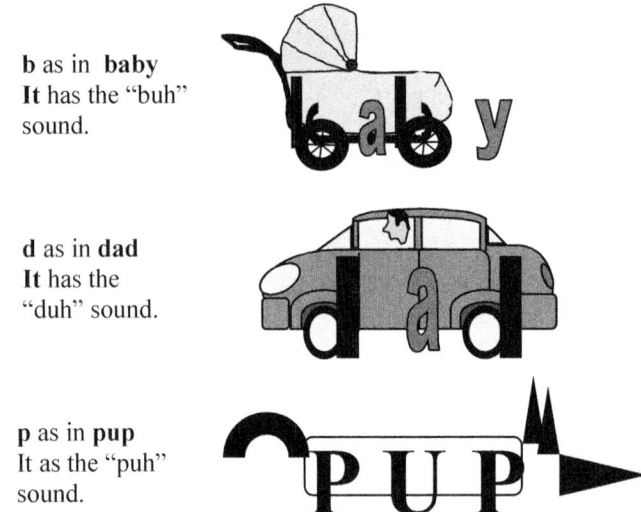

b as in **baby**
It has the "buh" sound.

d as in **dad**
It has the "duh" sound.

p as in **pup**
It as the "puh" sound.

Sometimes the letter **q** can be confused as well. It has the "kwuh" sound and is usually combined with the letter **u.**

THIRTEEN LETTERS THAT VARY in shape between the upper and lower case forms are as follows:

Aa = 3 sounds — a̅ as in ace,   a as in hat,   and a as in ball.

Ee = 2 sounds — e̅ as in eel,   and ĕ as in bed .

Ff as in fish. Pronounced "fuh".

Gg = 2 sounds — hard g = "guh" as in goat,   and soft g = "juh" as in gems.

Hh as in hat. Has a "huh" sound.

Ii = 2 sounds ī as in   ice,   and ĭ as in pin.

Jj as in jack. Has a "juh" sound.

Ll as in lamp. Has a "luh" sound.

Mm as in man. Has a "muh" or "mm" sound.

Nn as in nut. Has a "nuh" or "nn" sound.

Rr as in ring. Has a "ruh" or "rr" sound.

Tt as in tack. Has a "tuh" sound.

Yy = 2 sounds — the yuh sound or the e̅ sound as in yo-yo,   and the ī sound as in fly.

TEN UPPER AND LOWER CASE LETTERS RESEMBLE ONE ANOTHER IN FORM

c has 2 sounds — hard "kuh" as in cat,   and soft "s" as in cereal.

k = "kuh"

o has 3 sounds — ō as in boat,   o as in   dog,   and o "uh" as in ton.

p = "puh"

s = "suh" or "ss".

u has 2 sounds — ū as in glue,   and ŭ as in tub.

v = "vuh"

w = "wuh"

x = "ks" — most often used within or at the end of a word as in box.

z = "zuh" or "zz" as in zipper.

7

COMMON BEGINNING BLENDS AND DIGRAPHS

bl = "bluh" as in block

br = "bruh" as in brick

ch = 3 sounds — "chuh" as in chest,   "kuh" as in choir   and "sh" as in chef.

cl = "cluh" as in clock.

cr = "cruh" as in crate.

dr= "druh" as in drink.

fl = "fluh" as in fly.

fr = "fruh" as in frog.

gl = "gluh" as in glass.

gr = "gruh"as in grater.

pl = "pluh" as in plate.

pr = "pruh" as in prince.

qu = "kwuh" as in queen.

sc = "skuh" as in scarf.

sch = "skuh" as in school.

scr = "scruh" as in screw.

sh = "sh" as in shoe.

shr= "shruh" as in shrimp

sk = "skuh" as in skis.

sl = "sluh" as in sled.

sm = "smuh" as in smoke.

sn = "snuh" as in snow.

sp = "spuh" as in spoon.

squ = "skwuh" as in squash.

spl = "spluh" as in split. (banana).

spr = "spruh" as in spring.

st = "stuh" as in star.

str = "struh" as in string.

sw = "swuh" as in swing.

th = 2 sounds — soft sound as in thumb,   hard sound as in **the**.

thr = "thruh" as in three . **3**

tr = "truh" as in truck.

wh = "hwuh" as in whale.

8

UPPER AND LOWER CASE ALPHABET

Ready-made cards (commercially published and sold in stores) usually display the upper and lower case letters. Game card sets will generally contain one picture of an animal or object that will match the sound made by one of the first letters of each letter card. When the letter "X" is represented by a picture, that word will use the "X" within or at the end of the word. Alphabet matching games can be found in most learning/educational supply stores as well as in many department stores.

GAME ONE: If you purchase a commercial set of matching cards, rules will accompany the game. Generally to play a game, turn just the letter cards face down. Start with six or eight card sets to start, and then eventually work up to all the cards. The child turns up a letter card; the parent or teacher says the letter's name and helps the child match the letter and the animal/object. Play this way until the child begins to match them correctly. Then allow the child to play with less and less assistance. Finally, both letter cards and picture cards can be turned face down when the child has become proficient at matching the letters and objects.

GAME TWO: Now let the child play the game in the book. You may need to pronounce the letters and point to them for awhile until he/she catches on. ODD-MAN-OUT —The child is to point to the picture that does not match the initial letter. This game is more difficult because the child must discriminate between first letter sounds.

ODD-MAN-OUT

ALPHABET

Aa

ALPHABET

Bb

ALPHABET

Cc

ALPHABET

Dd

10

Directions: Three of the four objects begin with the same letter sound. Choose the one that does not begin the same.

ALPHABET

Ee

ALPHABET

Ff

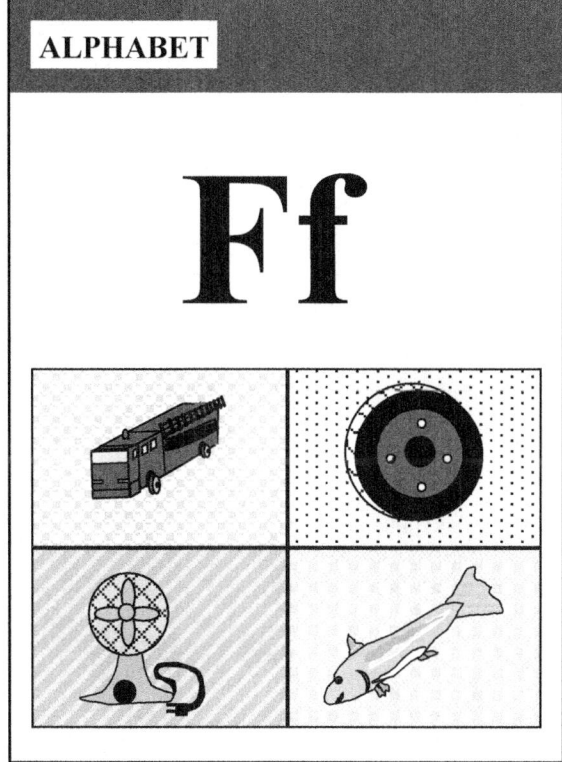

ALPHABET

Gg

ALPHABET

Hh

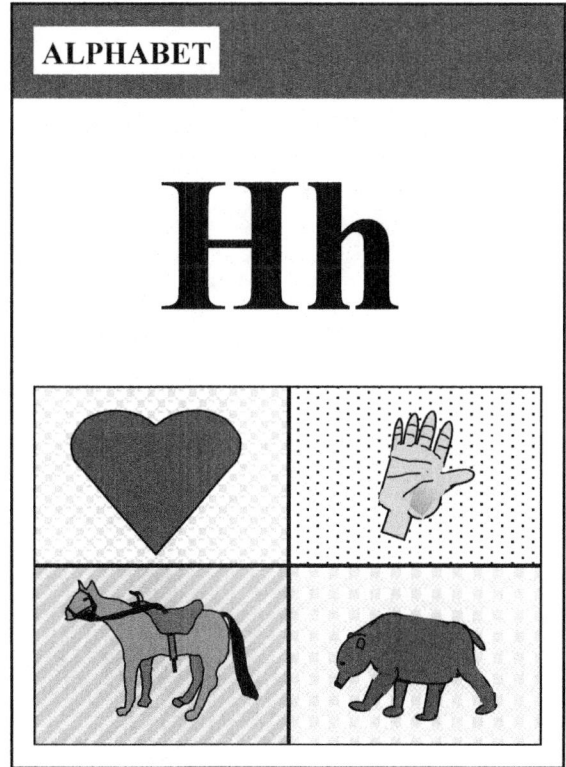

11

ODD-MAN-OUT

Directions: Three of the four objects begin with the same letter sound. Choose the one that does not begin the same.

ALPHABET

Ii

ALPHABET

Jj

ALPHABET

Kk

ALPHABET

Ll

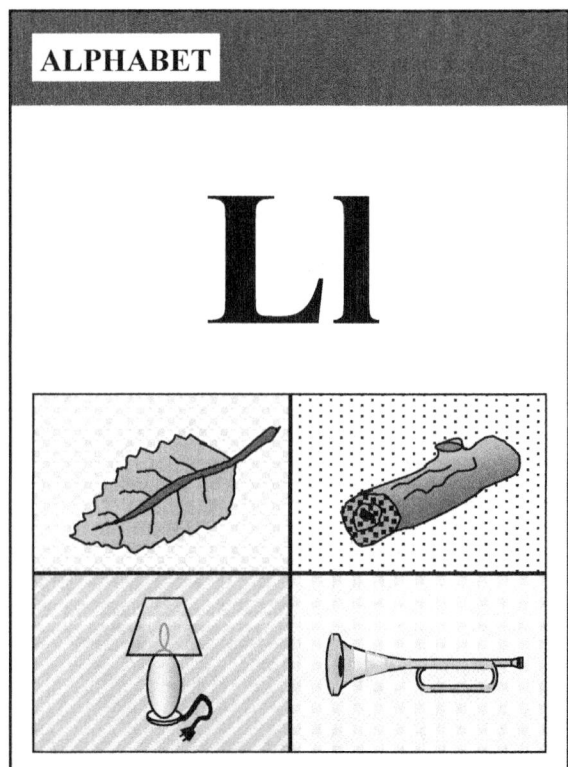

12

Directions: Three of the four objects begin with the same letter sound. Choose the one that does not begin the same.

ALPHABET

Mm

ALPHABET

Nn

ALPHABET

Oo

ALPHABET

Pp

13

ODD-MAN-OUT

ALPHABET

Qq

ALPHABET

Rr

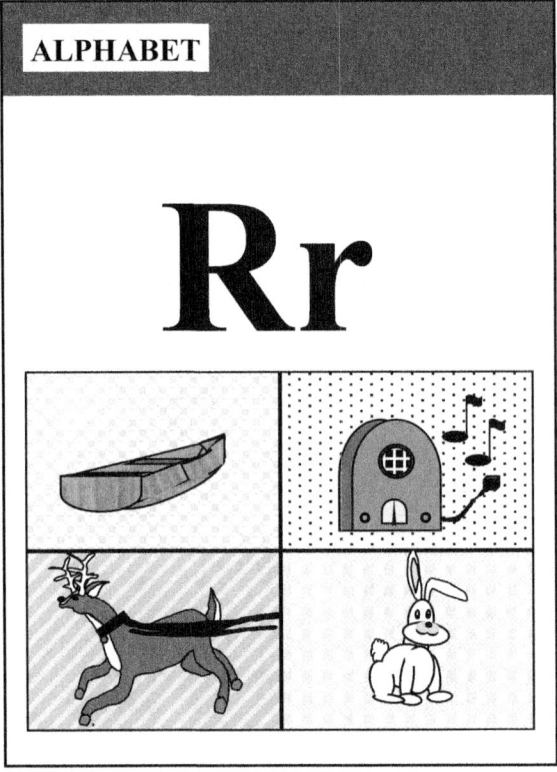

ALPHABET

Ss

ALPHABET

Tt

ODD-MAN-OUT

Directions: Three of the four objects begin with the same letter sound. Choose the one that does not begin the same.

ALPHABET

Vv

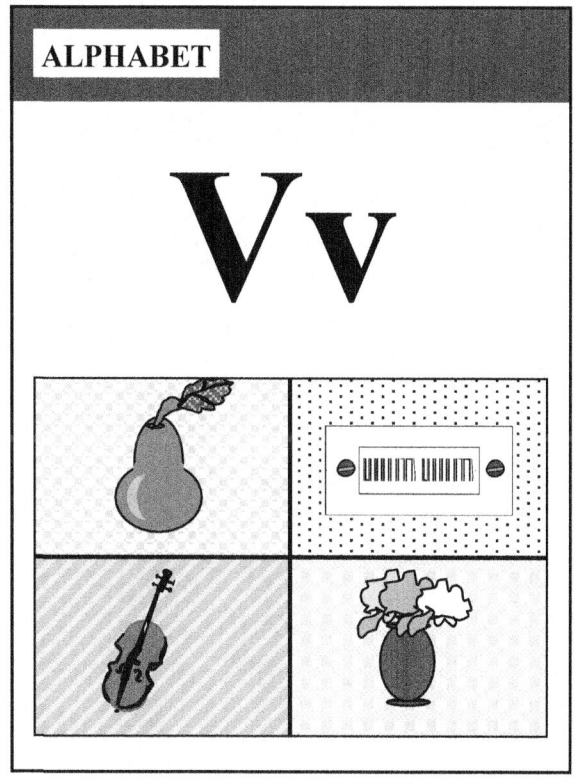

ALPHABET

Ww

ALPHABET

Yy

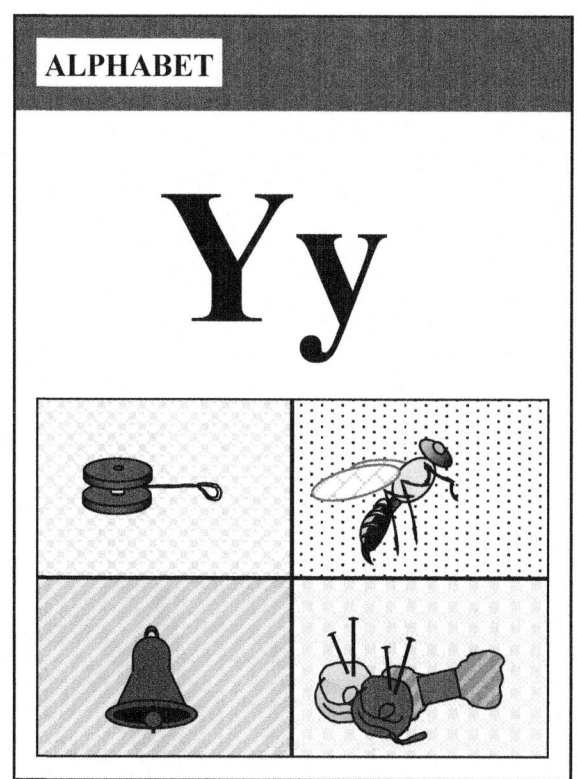

ALPHABET

Zz

BEGINNING CONSONANT CLUSTERS

Clusters include two kinds of blends: (1) letter groups that pronounce all letters such as b and l as in the word **blend** or **block,** and (2) digraphs like **ch** and **sh** as in the words **ship** and **church** in which the combined letters are pronounced different from the individual letters. Commercial game card decks can be purchased from educational supply stores to help a child learn consonant clusters. These games generally allow the child to match these blends with pictures.

GAME ONE: Start with six or eight card sets, and then finally use all the cards. As the child picks up a cluster card, you may pronounce it and help him/her to match it to a picture that begins with that cluster. Continue this method of play until the child has gained proficiency. Then let the child play without assistance. Finally, turn both sets of cards over for the more difficult form of matching game.

GAME TWO: <u>ODD-MAN-OUT</u> — Play the blending game on the following pages in which the child is to pick out three objects that begin with the cluster; one cluster will not have a match. This game is more difficult because the child must discriminate between cluster sounds.

Directions: Three of the four objects begin with the same letter blend sound. Choose the one that does not begin the same.

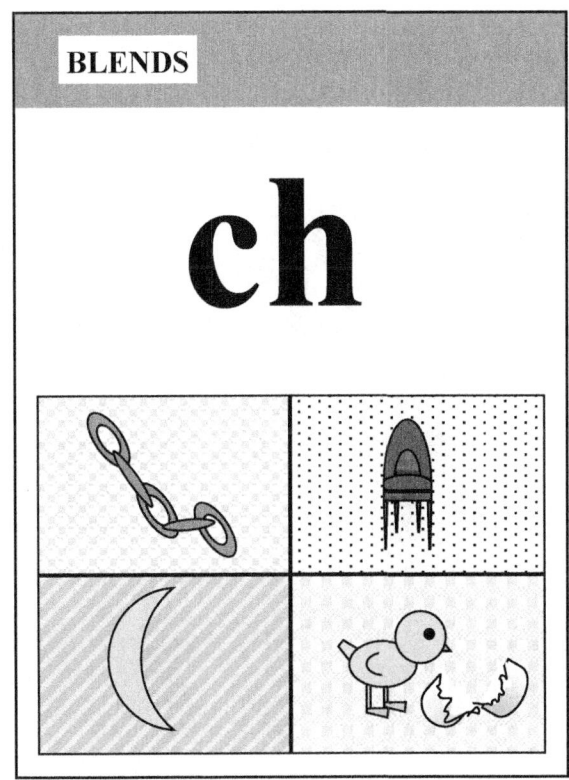

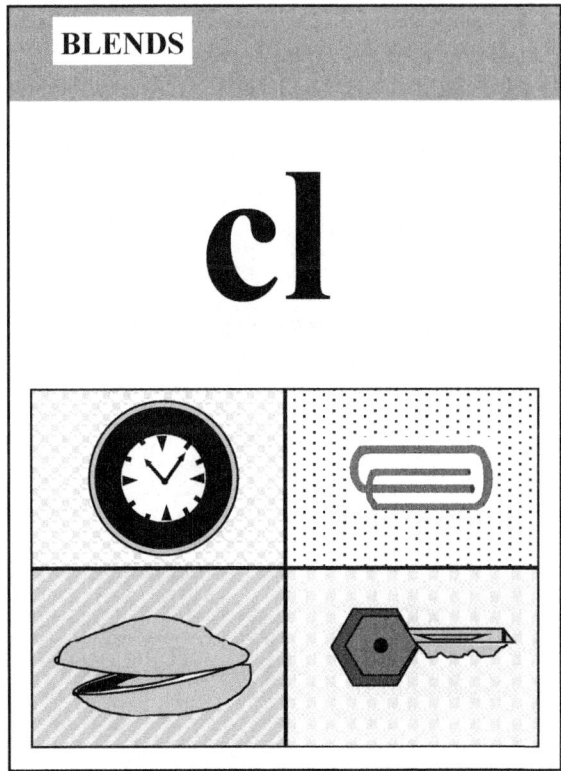

ODD-MAN-OUT

Directions: Three of the four objects begin with the same letter blend sound. Choose the one that does not begin the same.

BLENDS

cr

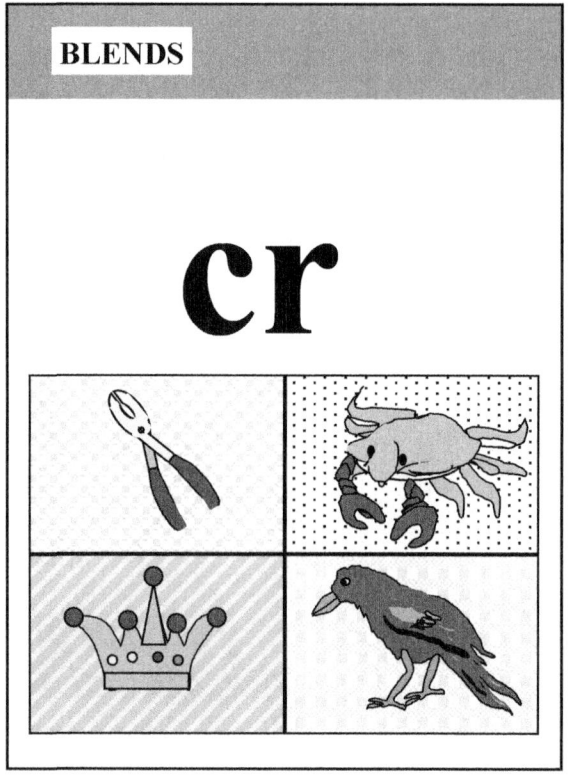

BLENDS

dr

BLENDS

fl

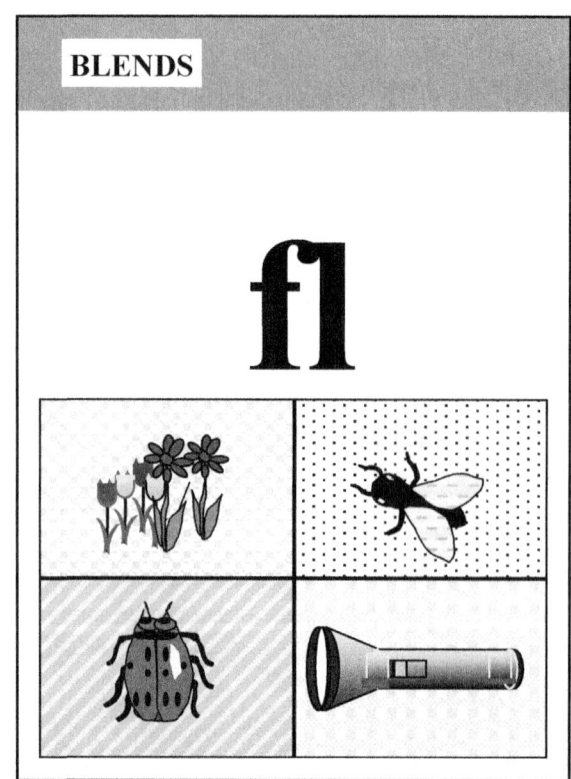

BLENDS

fr

18

ODD-MAN-OUT

Directions: Three of the four objects begin with the same letter blend sound. Choose the one that does not begin the same.

BLENDS

gl

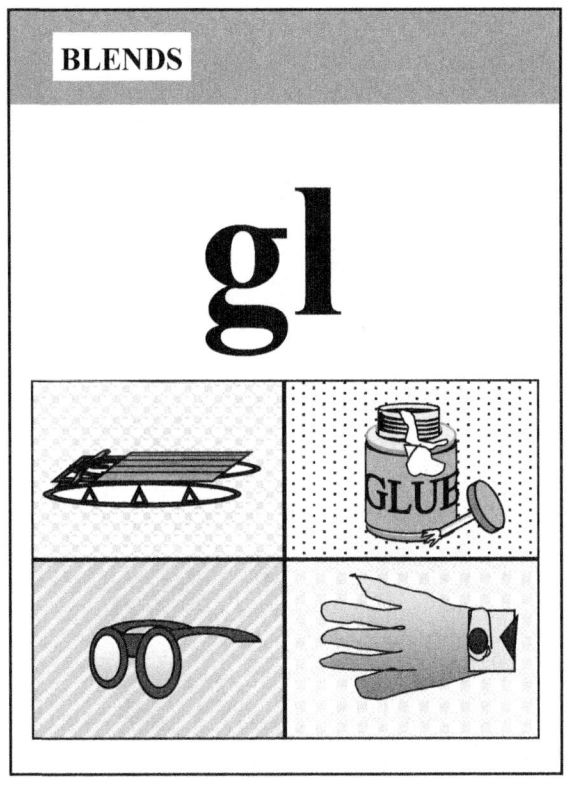

BLENDS

gr

BLENDS

kn

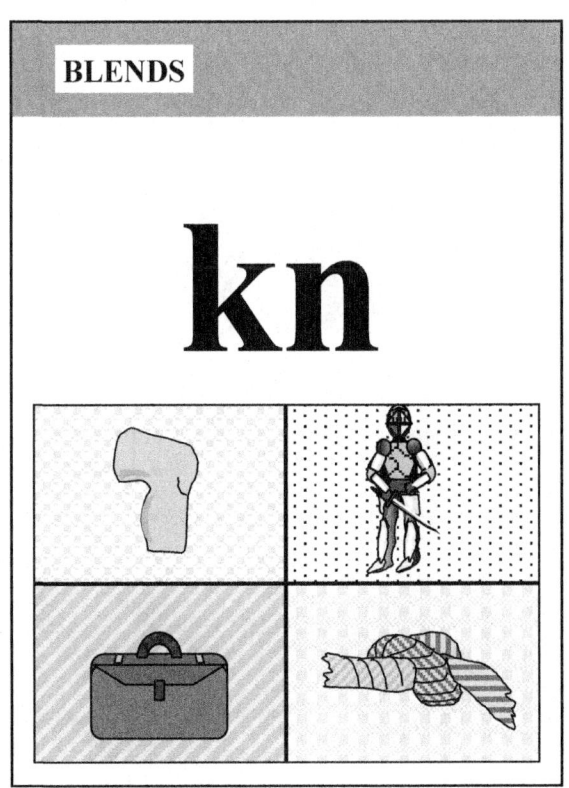

BLENDS

pl

ODD-MAN-OUT

Directions: Three of the four objects begin with the same letter blend sound. Choose the one that does not begin the same.

BLENDS

pr

BLENDS

qu

BLENDS

sc

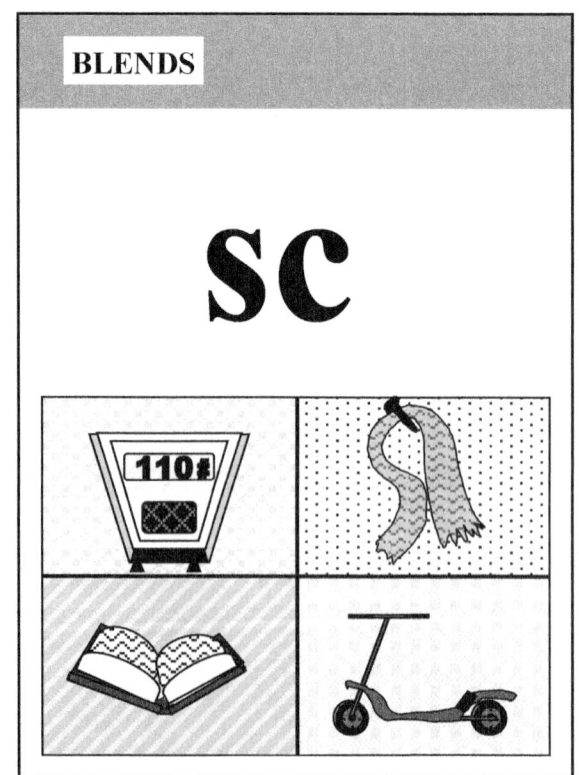

BLENDS

scr

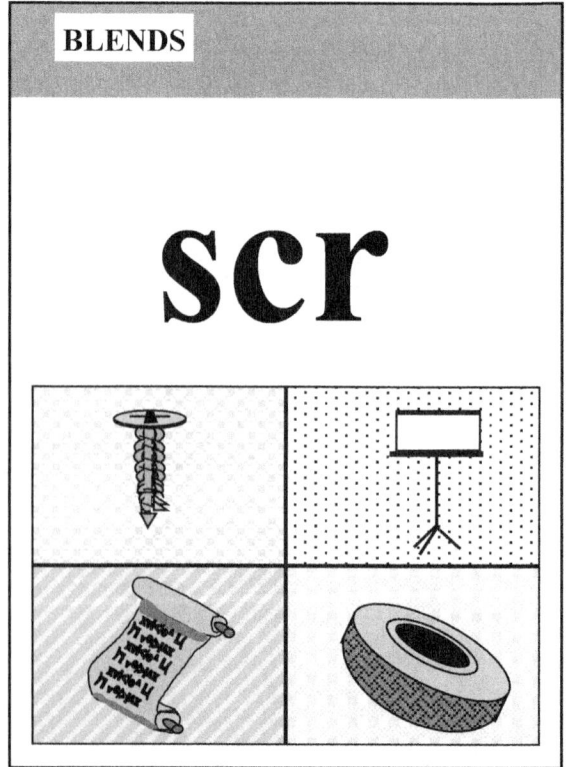

ODD-MAN-OUT

BLENDS

sh

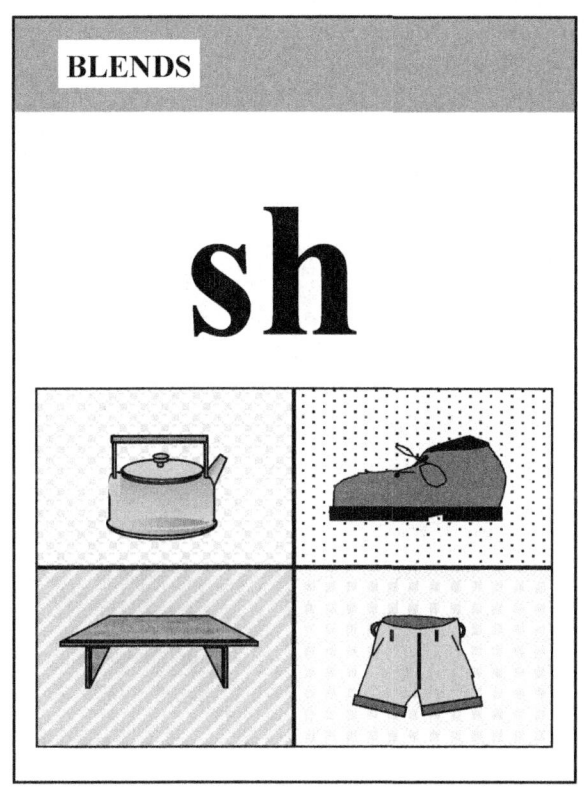

BLENDS

sk

BLENDS

sl

BLENDS

sn

Directions: Three of the four objects begin with the same letter blend sound. Choose the one that does not begin the same.

BLENDS

sp

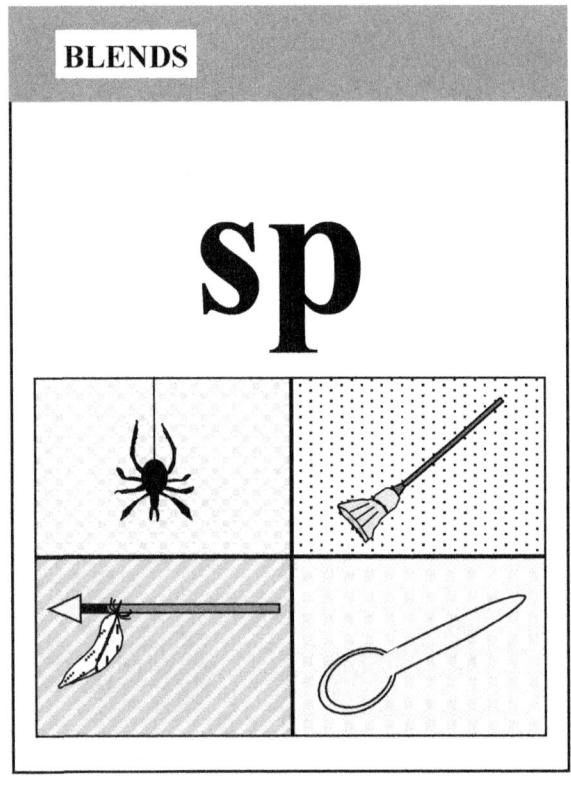

BLENDS

spr

BLENDS

squ

BLENDS

st

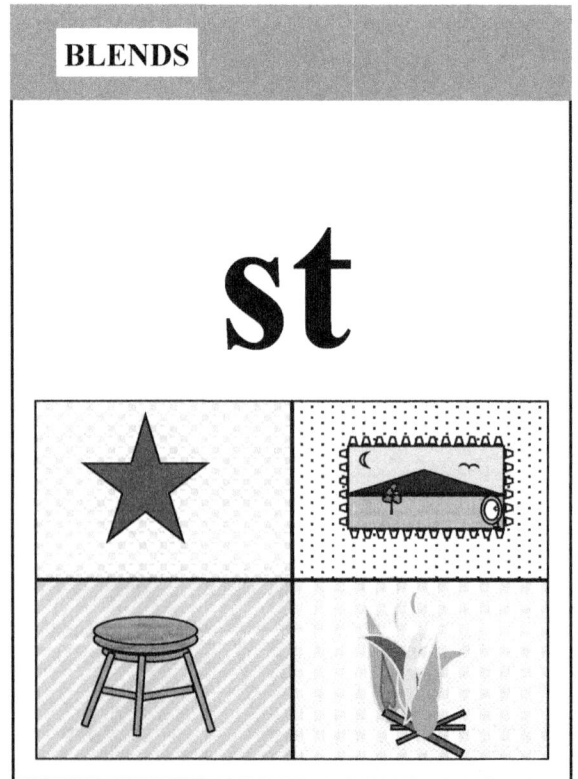

Directions: Three of the four objects begin with the same letter blend sound. Choose the one that does not begin the same.

BLENDS

str

BLENDS

sw

BLENDS

th

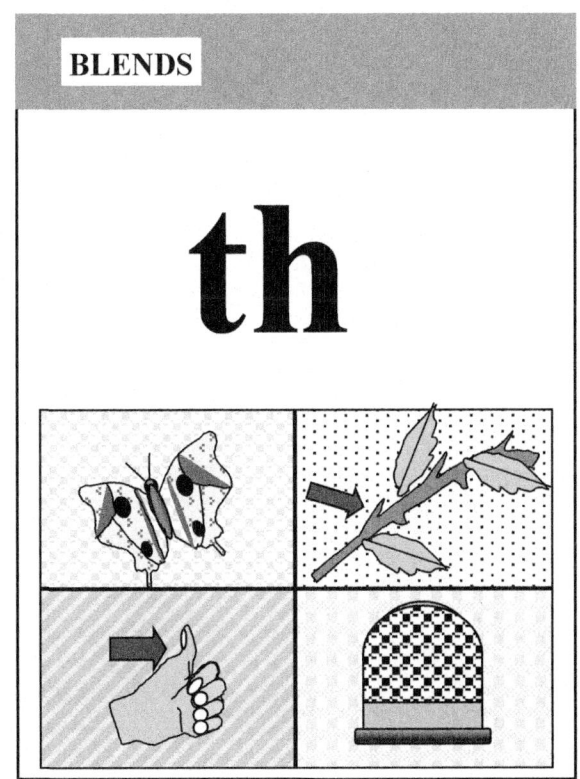

BLENDS

thr

ODD-MAN-OUT

BLENDS

tr

BLENDS

tw

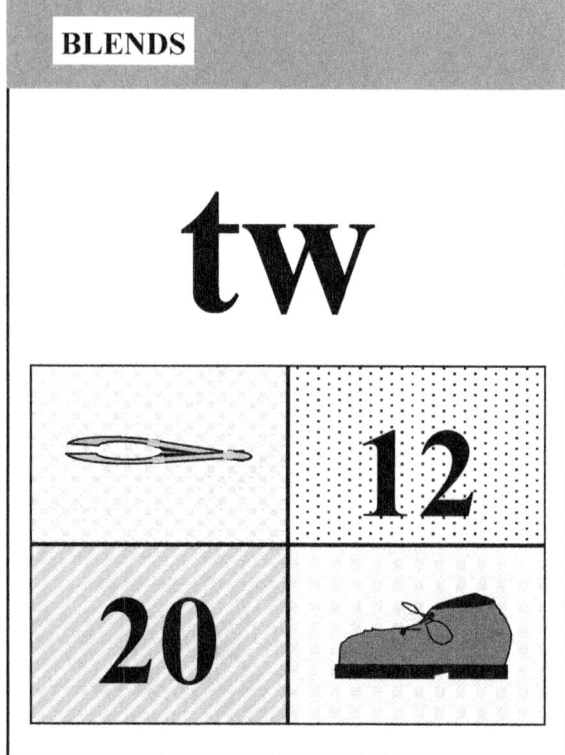

BLENDS

wh

24

RHYME ENDINGS

ODD-MAN-OUT — The activities in this section require the student to recognize the three objects in each game that have the same rhyming ending and then pick out the one that does not rhyme. When first attempting this activity, the teacher or parent should point to the rhyming letters and indicate to the child the sound they make, and then ask him/her to say aloud the four pictured objects and determine which one does not rhyme. Eventually, the child should be able to correctly identify the sounds each set of letters makes and, finally, to do the game completely by himself or herself.

The games in this section begin with short vowel sounds and at the end the long vowel sounds.

Directions: Three of the four objects in each section have the same ending. The one that does not is the Odd Man Out.

RHYME END -SHORT

ack

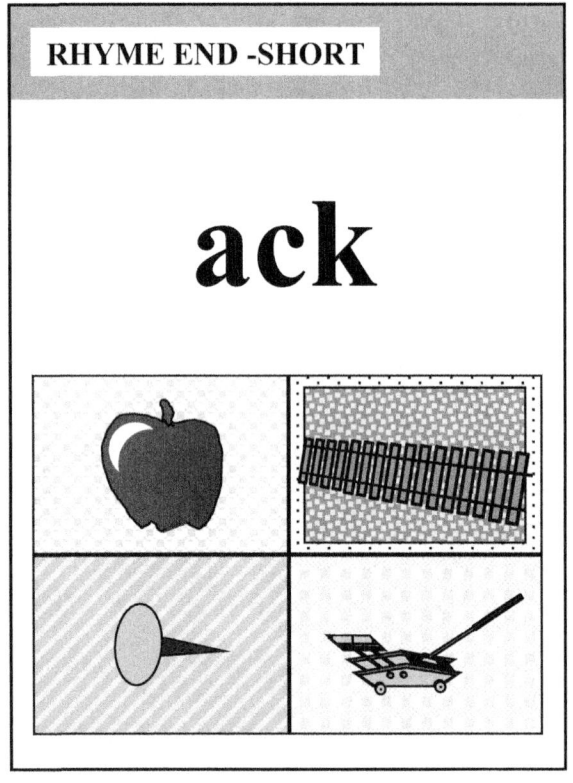

RHYME END -SHORT

ag

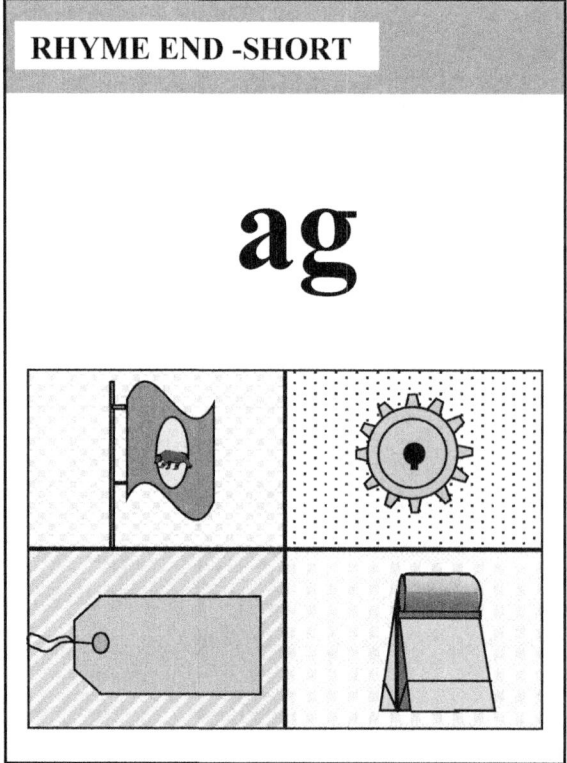

RHYME END -SHORT

am

RHYME END -SHORT

amp

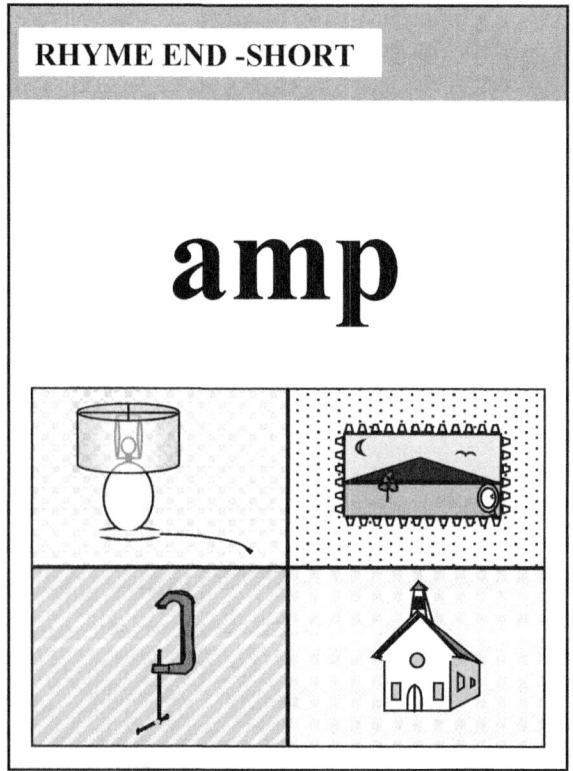

Directions: Three of the four objects in each section have the same ending. The one that does not is the Odd Man Out.

RHYME END -SHORT

an

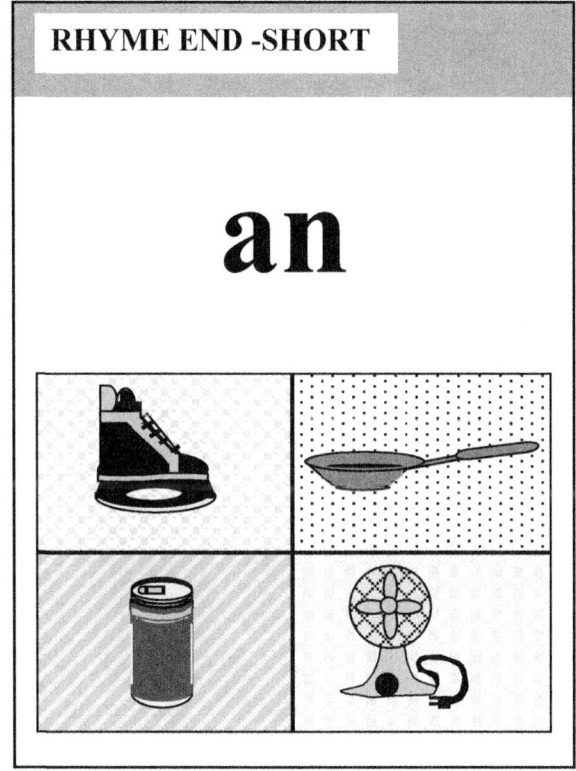

RHYME END -SHORT

and

RHYME END -SHORT

ap

RHYME END -SHORT

at

27

Directions: Three of the four objects in each section have the same ending. The one that does not is the Odd Man Out.

RHYME END -SHORT

acks
ax

RHYME END -SHORT

ead
ed

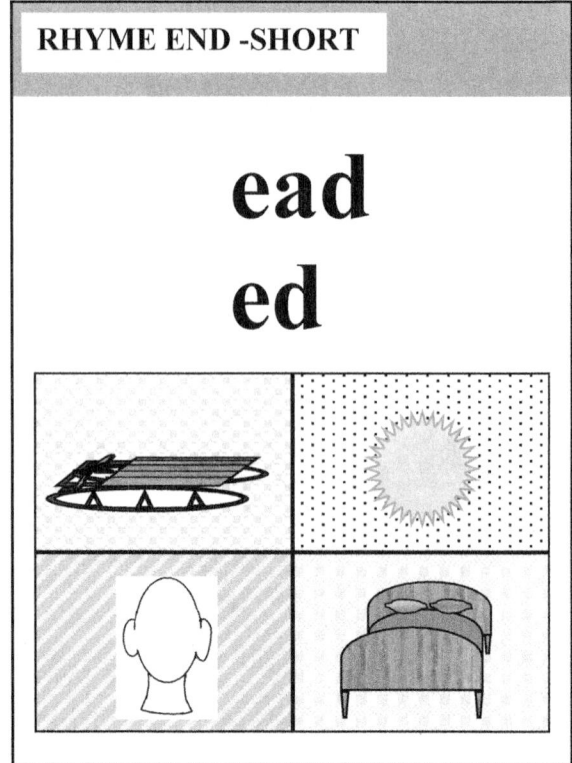

RHYME END -SHORT

ell

RHYME END -SHORT

en

28

ODD-MAN-OUT

Directions: Three of the four objects in each section have the same ending. The one that does not is the Odd Man Out.

RHYME END -SHORT

ick

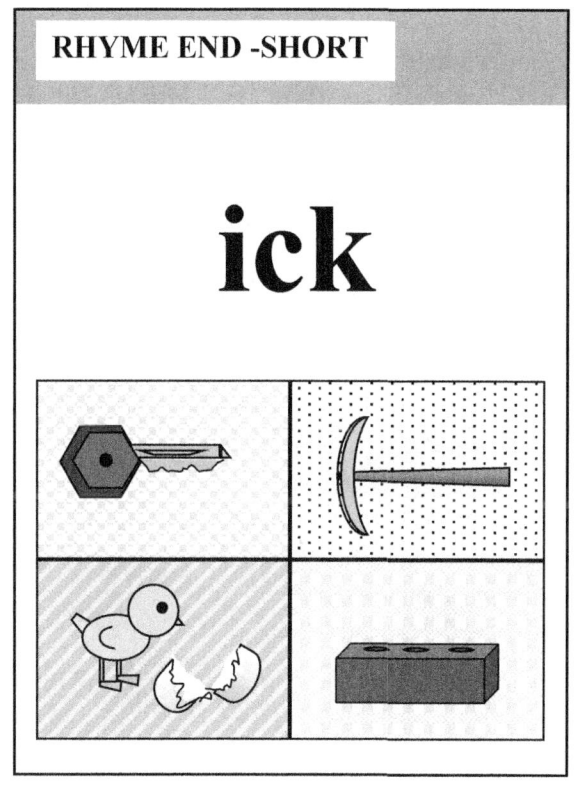

RHYME END -SHORT

in

RHYME END -SHORT

ing

RHYME END -SHORT

ink

Directions: Three of the four objects in each section have the same ending. The one that does not is the Odd Man Out.

RHYME END -SHORT

icks
ix

RHYME END -SHORT

og

RHYME END -SHORT

ot

RHYME END -SHORT

ug

30

Directions: Three of the four objects in each section have the same ending. The one that does not is the Odd Man Out.

RHYME END -SHORT

one
un

RHYME END -SHORT

art

Directions: Three of the four objects in each section have the same ending. The one that does not is the Odd Man Out.

RHYME END -LONG

ace
ase

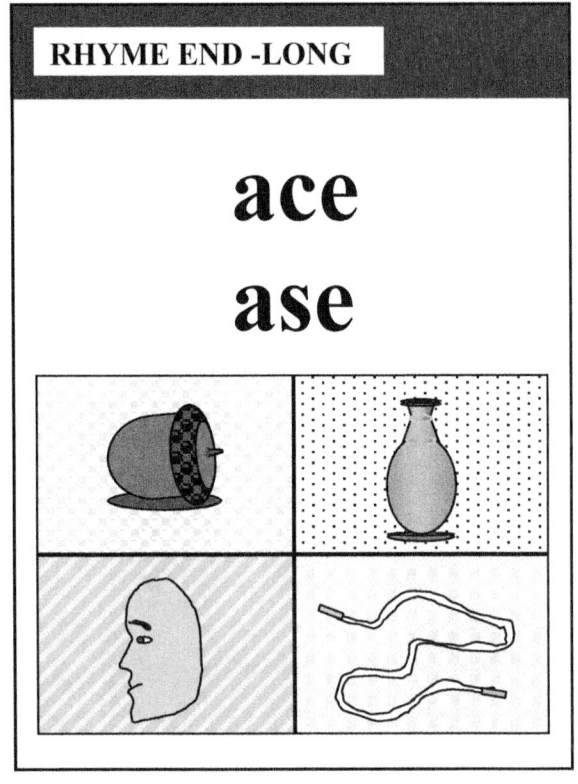

RHYME END -LONG

age

RHYME END -LONG

ail
ale

RHYME END -LONG

ait
ate
eight

Directions: Three of the four objects in each section have the same ending. The one that does not is the Odd Man Out.

RHYME END -LONG

ake
eak

RHYME END -LONG

ea
ee
ey

RHYME END -LONG

eas
ease
eese
ees

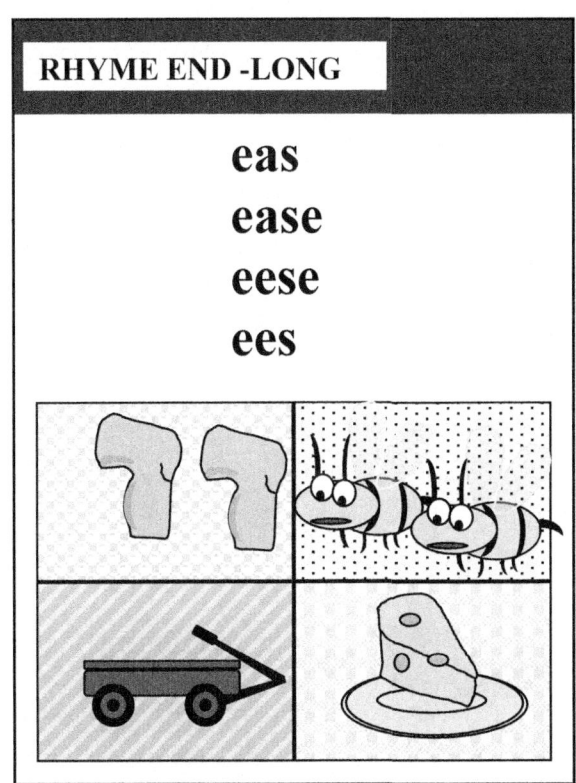

RHYME END -LONG

eat
eet

33

Directions: Three of the four objects in each section have the same ending. The one that does not is the Odd Man Out.

RHYME END -LONG

ice
ise

RHYME END -LONG

eye
ie
igh
uy
y

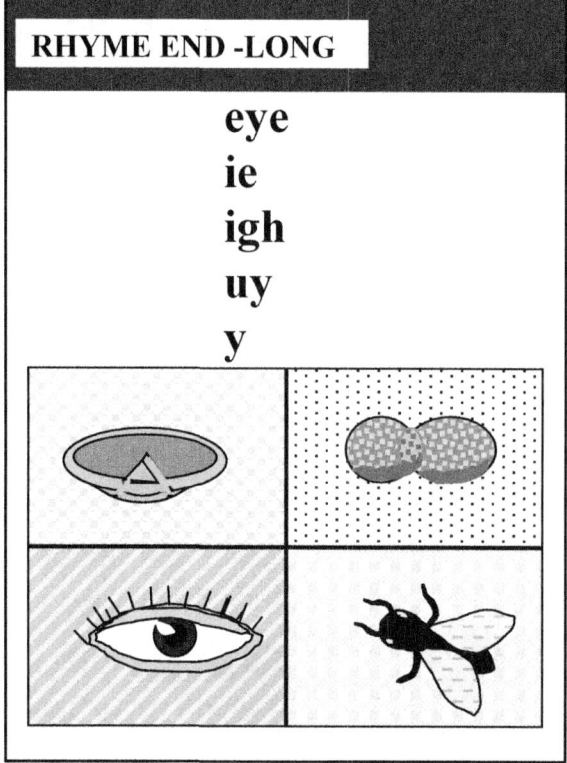

RHYME END -LONG

iers
ires

RHYME END -LONG

ies
ise

34

Directions: Three of the four objects in each section have the same ending. The one that does not is the Odd Man Out.

RHYME END -LONG

ight
ite

RHYME END -LONG

oal
ole
oll
owl

RHYME END -LONG

oan
one

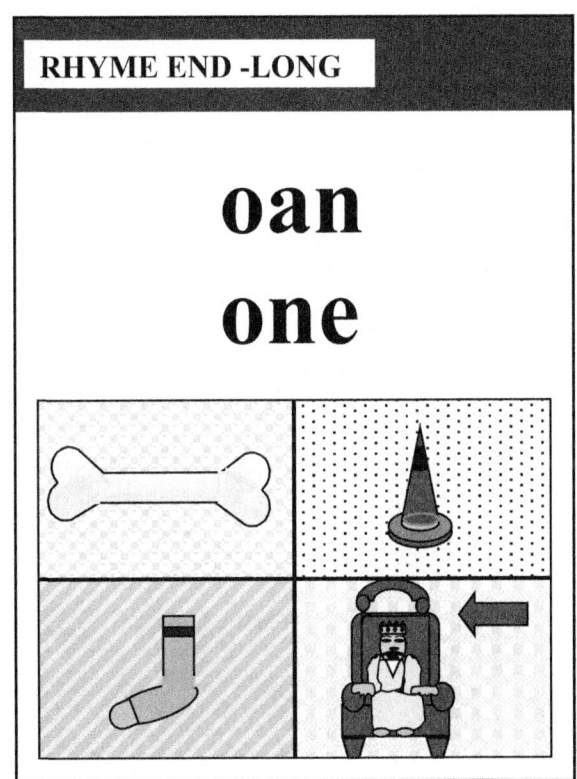

RHYME END -LONG

oat
ote

Directions: Three of the four objects in each section have the same ending. The one that does not is the Odd Man Out.

RHYME END -LONG

o
oa
oe
ough
ow

RHYME END -LONG

oes

ose

ows

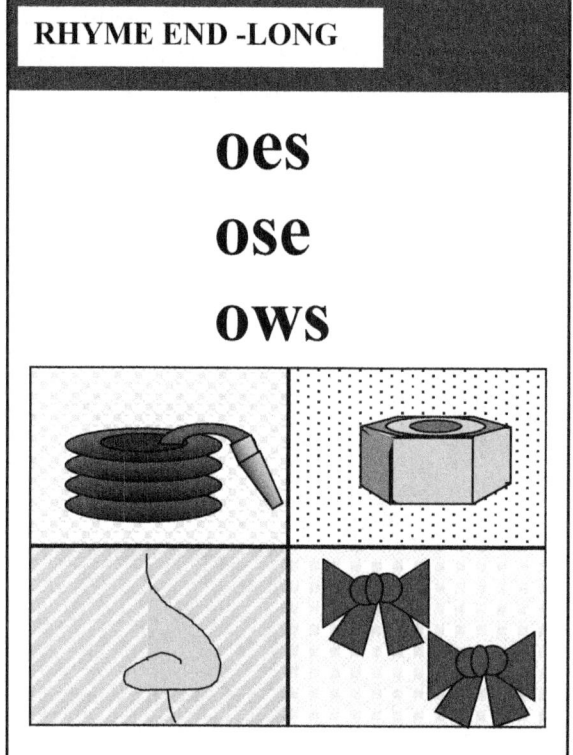

RHYME END -LONG

ew
o
oe
oo
ue

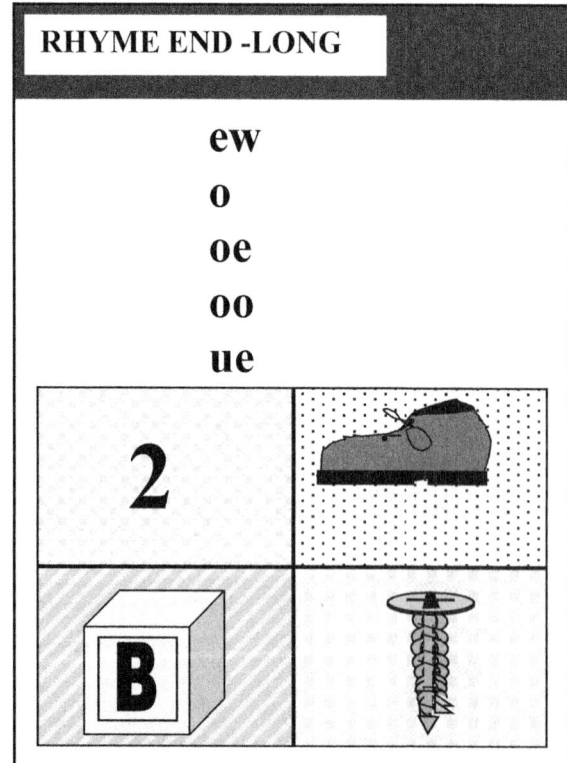

RHYME END -LONG

ews
oes
uise
use
ues

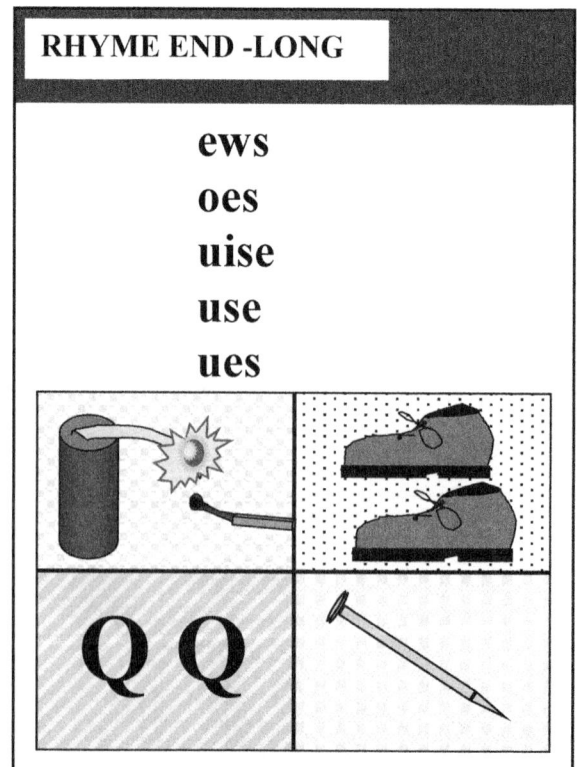

ONSET/RIME

The activities in the following section will require the student to pronounce words that have the same rhyming ending (sometimes called **rime**) but different initial (OR BEGINNING) letters (referred to as **onset**). The parent or teacher may begin by demonstrating how to combine the onset and the rime by pronouncing the initial letters and following that with the rhyming ending; such as, saying "kuh" followed by "at" for "c" + "at" for the word "cat". A "PLUS" sign (+) is used to show the addition (blending) of the letter or letters to the ending. The parent or teacher starts by pronouncing the onset letter and then the rhyme ending and pronouncing them slowly as they are brought together to form a single sound unit which also forms the entire single syllable word.

ONSET/RIME

j +
s +
t +   **ack**

ONSET/RIME

b +
fl +
t +   **ag**

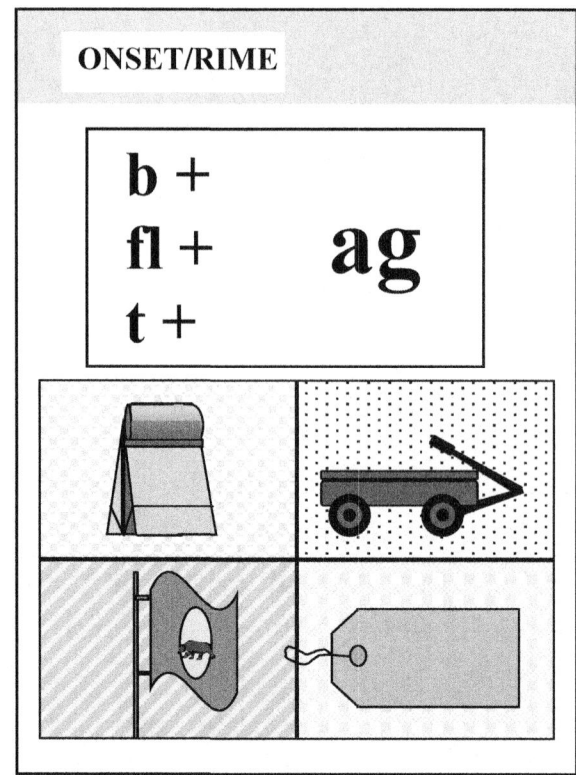

ONSET/RIME

cl +
l +
st +   **amp**

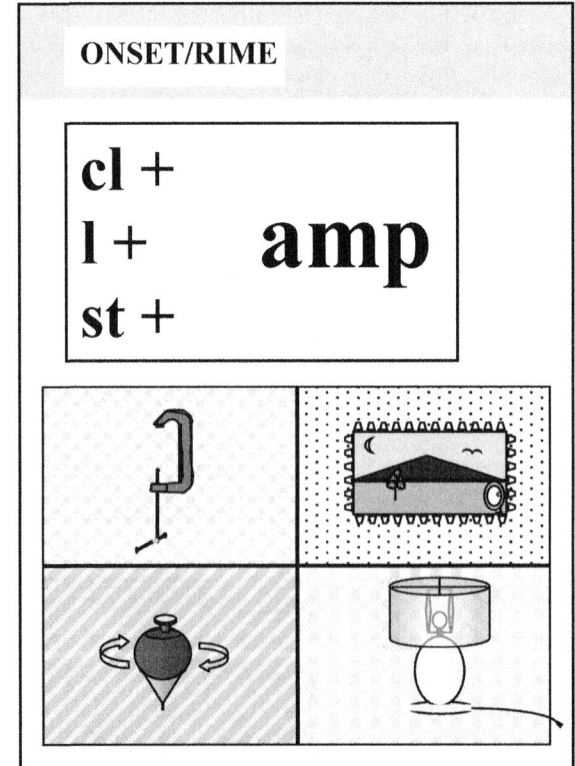

ONSET/RIME

cl +
h +
r +   **am**
        amb

38

Directions: Three of four of the objects on each card have the same rhyme ending. Choose the one that does not rhyme.

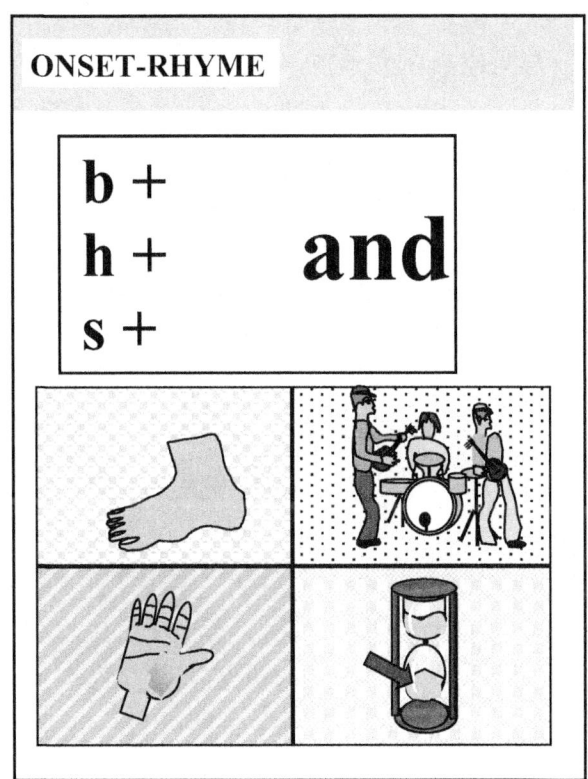

ONSET-RHYME

b +
h +
s + **and**

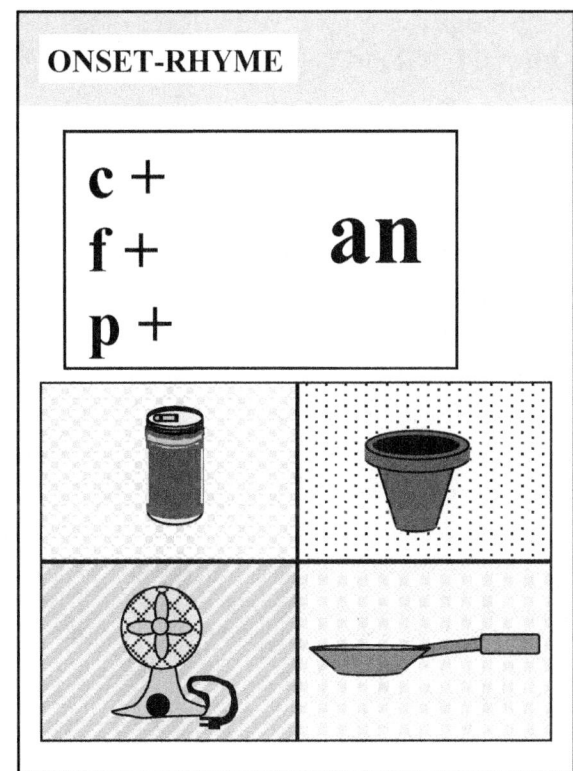

ONSET-RHYME

c +
f +
p + **an**

ONSET-RHYME

b +
c +
h + **at**

ONSET-RHYME

c +
m +
tr + **ap**

ONSET-RHYME

j +
s +   acks
t +

ONSET-RHYME

b +
br +   ead
sl +   ed

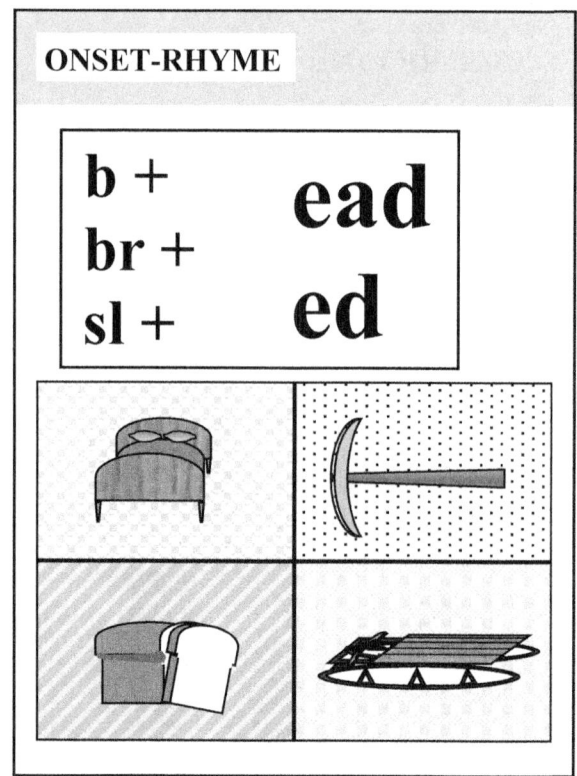

ONSET-RHYME

b +
sh +   ell
w +

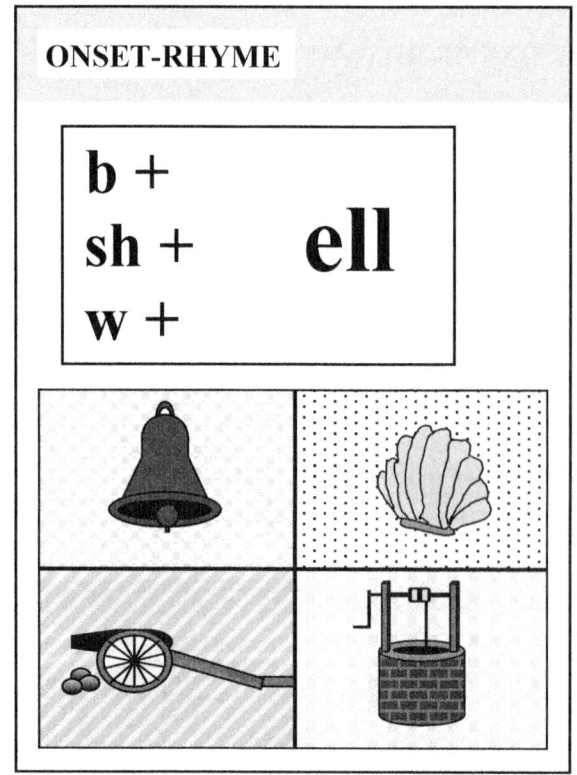

ONSET-RHYME

h +
m +   en
p +

40

ONSET-RHYME

ch +
n + **est**
v +

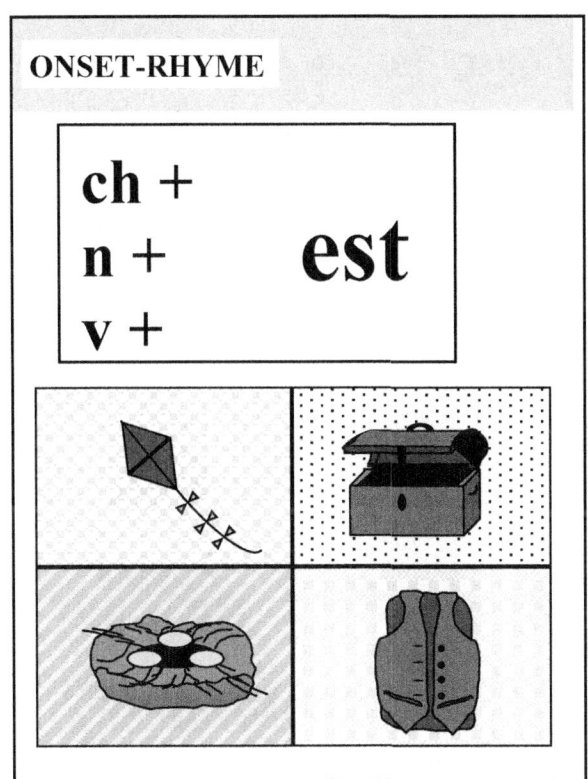

ONSET-RHYME

br +
p + **ick**
ch+

ONSET-RHYME

p +
f + **in**
sh +

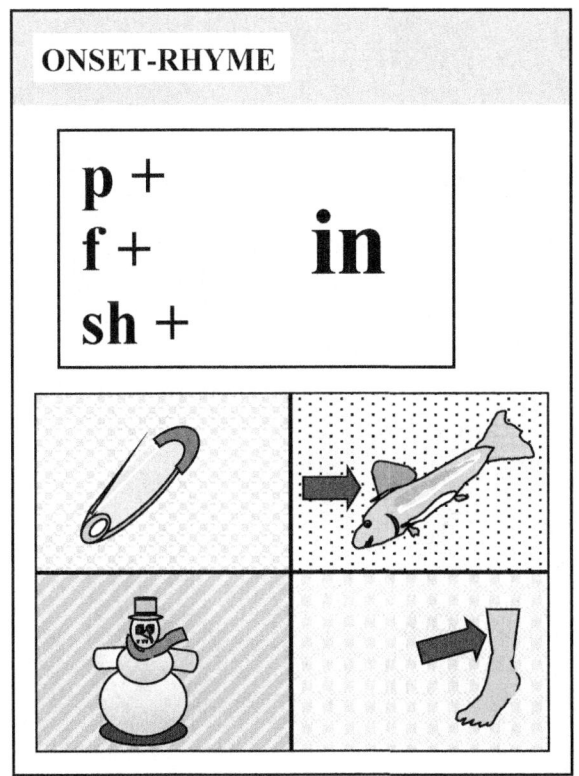

ONSET-RHYME

k +
r + **ing**
sw +

41

ONSET-RHYME

ch +
p +
t +
icks

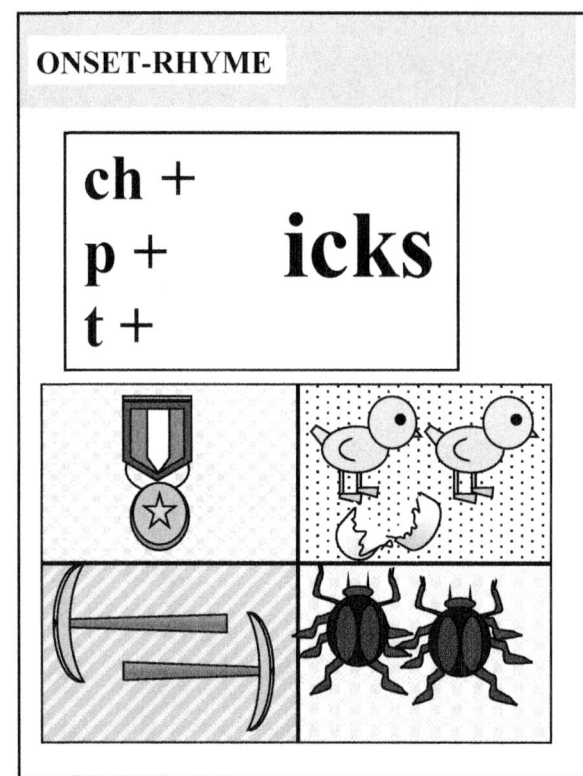

ONSET-RHYME

cl +
h +
sh +
ip

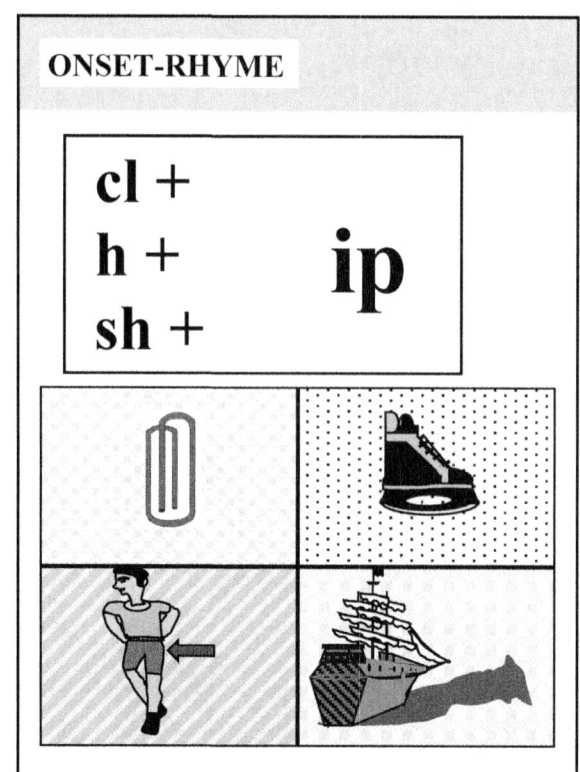

ONSET-RHYME

m +
p +
t +
op

ONSET-RHYME

c +
d +
fr +
og

42

Directions: Three of four of the objects on each card have the same rhyme ending. Choose the one that does not rhyme.

ONSET-RHYME

b +
d +   **uck**
tr +

ONSET-RHYME

c +
kn +   **ot**
p +

ONSET-RHYME

b +
sk +   **unk**
tr +

ONSET-RHYME

b +
j +   **ug**
m +

43

Directions: Three of four of the objects on each card have the same rhyme ending. Choose the one that does not rhyme.

ONSET-RHYME

h +
m +
p +   ail

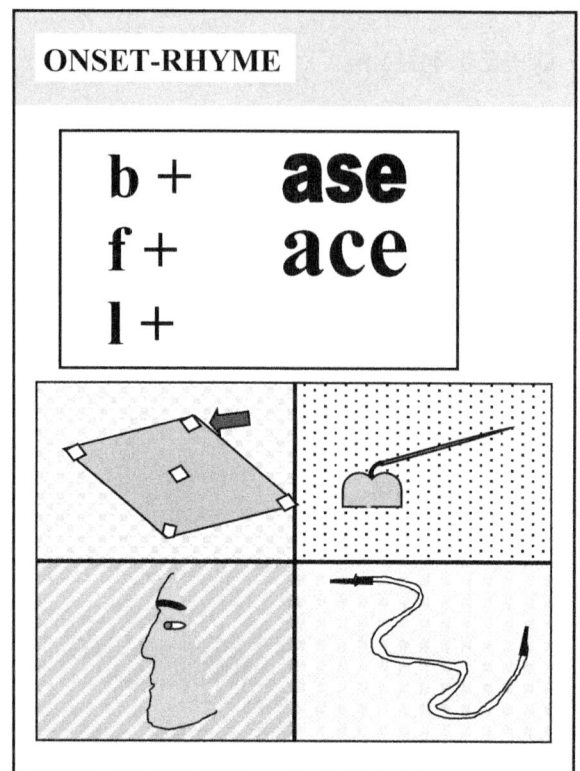

ONSET-RHYME

b +   **ase**
f +   ace
l +

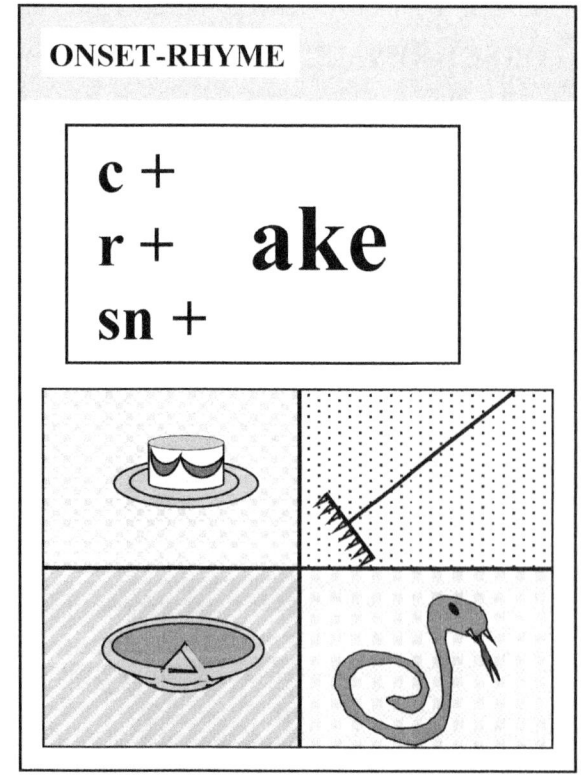

ONSET-RHYME

c +
r +   ake
sn +

ONSET-RHYME

cr +
g +   ate
pl +

44

ONSET-RHYME

c +
gr + **ape**
t +

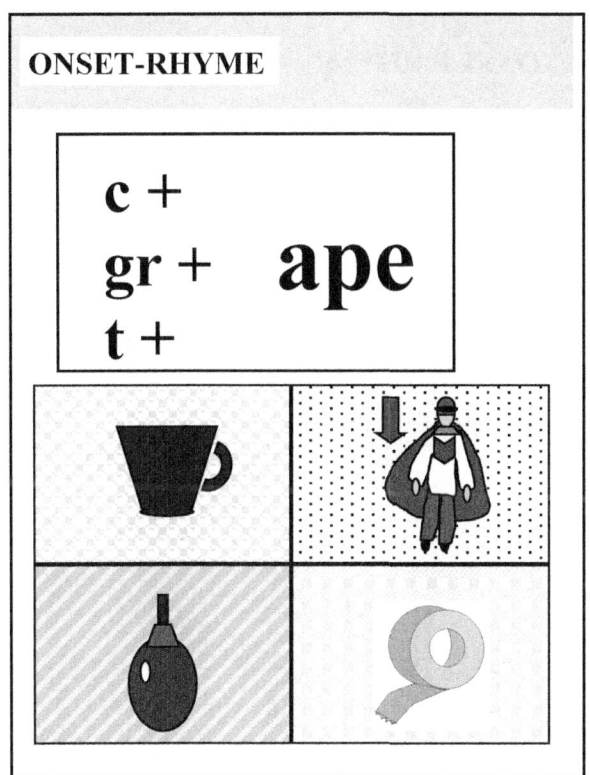

ONSET-RHYME

b +
kn + **ee**
tr +

ONSET-RHYME

b +
kn + **ees**
tr +

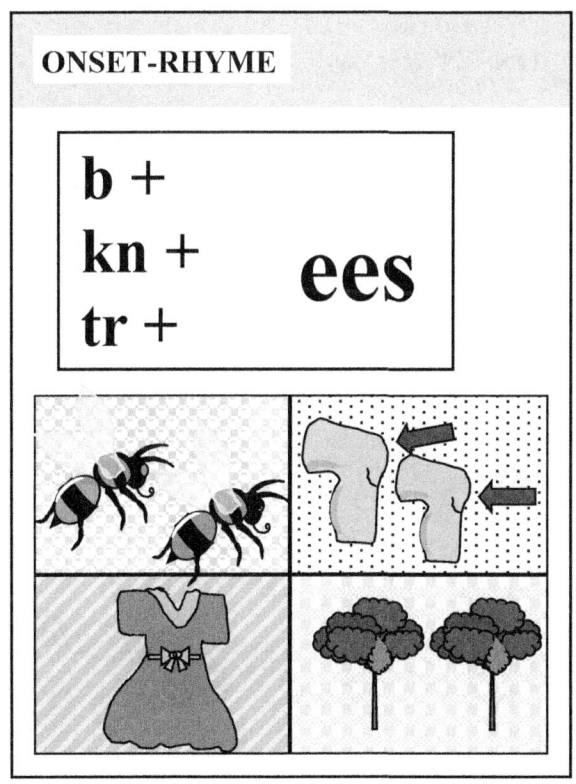

ONSET-RHYME

b +
f + **eet**
fl +

45

Directions: Three of four of the objects on each card have the same rhyme ending. Choose the one that does not rhyme.

ONSET-RHYME

f +
t +
w +   ire

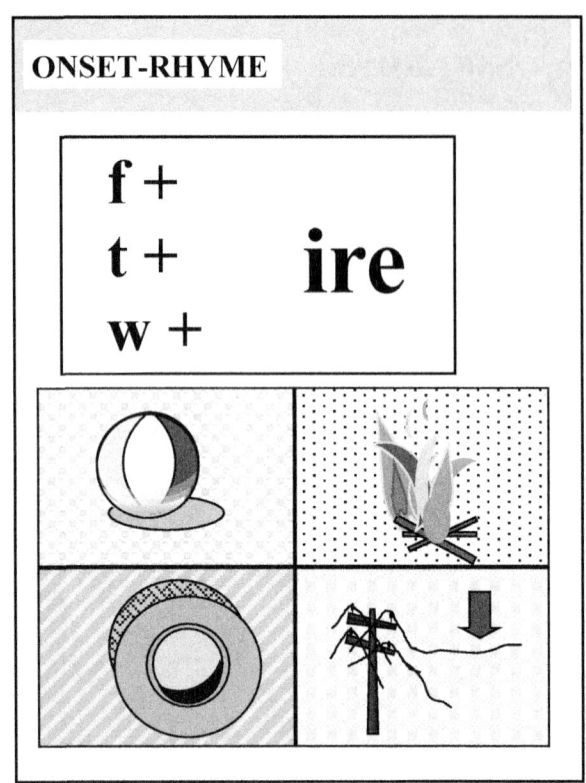

ONSET-RHYME

s +
tr +
wh +   eat

ONSET-RHYME

f +
sm +
t +   ile

ONSET-RHYME

fl +
p +
t +   ies

46

Directions: Three of four of the objects on each card have the same rhyme ending. Choose the one that does not rhyme.

ONSET-RHYME

b +
c +
thr +   **one**

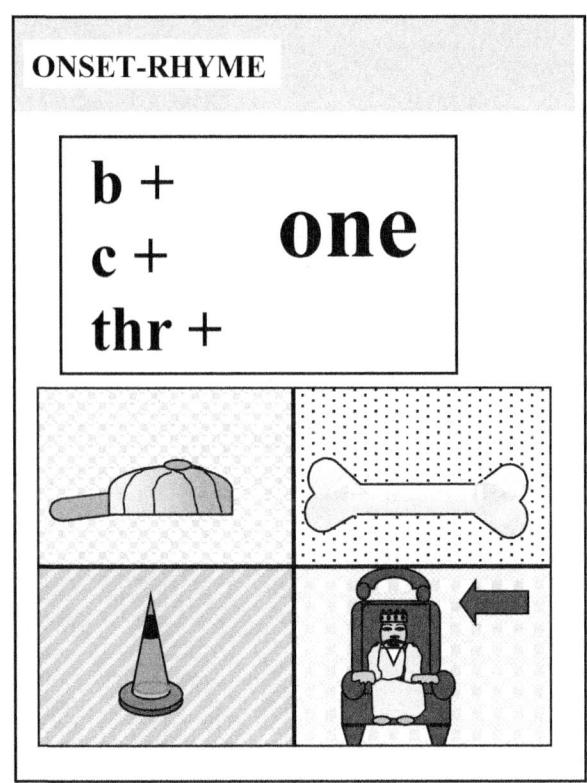

ONSET-RHYME

b +
c +
g +   **oat**

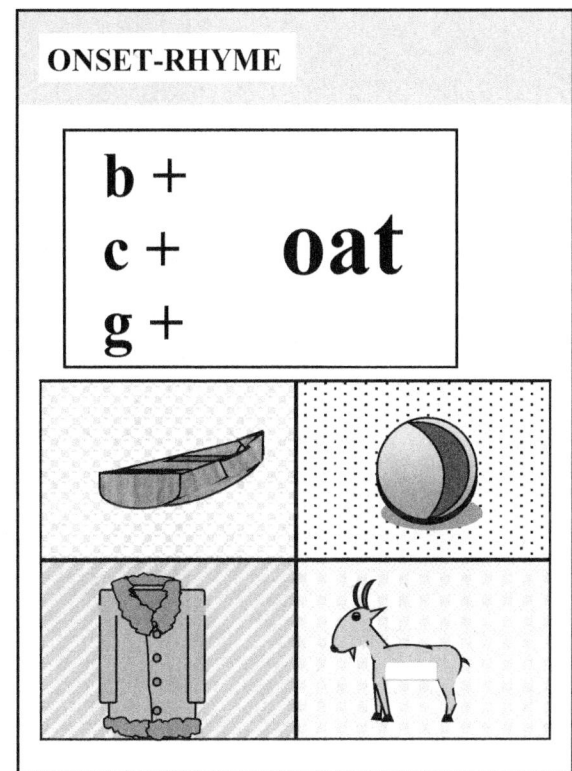

ONSET-RHYME

b +
cr +
sn +   **ow**

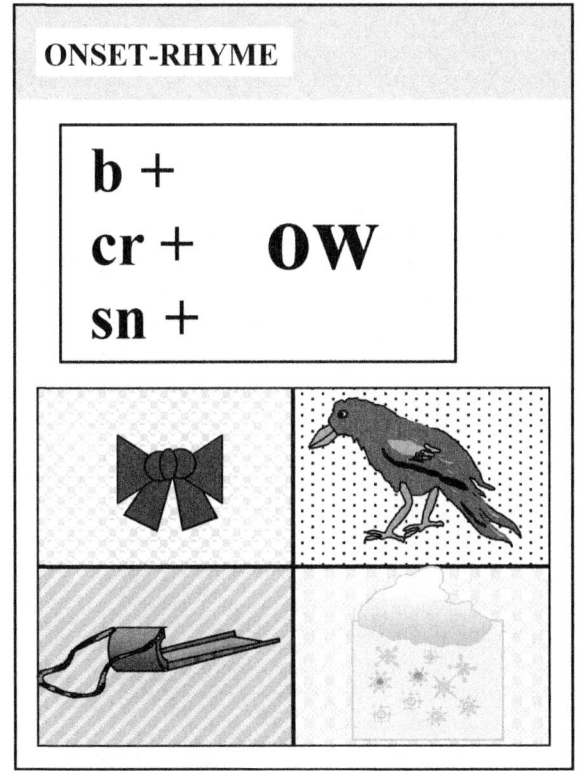

ONSET-RHYME

h +
n +
r +   **ose**

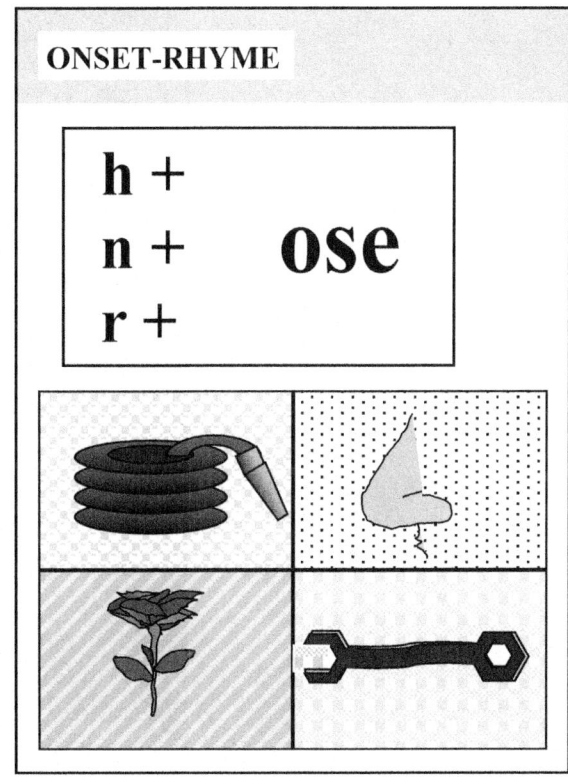

47

END BLENDS

End clusters are consonant groups or sets that appear at the end of a syllable or word. The following activities are among the more difficult for children to understand. If a student struggles with this section, skip it and return to it later when he/she has better reading proficiency. The parent or teacher will help the child by pronouncing the ending and asking the child to say the four objects in each game. Then determine which one of the objects does not end with the selected sound displayed above the objects. When the child is more proficient, allow him (her) to do the activities by himself (herself) while only indicating when the child is correct or incorrect.

END BLEND

SPRI
RI
STRI

ng

END BLEND

A
BA
HA

nd

END BLEND

LA
LI
CO

mb

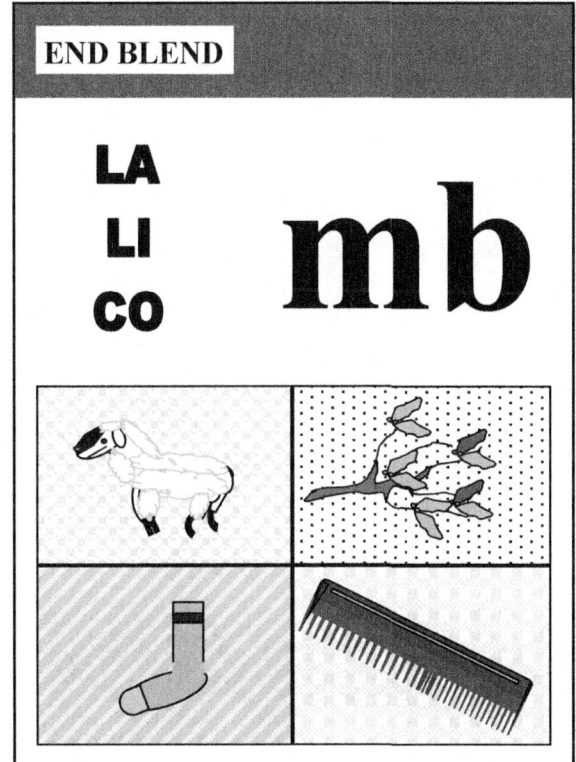

END BLEND

A
PAI
TE

nt

49

Directions: Three of the four objects begin with the same ending-letter blend sound. Choose the one that does not begin the same.

END BLEND

BA
I
SI
nk

END BLEND

FI
BRU
DI
sh

END BLEND

SHIE
MO
GO
ld

END BLEND

TOO
WREA
CLO
th

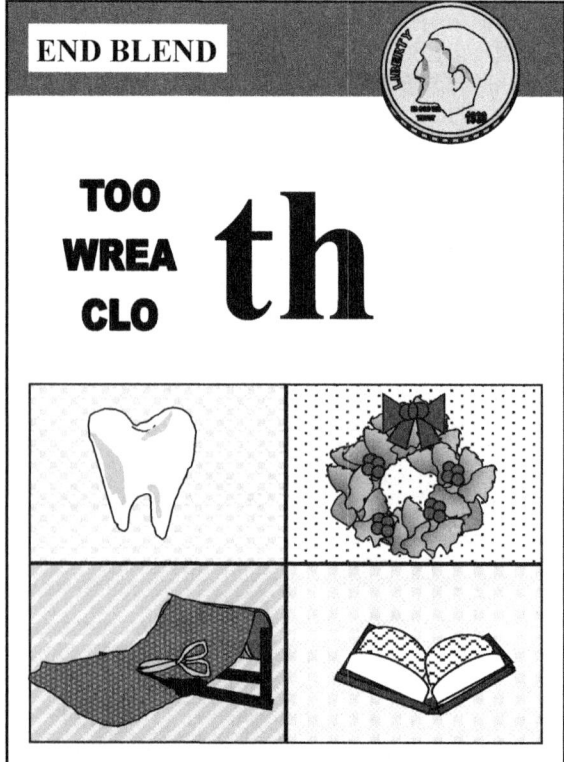

50

END BLEND

BLO
BRI
CLO

ck

END BLEND

WO
E
SHE

lf

END BLEND

ALA
A
WO

rm

END BLEND

PU
RA
WRE

nch

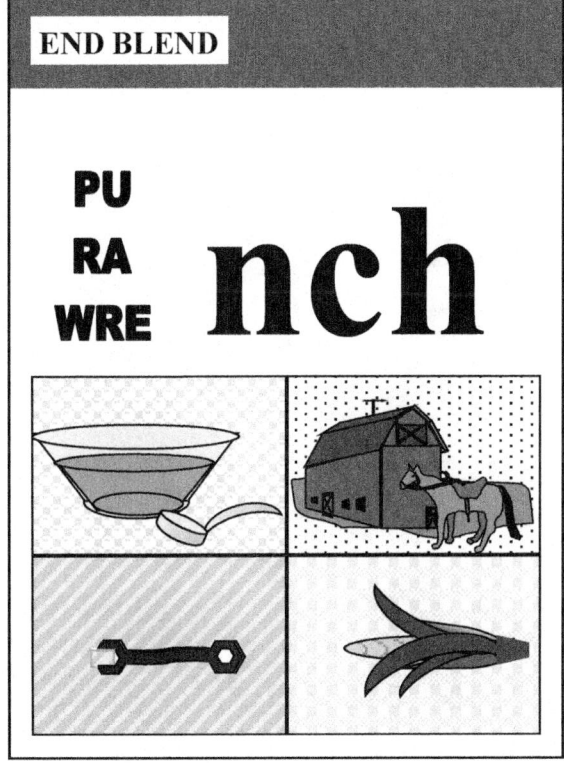

51

END BLEND

VE
WRI
CA
st

END BLEND

WA
WI
PA
tch

END BLEND

HO
BA
CO
rn

END BLEND

A
PO
TO
rch

52

END BLEND

boa
ca
swo

rd

END BLEND

de
di
ma

sk

END BLEND

ca
da
hea

rt

END BLEND

clo
cro
go

wn

53

END BLEND

co
fo
sha
rk

END BLEND

be
bo
co
lt

END BLEND

la
pu
sta
mp

END BLEND

ba
bri
ju
dge

54

END BLEND

pla
pri
ve
nt

END BLEND

i
sku
tru
nk

END BLEND

blo
ja
pi
ck

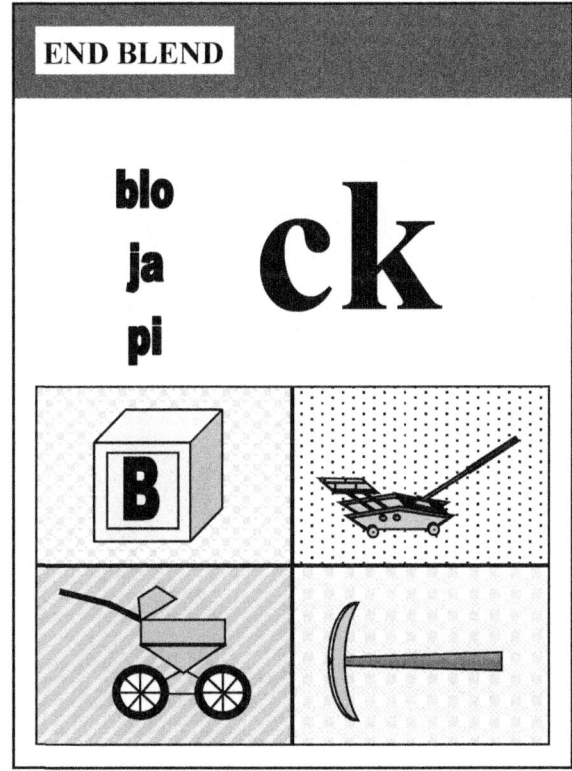

END BLEND

bi
boa
ca
rd

55

SYLLABICATION

This section requires the student to combine or add syllables together, from left to right, to form polysyllabic words. Many words in the English language are composed of more than one sound unit or syllable. For example, the word "car" is one syllable. If you combine it with the word "pet", you will form a two-syllable word with an entirely different meaning "carpet". Sometimes, two related words are added together to form what is referred to as a compound word. For example, if the word "cow" is combined with the word "boy", it forms the word "cowboy".

The following activities add together sound units consisting of objects and upper case letters which are pronounced as the name of the letter, not the sound it would make within a word. A plus sign (+) is used to indicate that you should join the sound units together. To help the teacher or parent to identify the objects that are incorrect, three of the four objects in each game begin with the same sound.

A parent or teacher should demonstrate how the sounds flow together to form a polysyllabic (POLY MEANS MANY.) word. Eventually, the child will be able to do the activity by himself. The parent or teacher should observe and correct only when necessary.

SYMBOL EYES

DECODING CLUES

TO DECODE: Each picture, symbol or letter represents a syllable. Pronounced in sequence, left to right, they form a word. PLUS signs link the sound units together.

EXAMPLE: R + 🐞 + L   =   ARTICLE

Occasionally, a picture or symbol may represent a phonic blend

Such as: ★ + 8 | For straight |

Some more common symbols used in rebuses are:

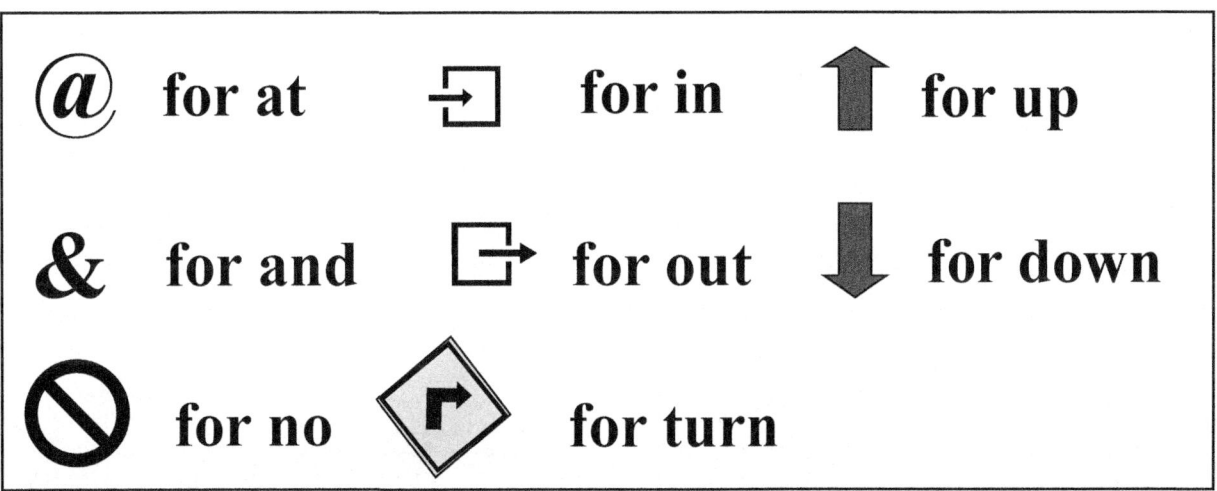

@ for at   ⊟ for in   ⬆ for up

& for and   ⬁ for out   ⬇ for down

🚫 for no   ◈ for turn

DOUBLE LETTERS are pronounced as plurals. For example,

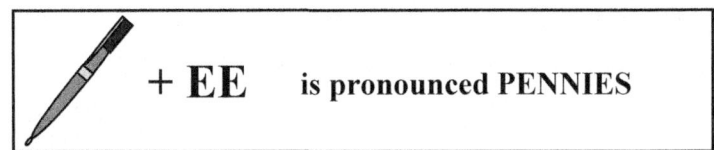

✒ + **EE**   is pronounced PENNIES

➡ A small arrow is used to point to or designate a part of an object.
A picture may refer to one of several possible words—generally single-syllable words. The more common form of the word will generally be used. For example, PIG or HOG will be used rather than sow, boar or swine. LOCALISM (colloquialism): Some objects have various pronunciations depending on its locality, such as: pop, soda, soft drink or phosphate. Generally, the shortest form will be used.

REBUS MATCH

Directions: Decode the rebus and match it to the correct object in the section below the rebus.

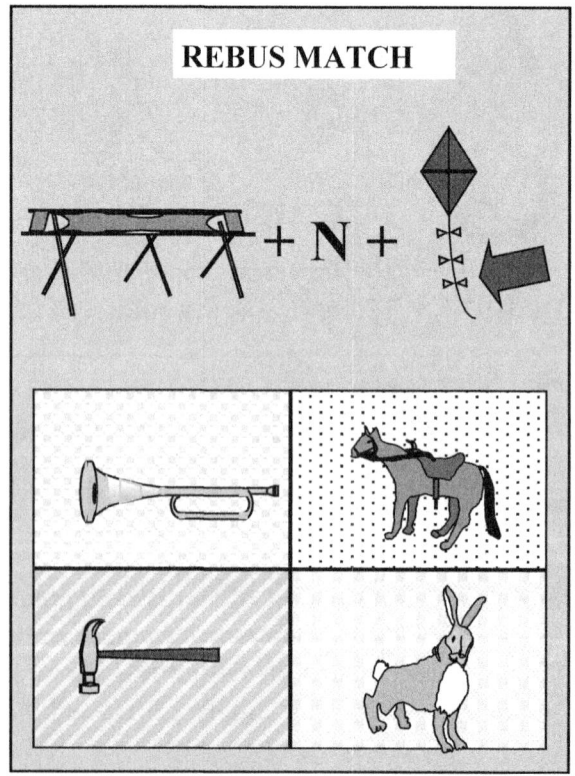

REBUS MATCH

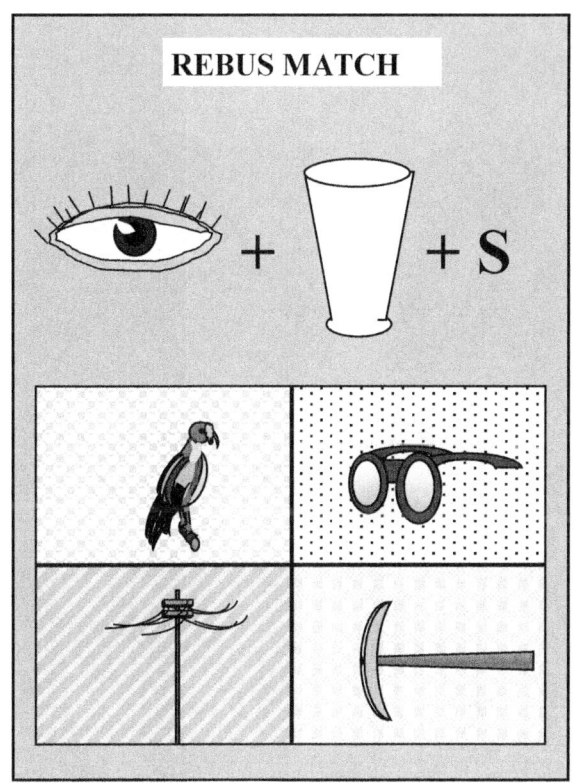

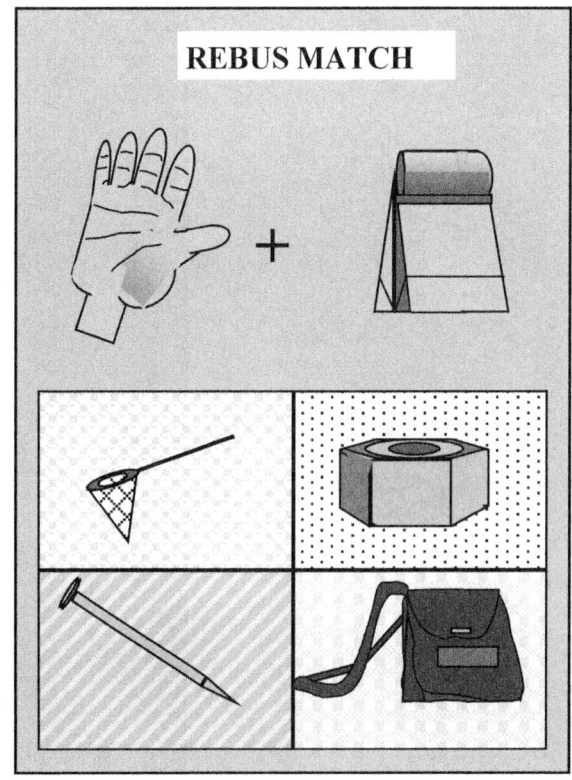

REBUS MATCH

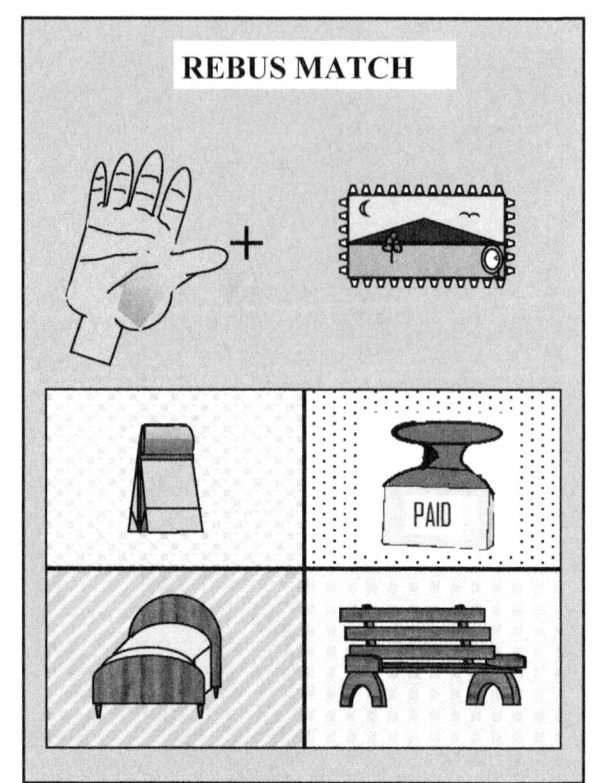

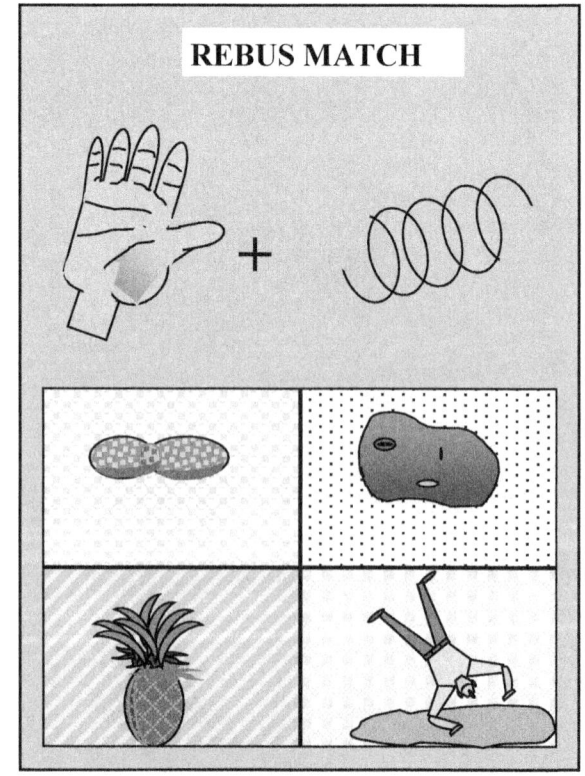

60

REBUS MATCH

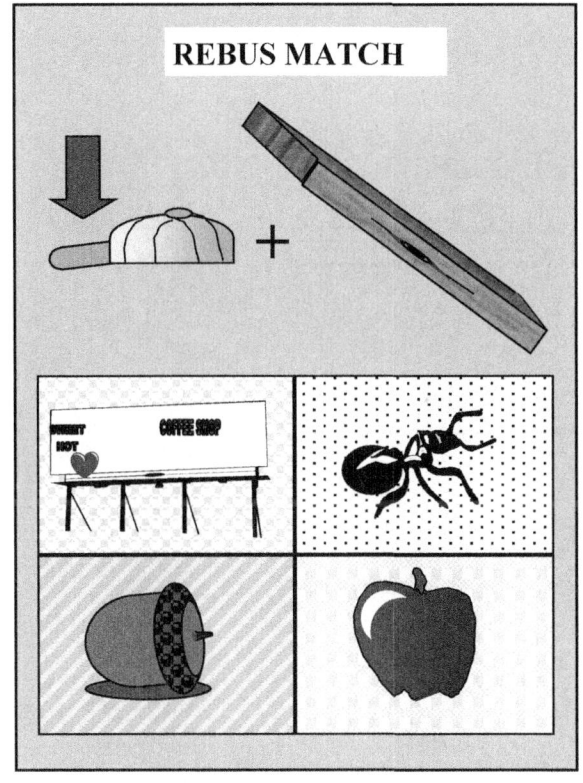

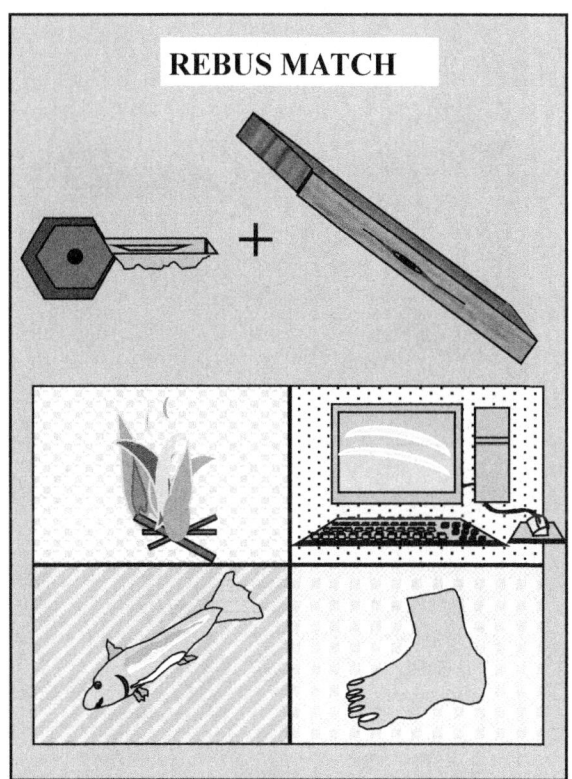

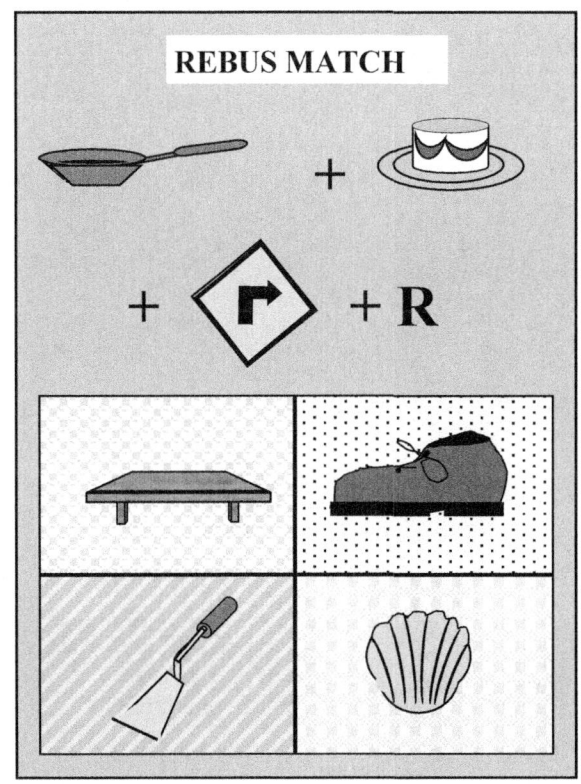

61

REBUS MATCH

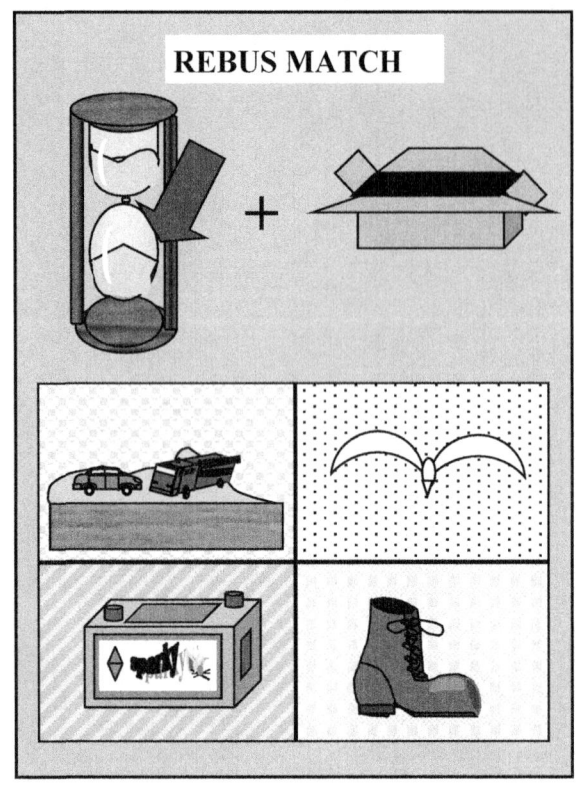

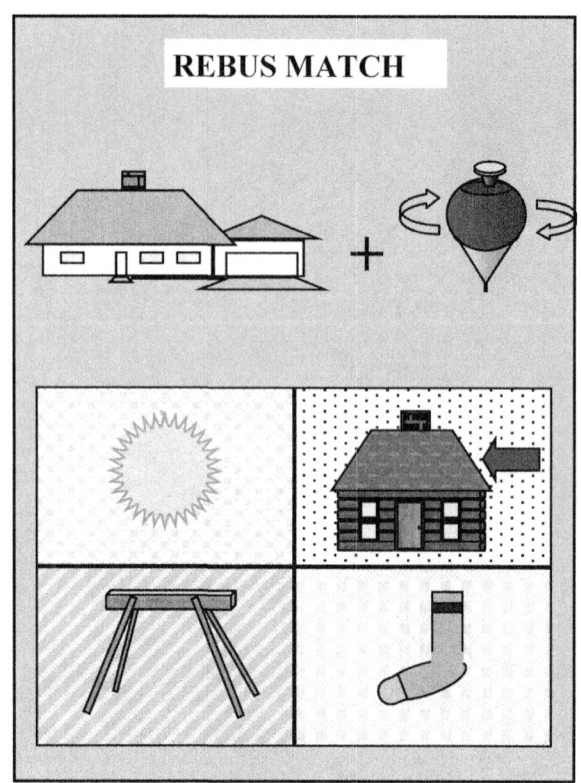

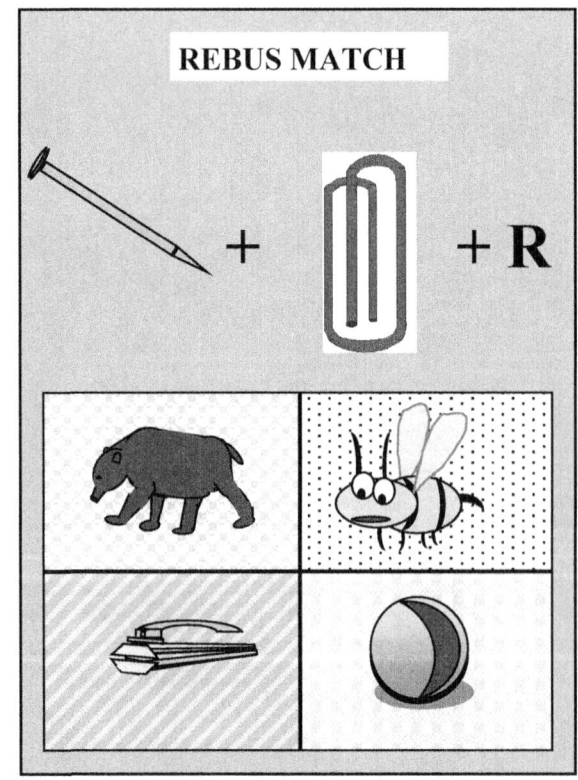

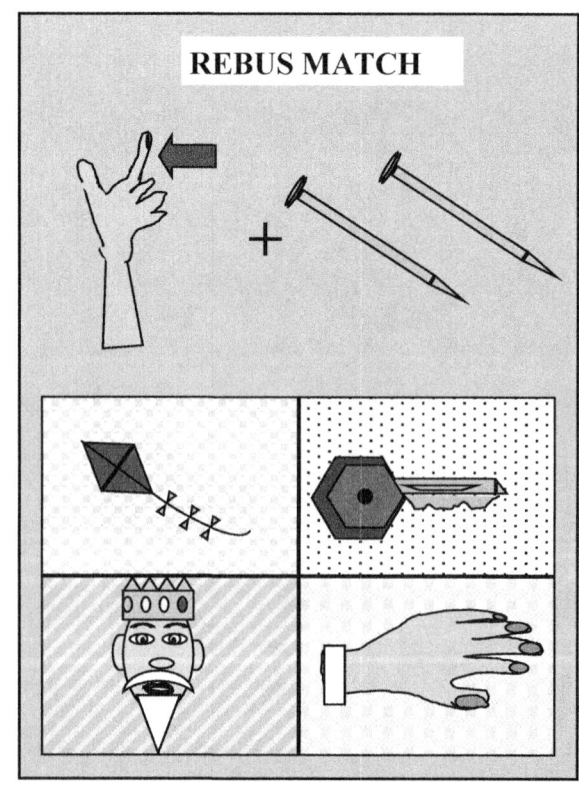

62

REBUS MATCH

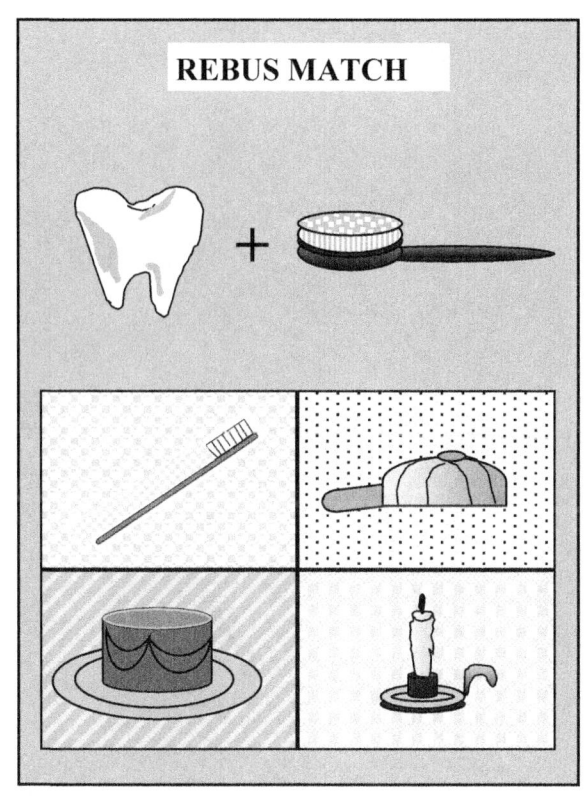

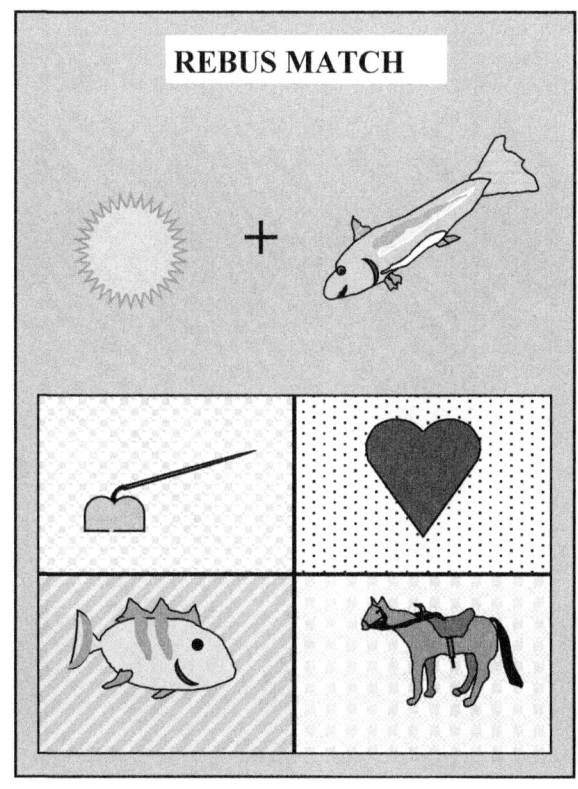

REBUS MATCH

Directions: Decode the rebus and match it to the correct object in the section below the rebus.

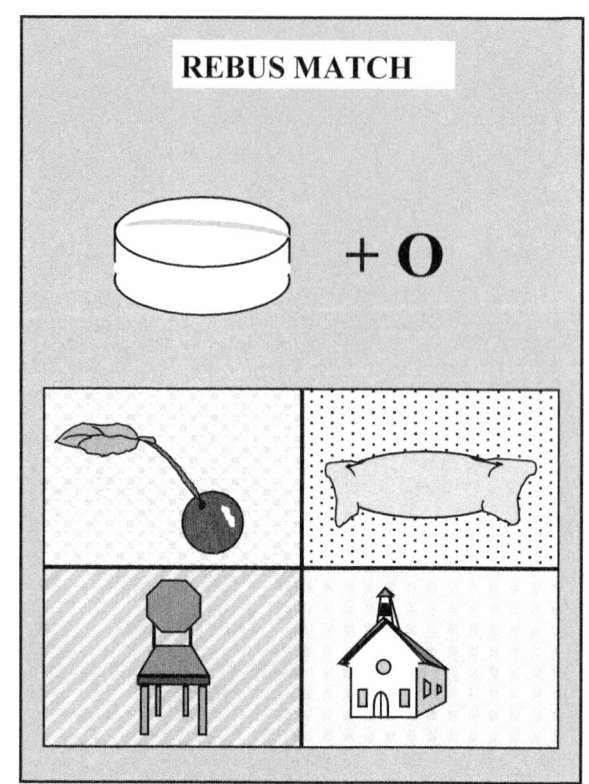

64

REBUS MATCH

Directions: Decode the rebus and match it to the correct object in the section below the rebus.

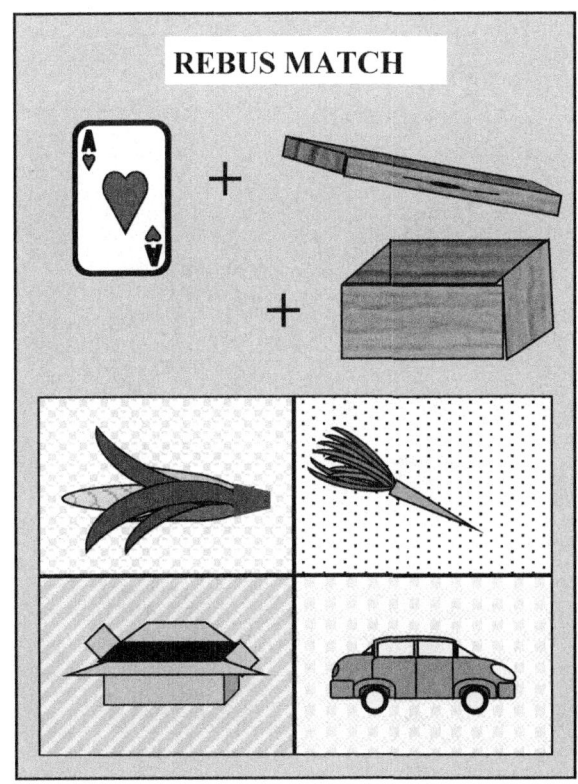

REBUS MATCH

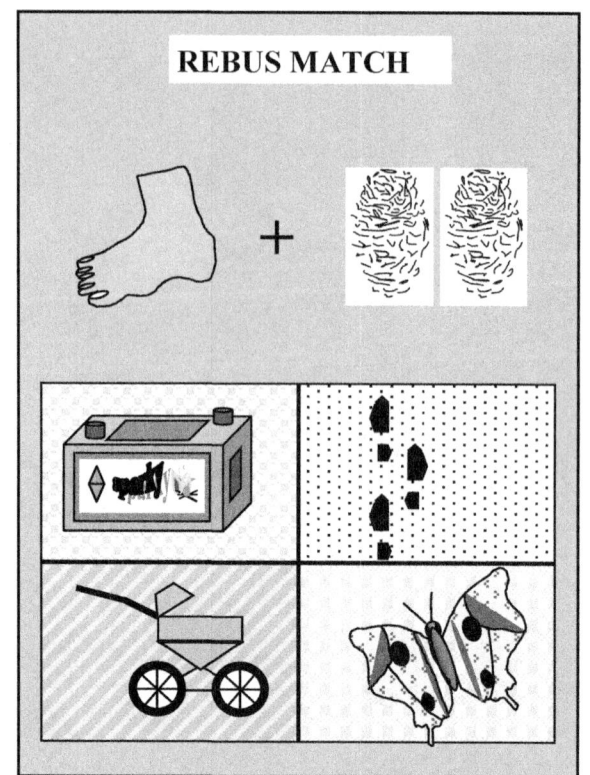

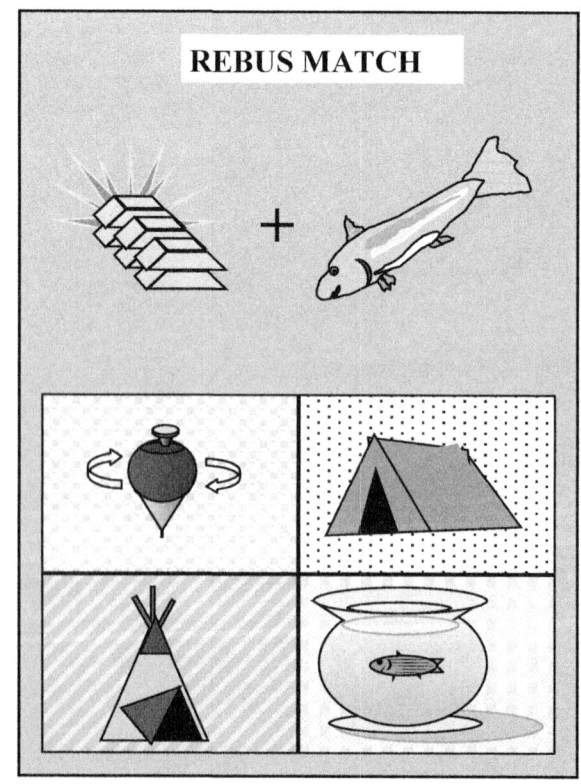

66

REBUS MATCH

Directions: Decode the rebus and match it to the correct object in the section below the rebus.

REBUS MATCH

REBUS MATCH

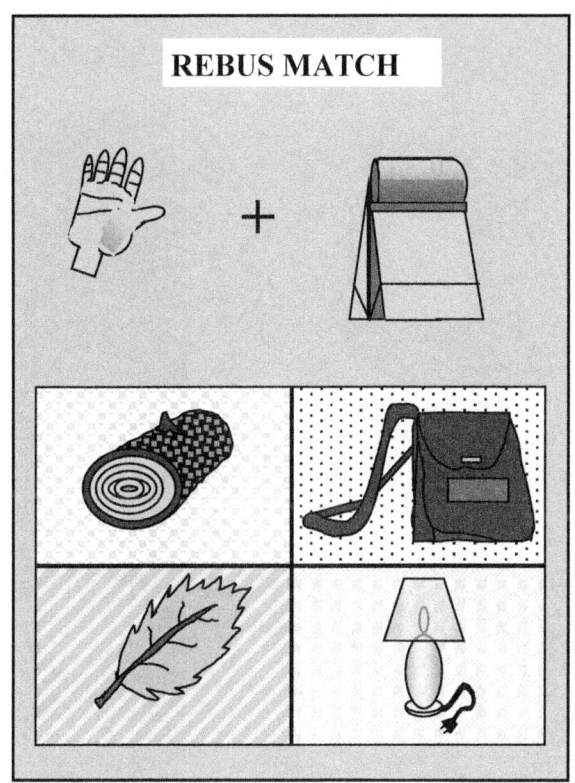

REBUS MATCH

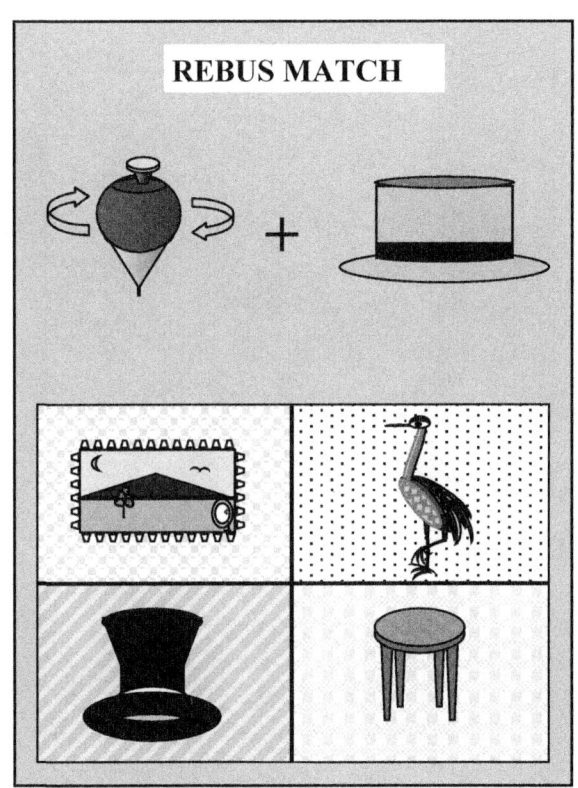

REBUS MATCH

REBUS MATCH

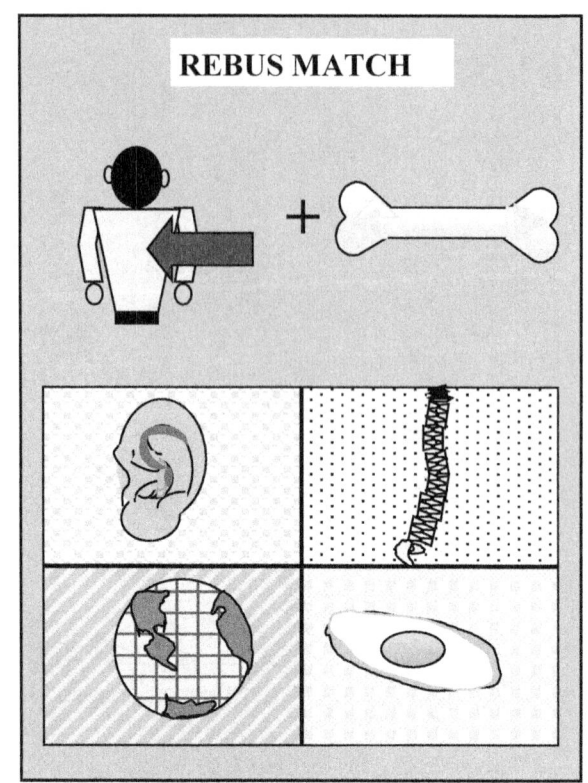

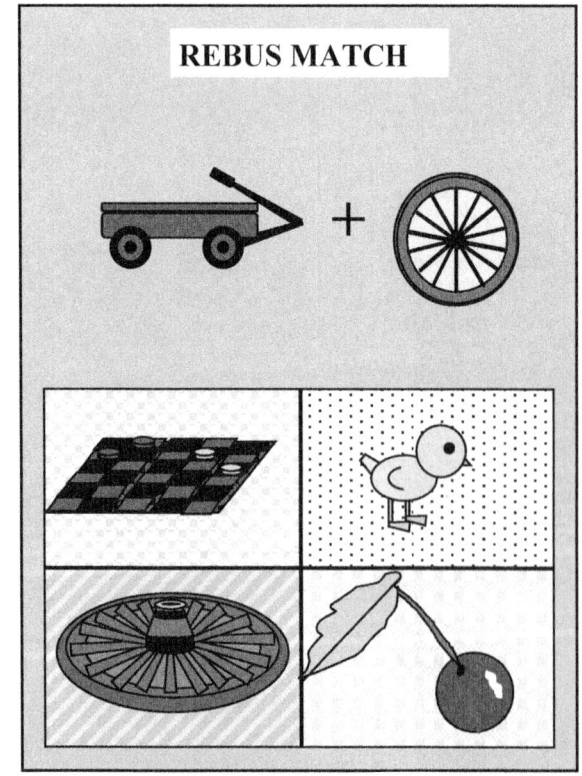

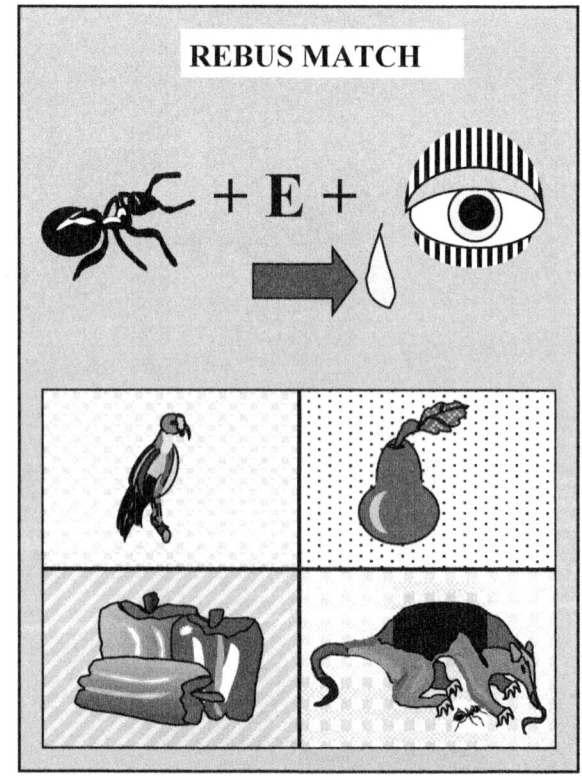

REBUS MATCH

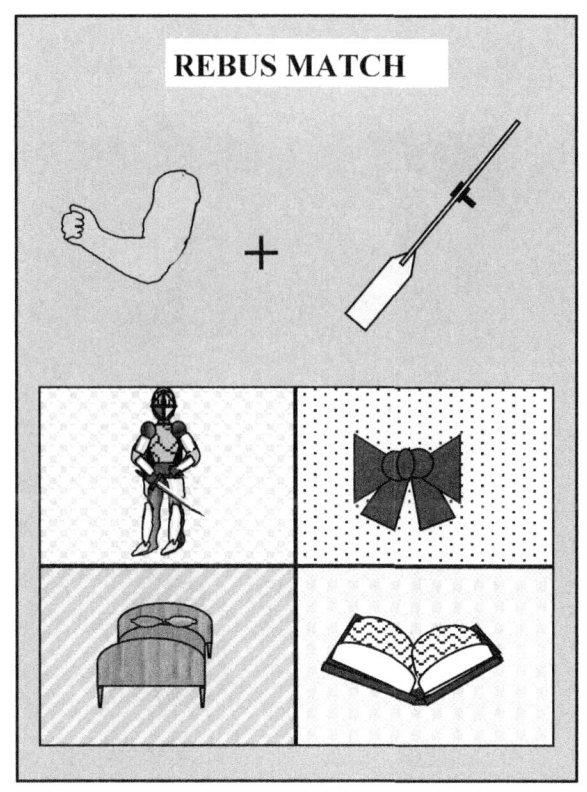

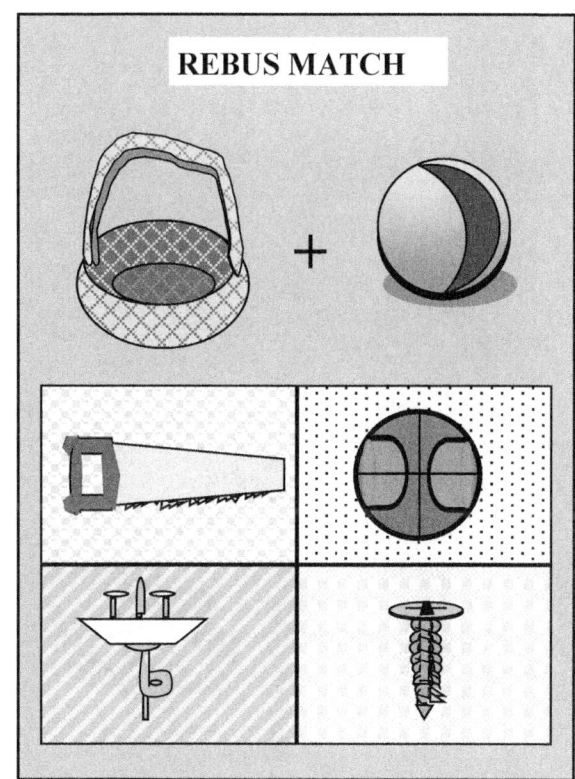

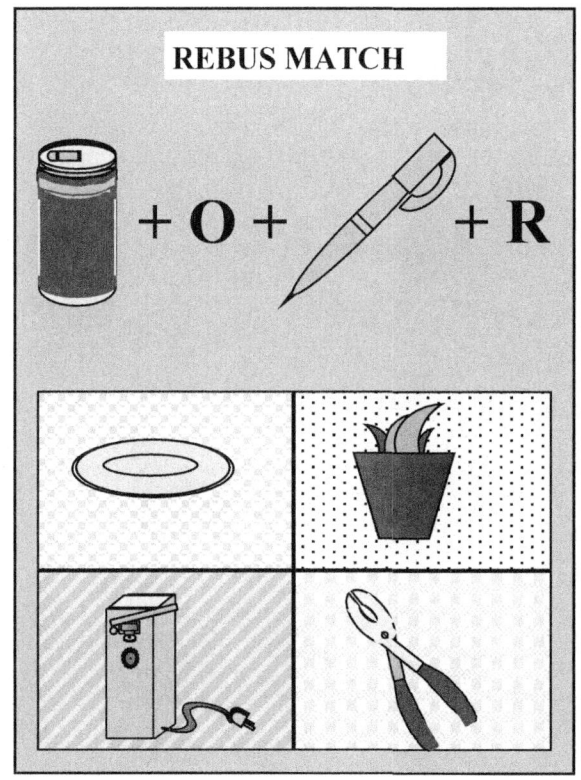

69

REBUS MATCH

Directions: Decode the rebus and match it to the correct object in the section below the rebus.

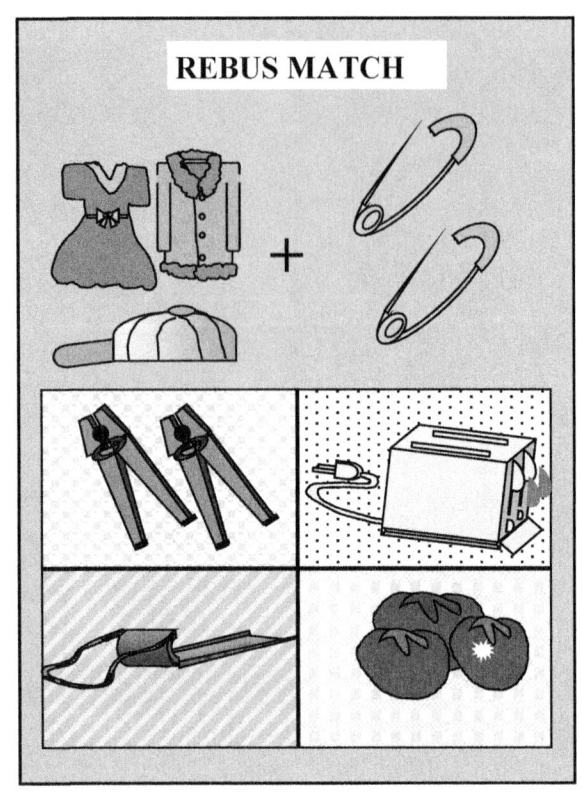

70

REBUS MATCH

Directions: Decode the rebus and match it to the correct object in the section below the rebus.

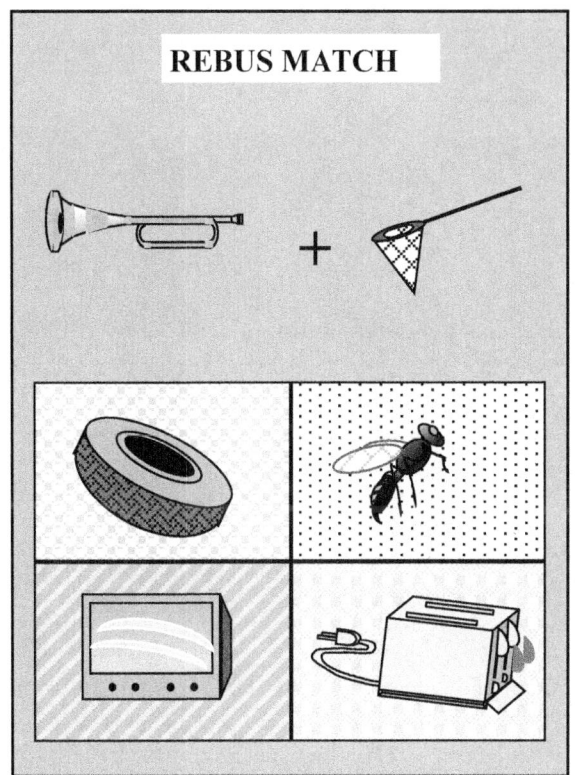

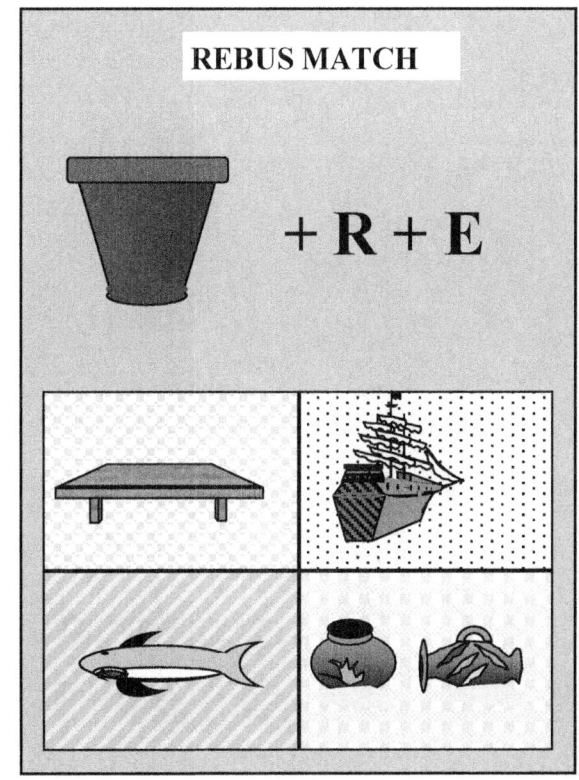

71

REBUS MATCH

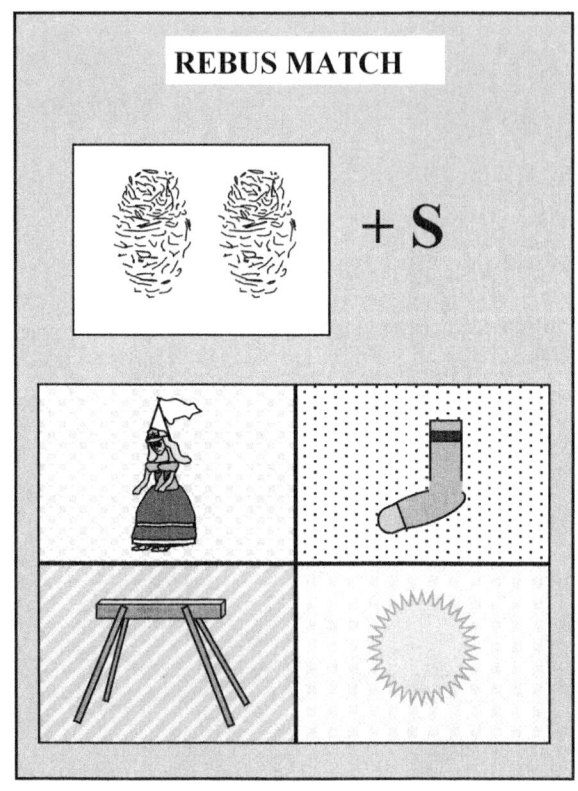

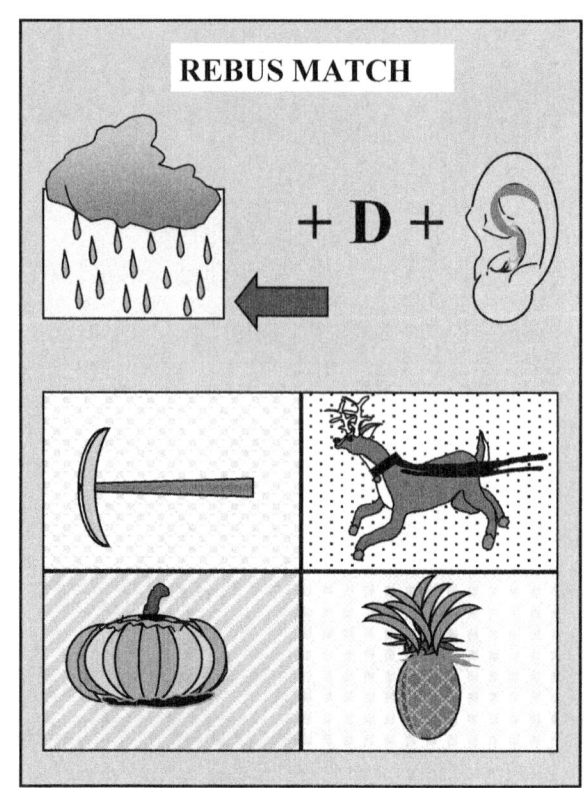

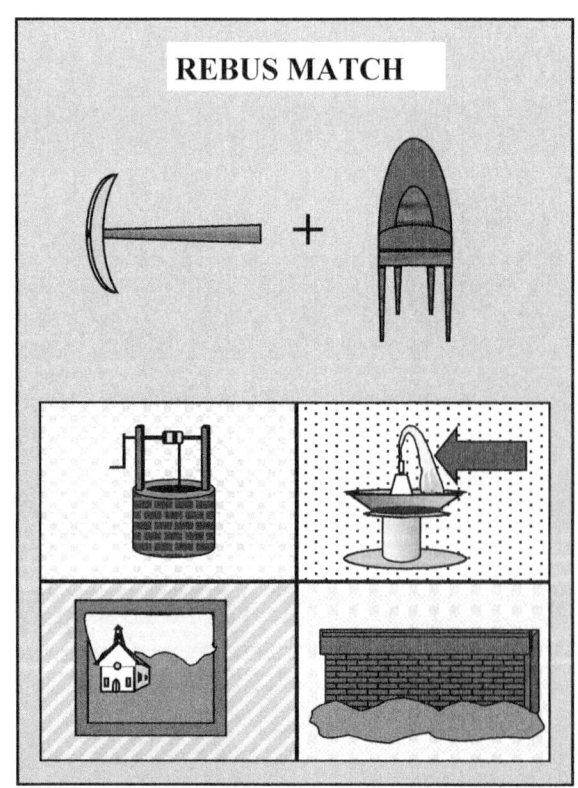

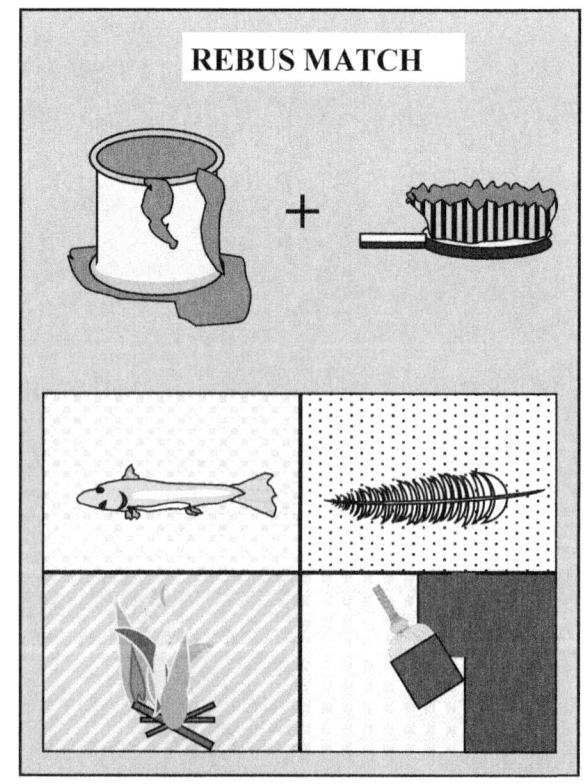

72

REBUS MATCH

Directions: Decode the rebus and match it to the correct object in the section below the rebus.

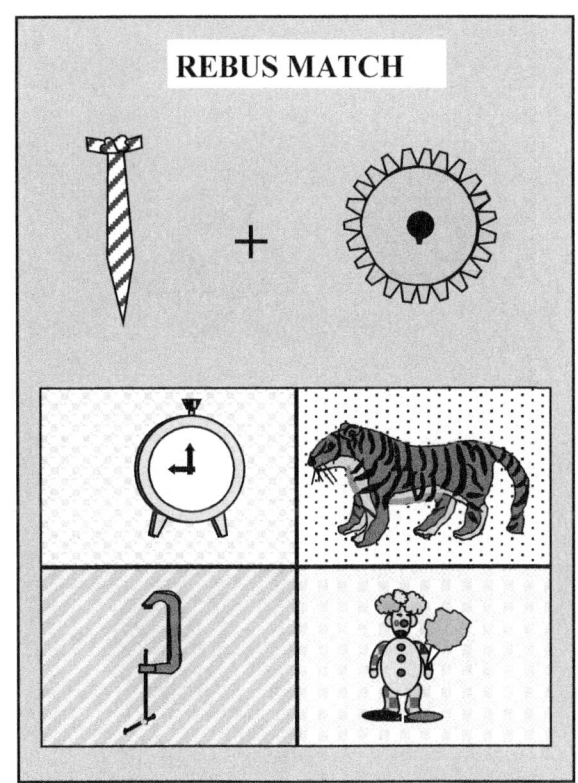

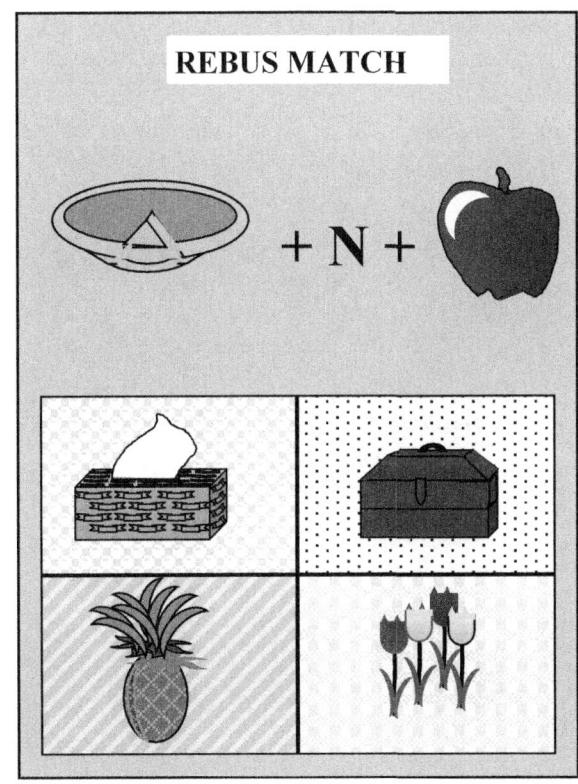

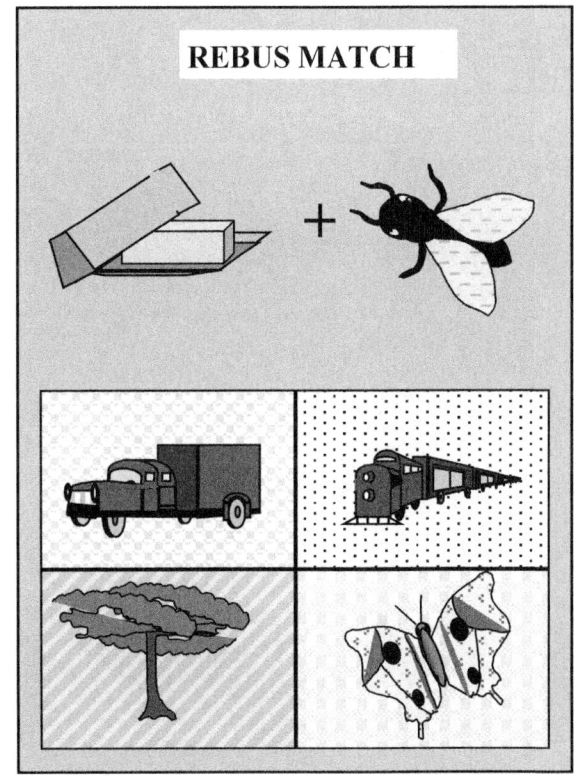

REBUS MATCH

Directions: Decode the rebus and match it to the correct object in the section below the rebus.

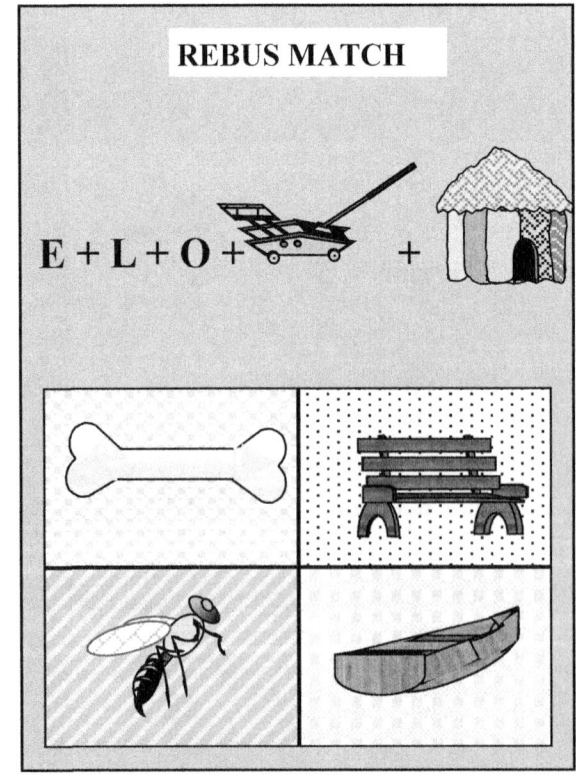

74

REBUS MATCH

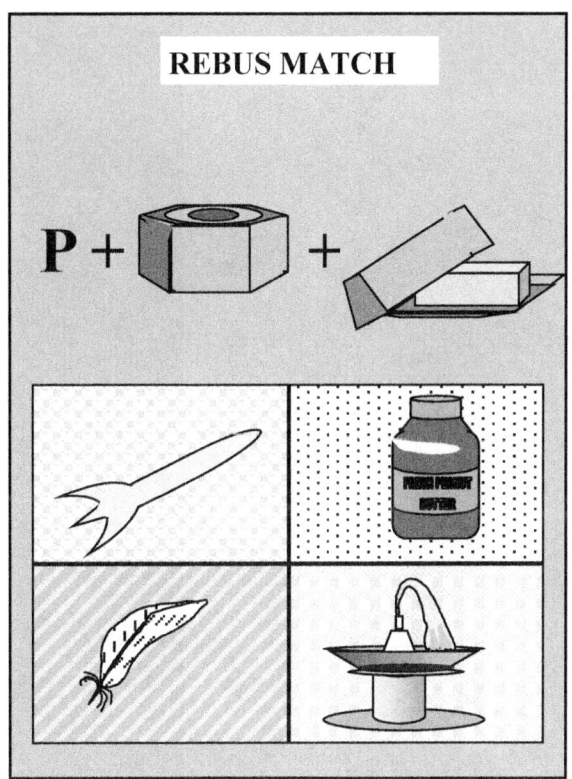

Directions: Decode the rebus and match it to the correct object in the section below the rebus.

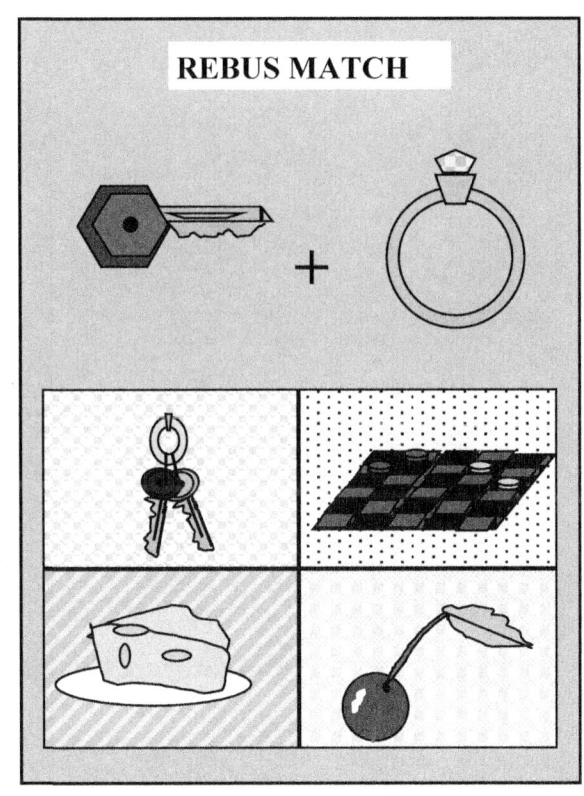

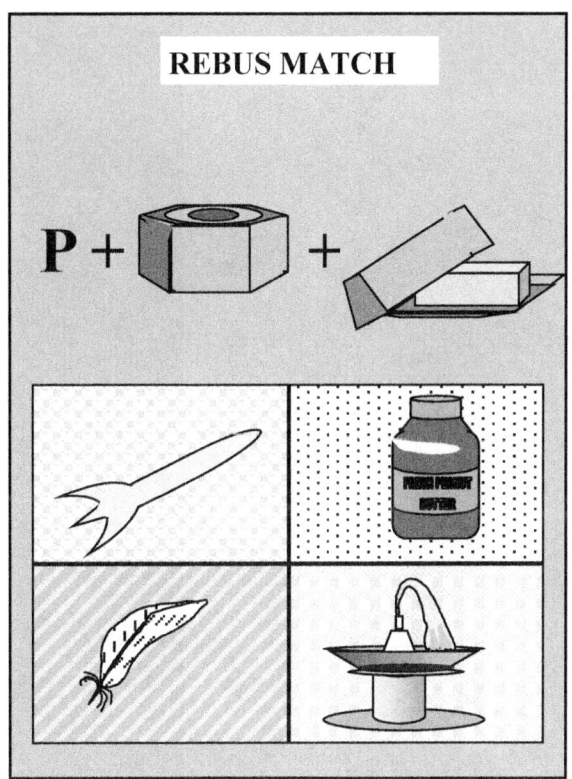

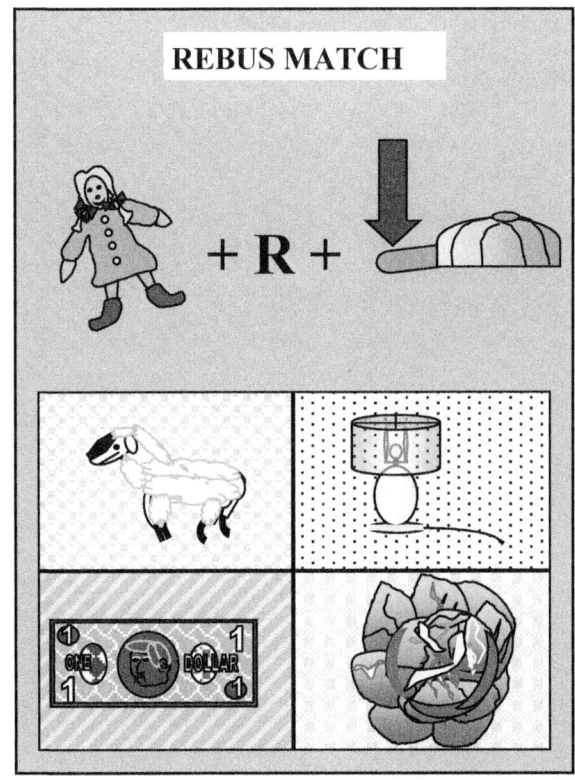

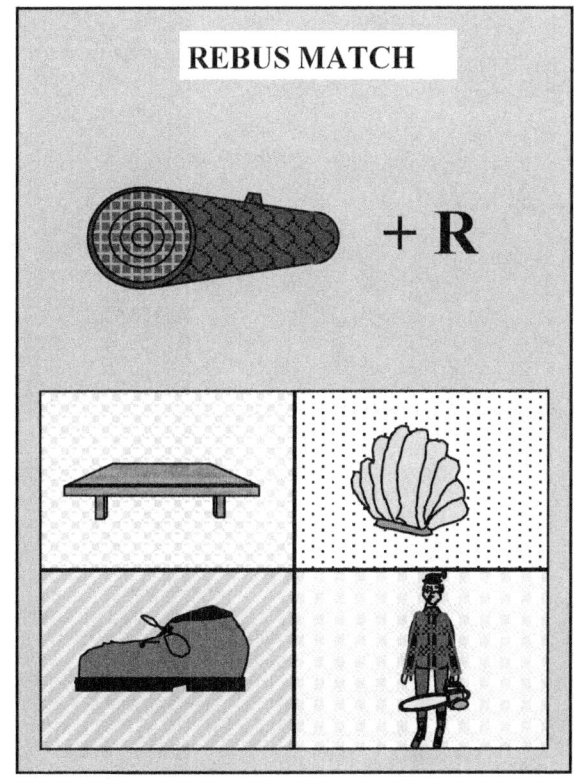

REBUS MATCH

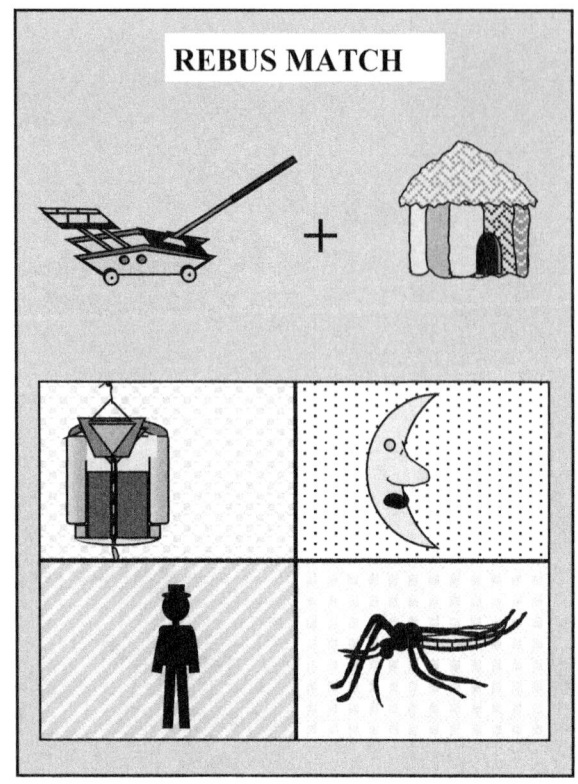

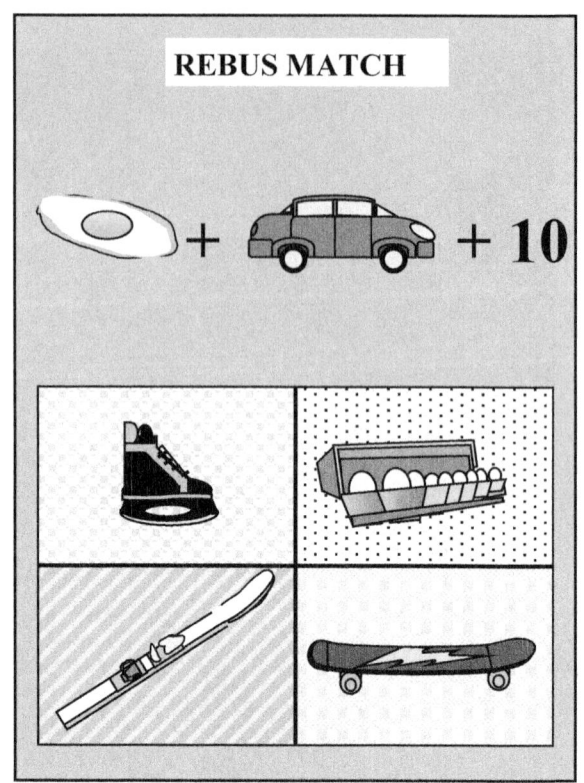

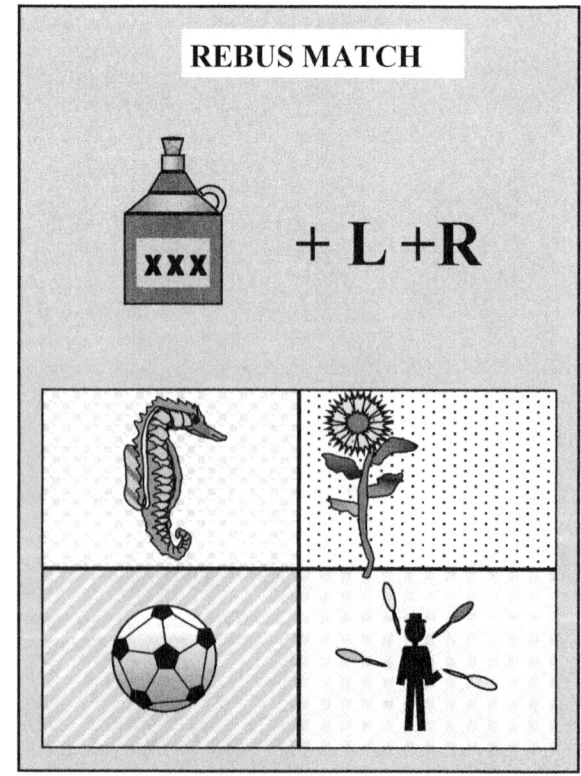

REBUS MATCH

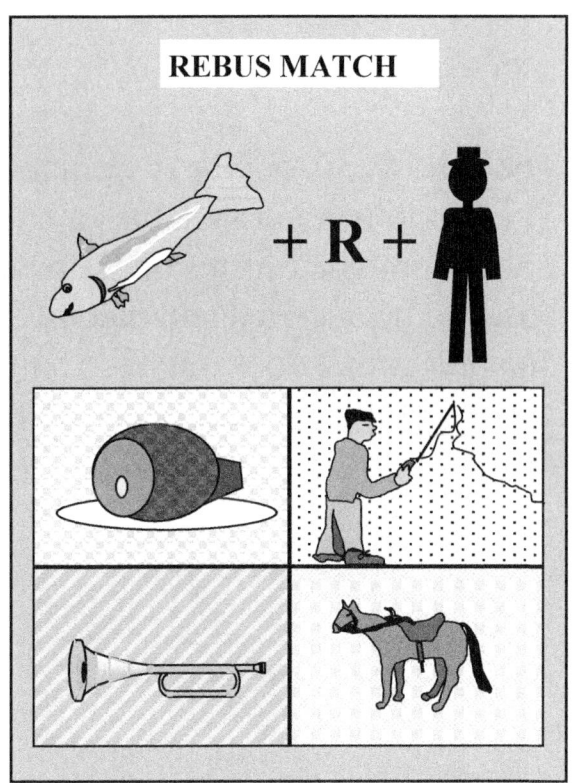

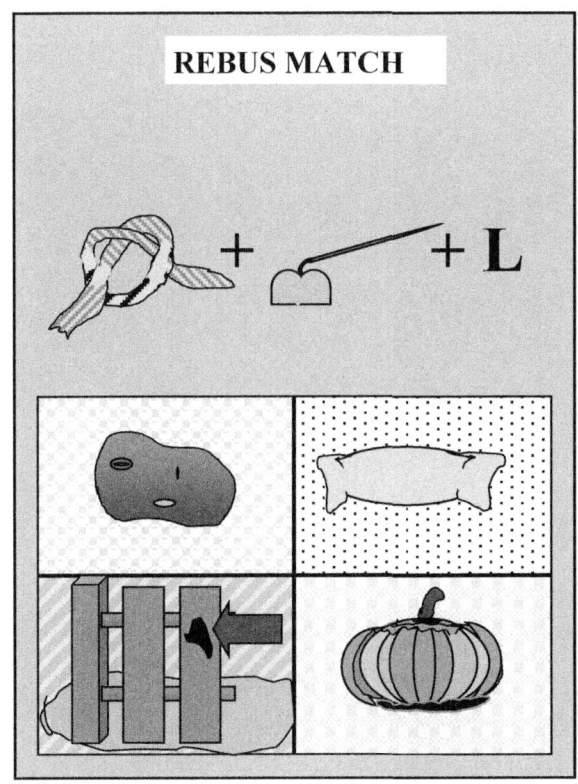

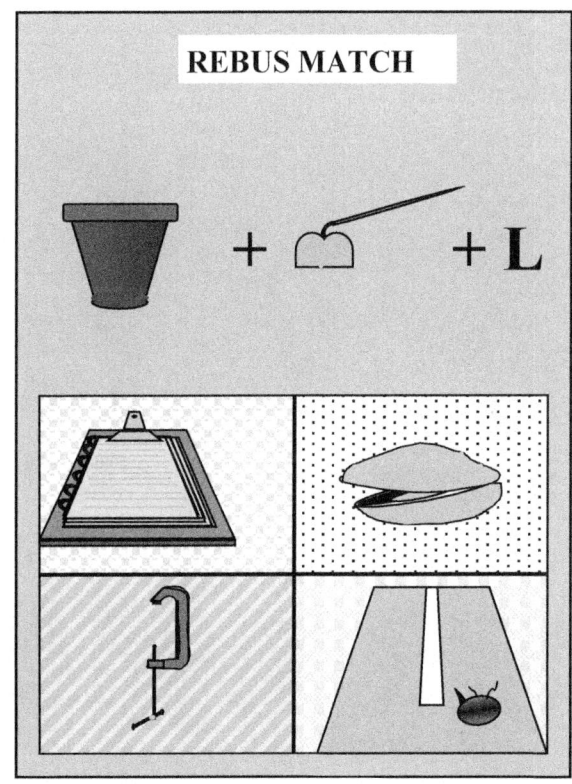

77

REBUS MATCH 2

The following activity is similar to the first REBUS MATCH game. The sound units or syllables are to be added together, left to right. These combined forms are known as rebuses. Each game has three rebuses to be decoded and matched to the objects below them. There is one object that does not have a matching rebus. The parent or teacher may want to help the child with these rebuses at first until he/ she understands.

REBUS MATCH 2

Directions: Decode the rebus words 1, 2 and 3, and match them to their objects to determine the object which does not have a matching rebus.

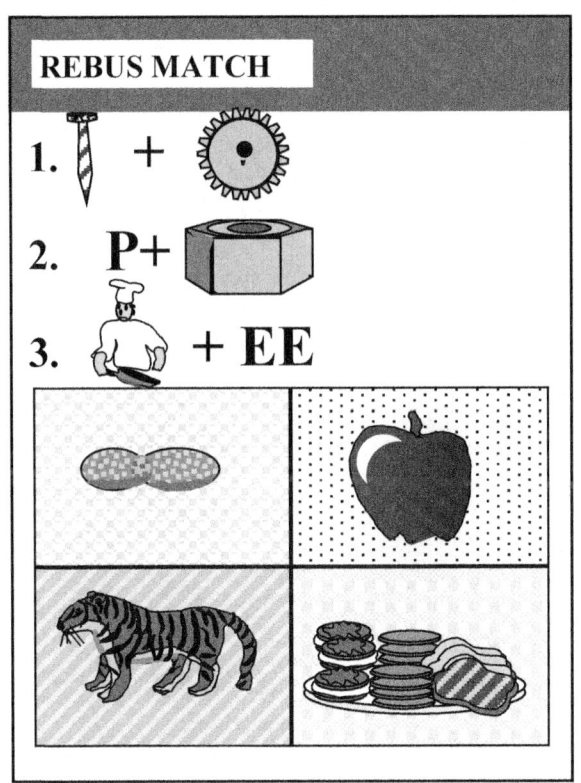

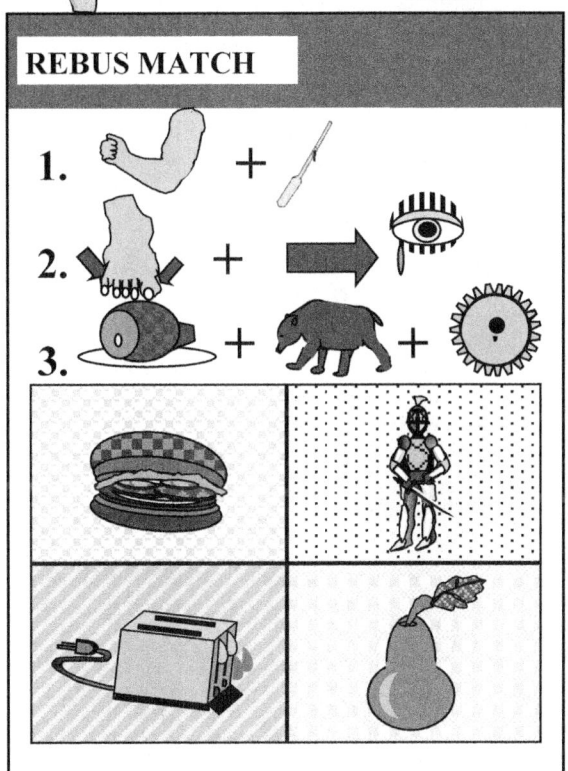

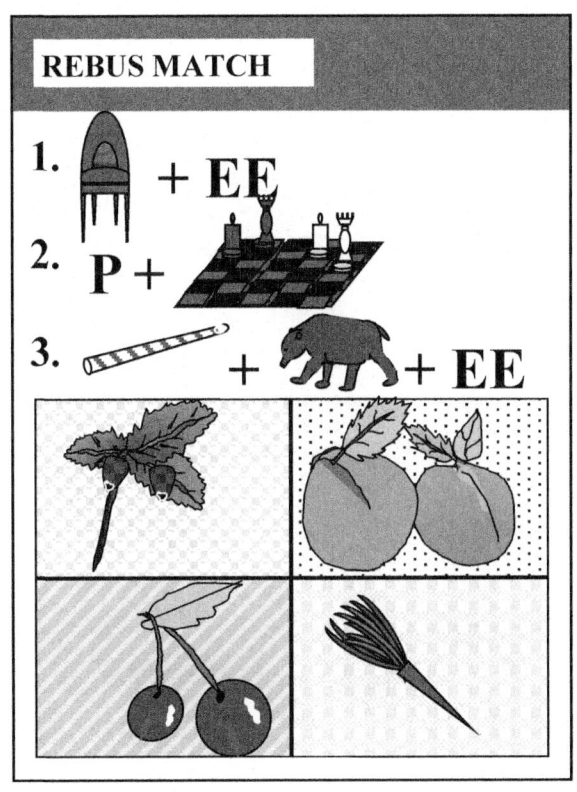

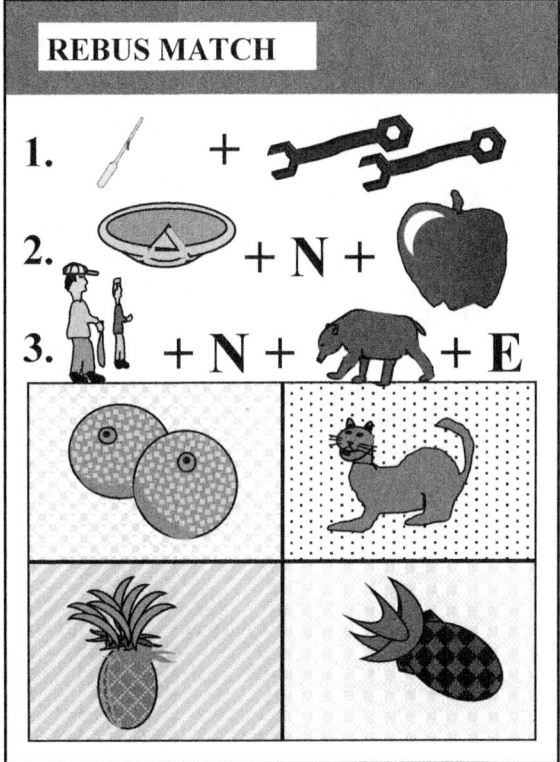

REBUS MATCH 2

Directions: Decode the rebus words 1, 2 and 3, and match them to their objects to determine the object which does not have a matching rebus.

 + O +  = bologna =

REBUS MATCH

1. Q +  +

2.  +

3. S +  +  + S

REBUS MATCH

1.  + L +  +

2.  +

3. C +  +

REBUS MATCH

1. 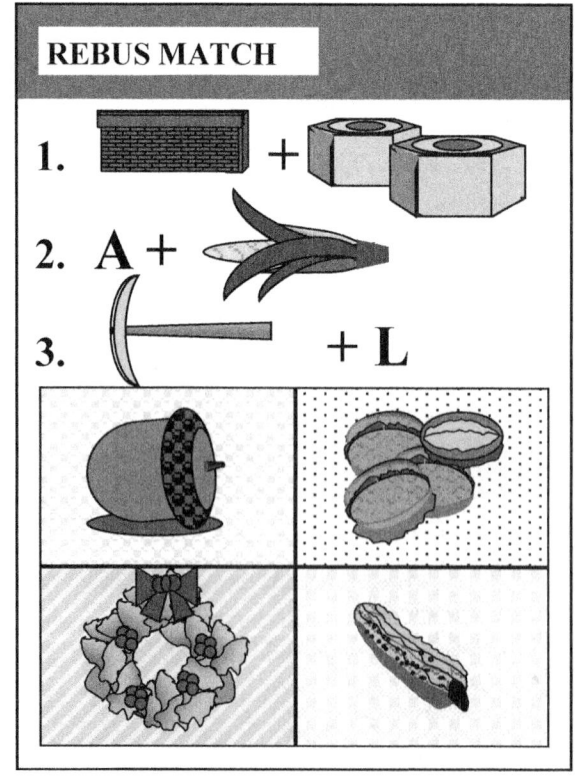 +

2. A +

3. + L

REBUS MATCH

1. L + F +

2.  +  + 8 +

3.  +  + E

80

REBUS MATCH 2

Directions: Decode the rebus words 1,2 and 3, and match them to their objects to determine the object which does not have a matching rebus.

🐂 + O + 🔨 ⬅ = bologna = 🌭

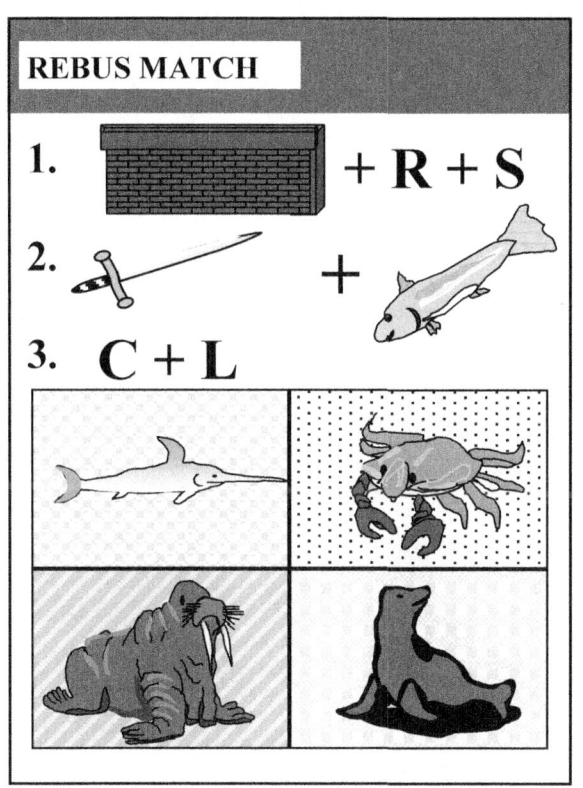

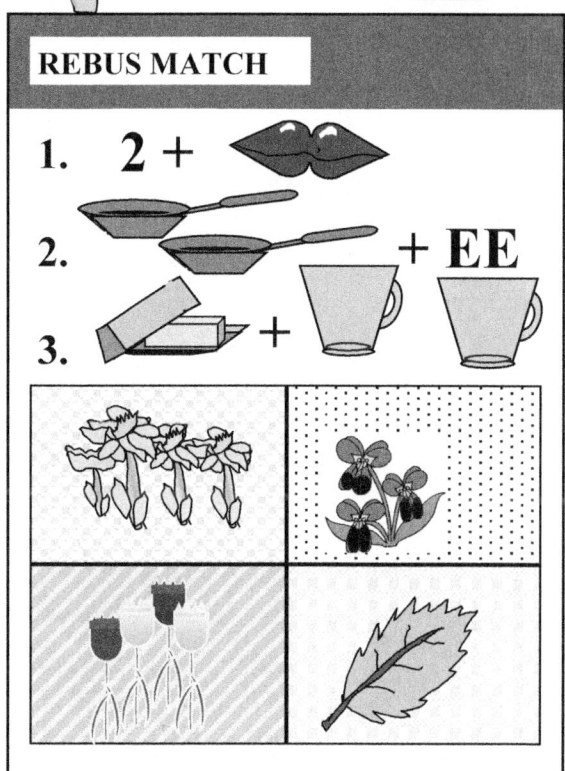

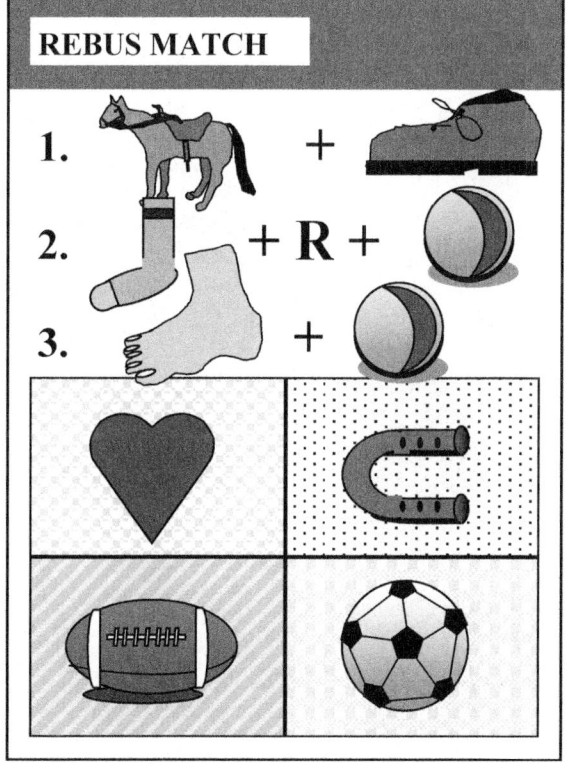

81

REBUS MATCH 2

Directions: Decode the rebus words 1,2 and 3, and match them to their objects to determine the object which does not have a matching rebus.

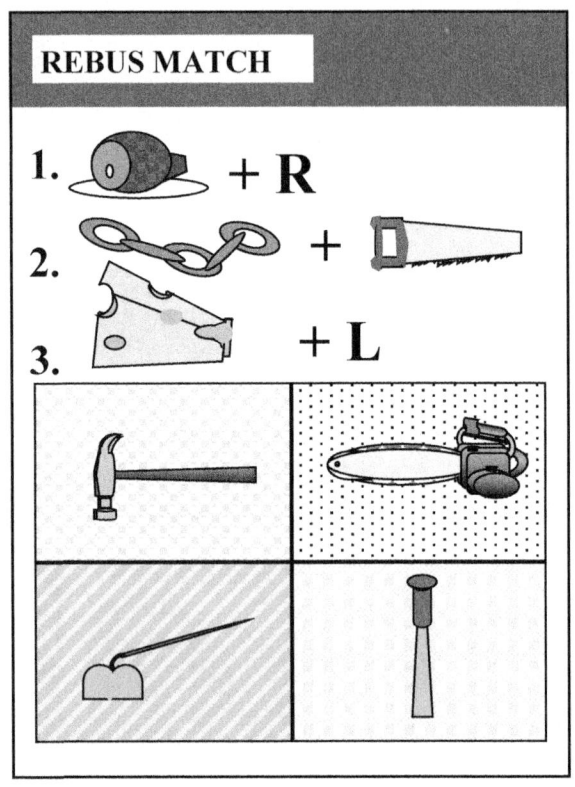

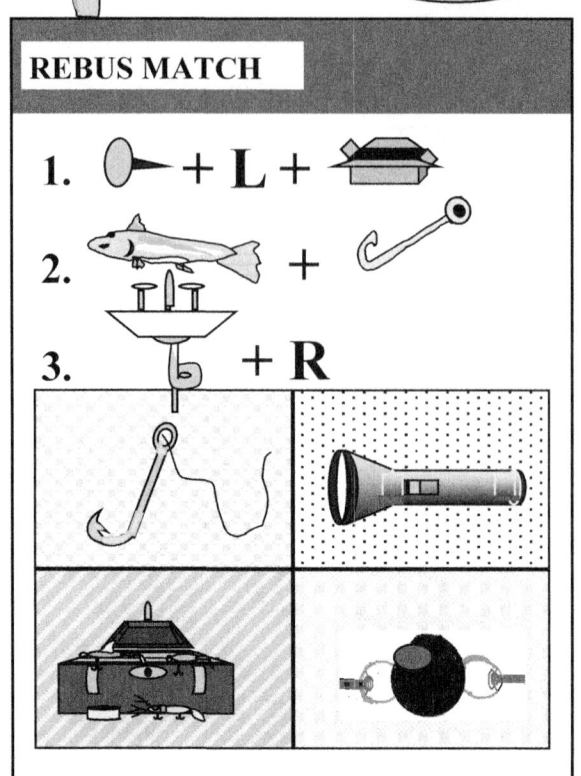

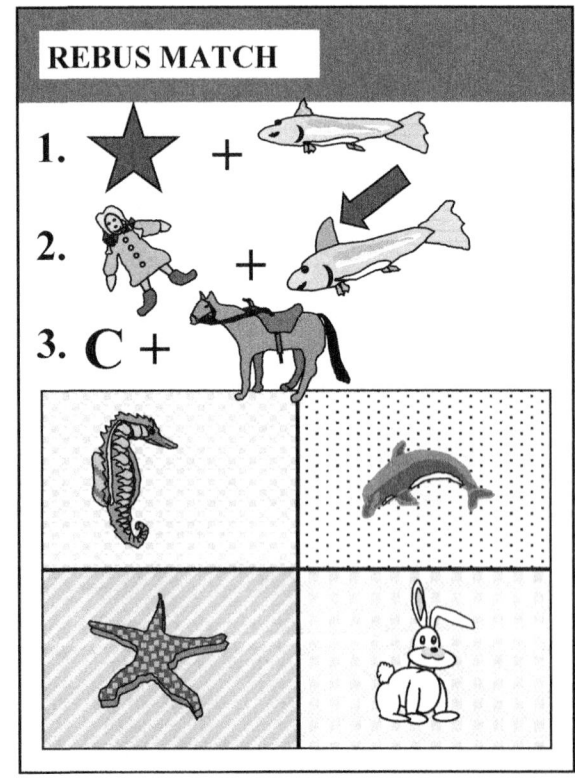

REBUS MATCH 2

Directions: Decode the rebus words 1,2 and 3, and match them to their objects to determine the object which does not have a matching rebus.

🐂 + O + 🔫 ⬅ = bologna = 🌭

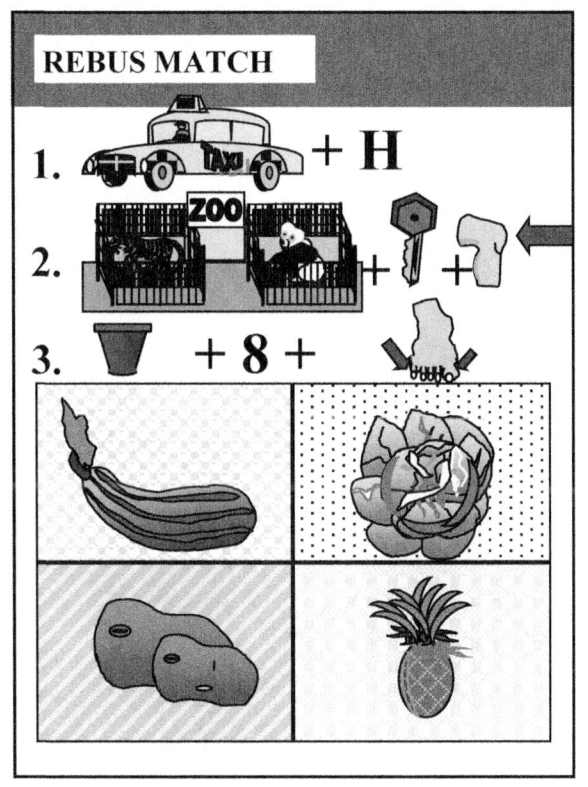

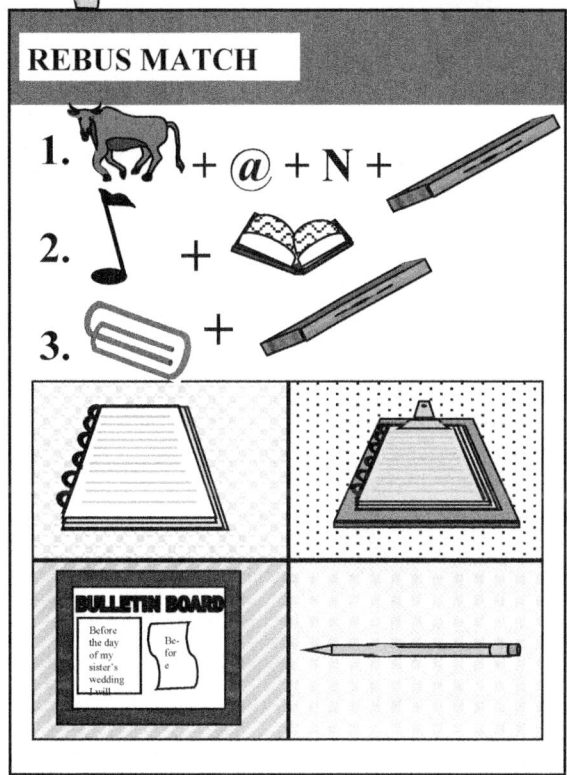

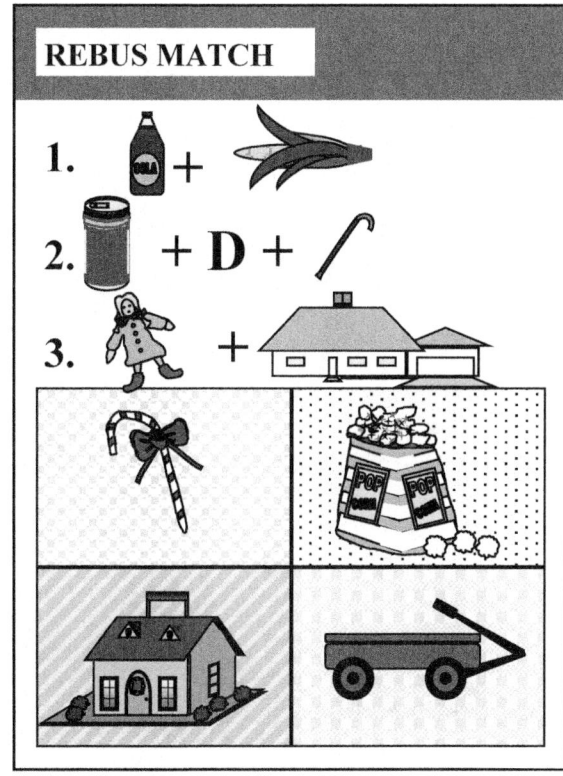

REBUS MATCH 2

Directions: Decode the rebus words 1,2 and 3, and match them to their objects to determine the object which does not have a matching rebus.

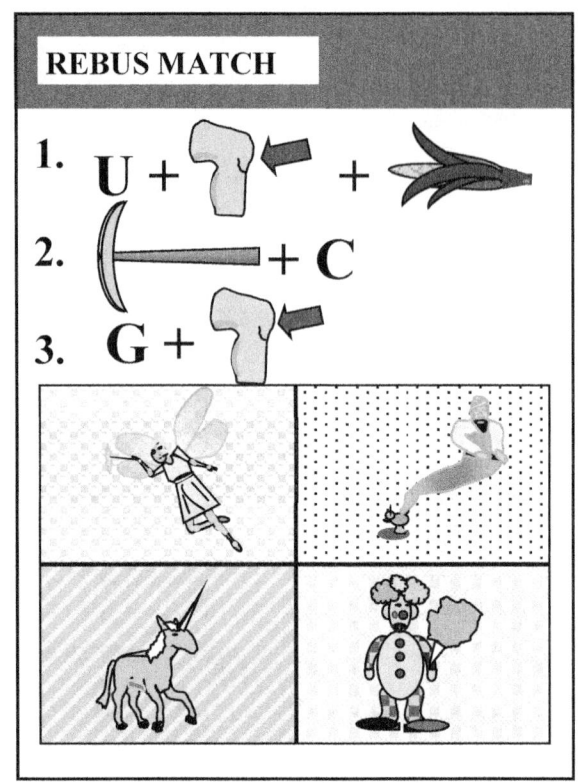

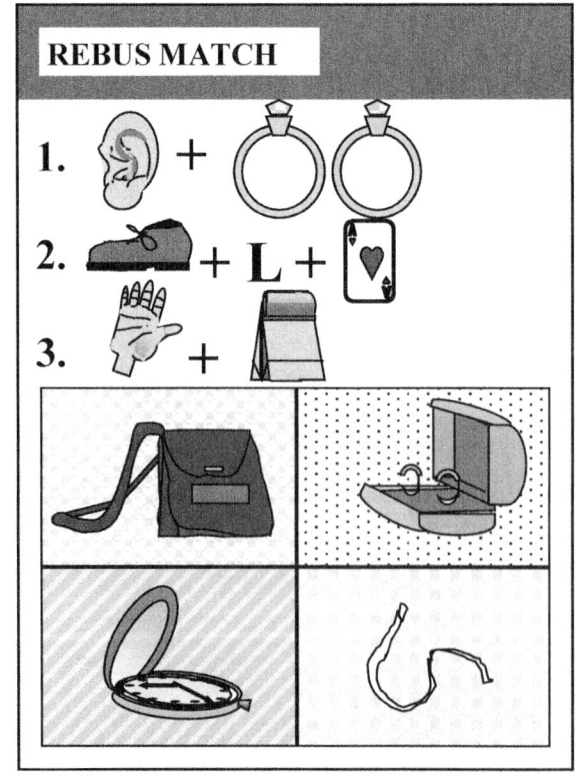

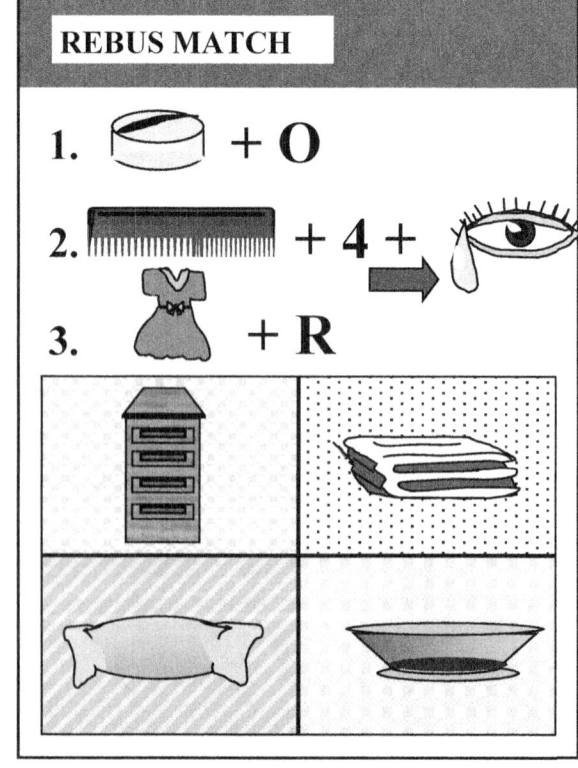

REBUS MATCH 2

Directions: Decode the rebus words 1, 2 and 3, and match them to their objects to determine the object which does not have a matching rebus.

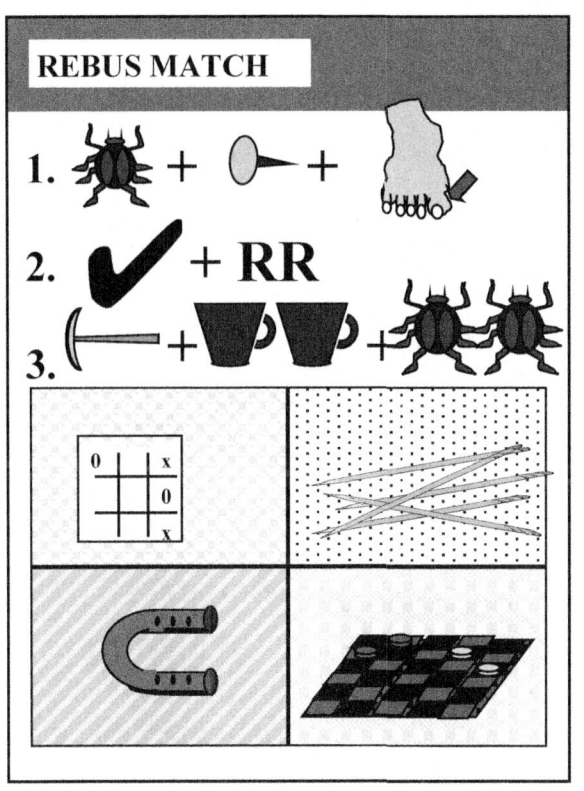 + O + 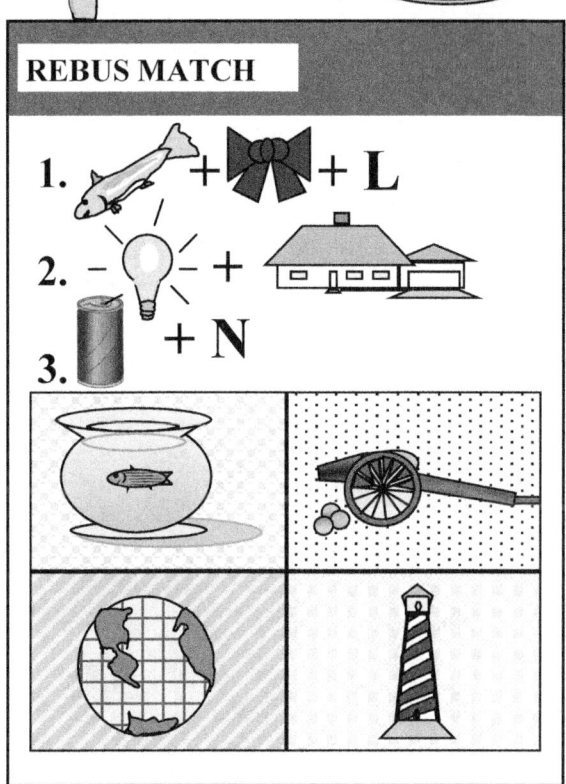 = bologna =

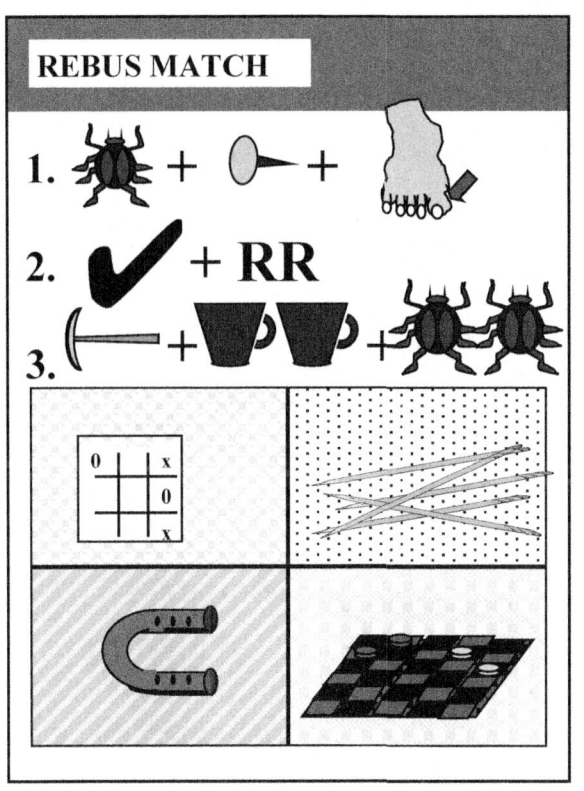

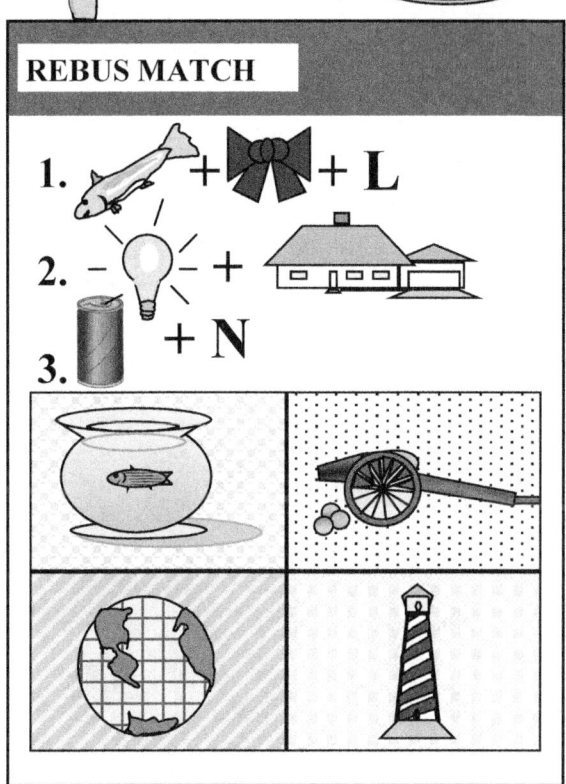

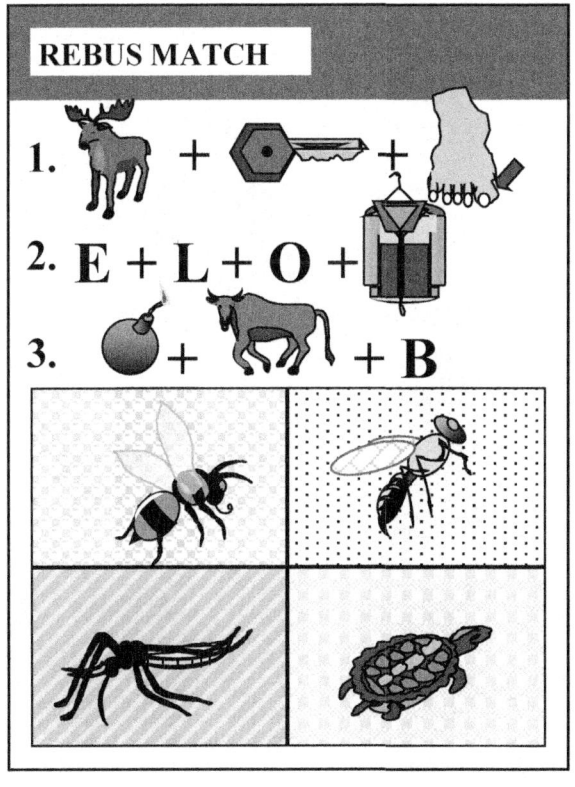

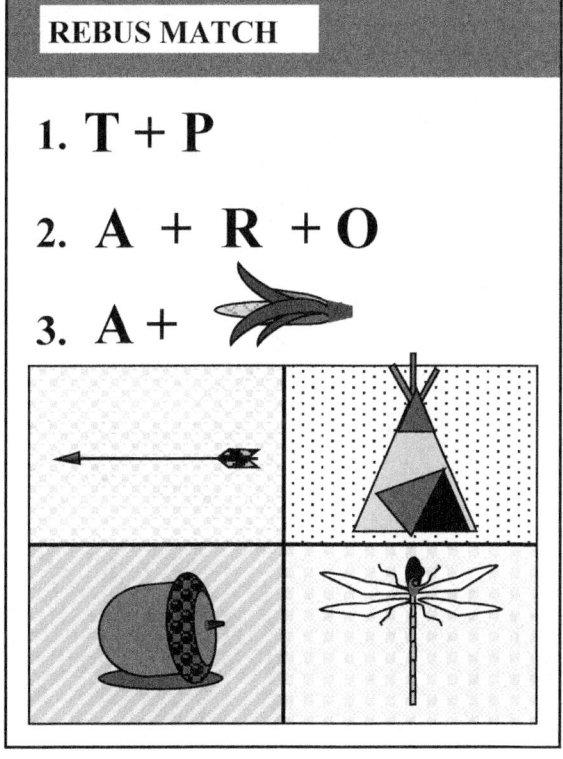

REBUS MATCH 2

Directions: Decode the rebus words 1, 2 and 3, and match them to their objects to determine the object which does not have a matching rebus.

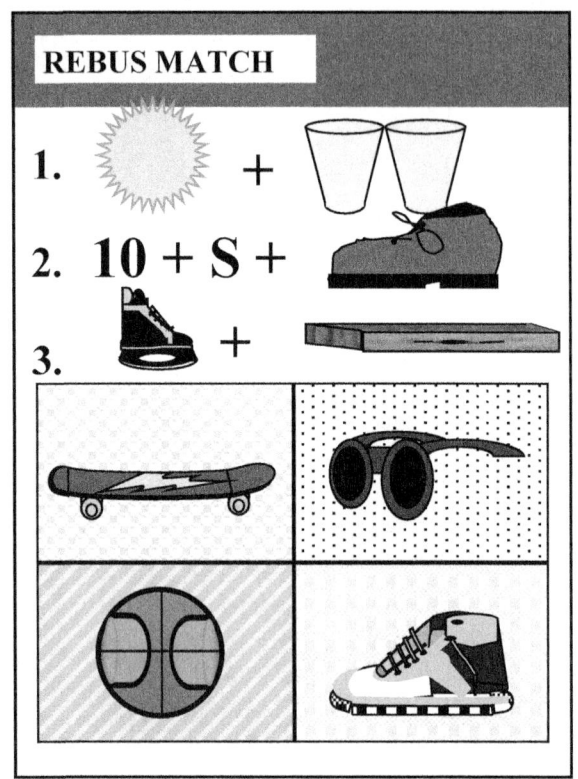

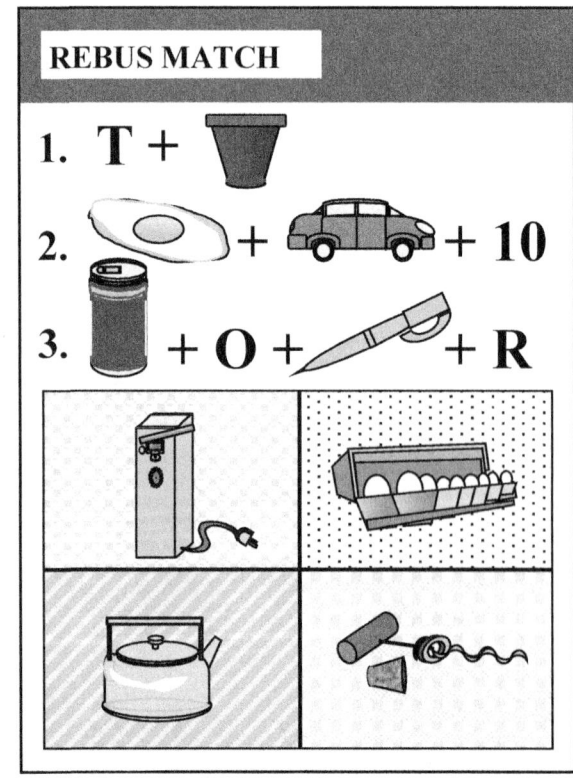

86

REBUS MATCH 2

+ O + ⬅ = bologna =

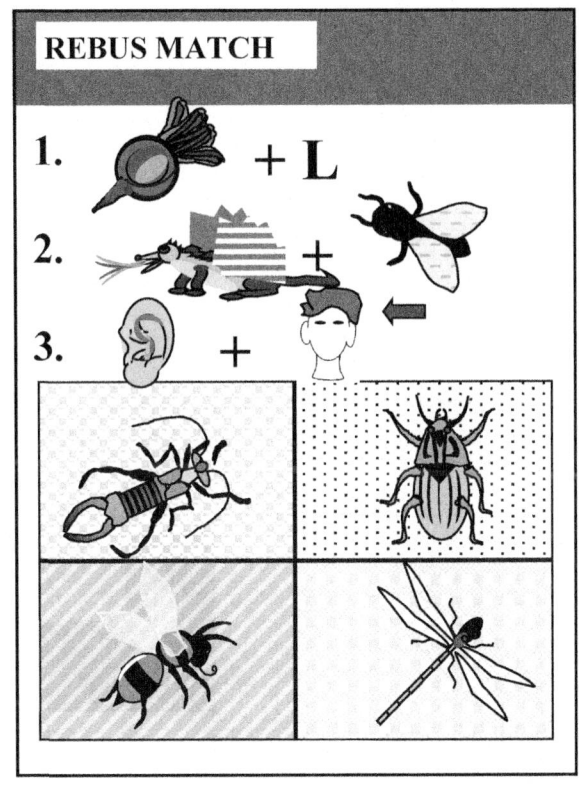

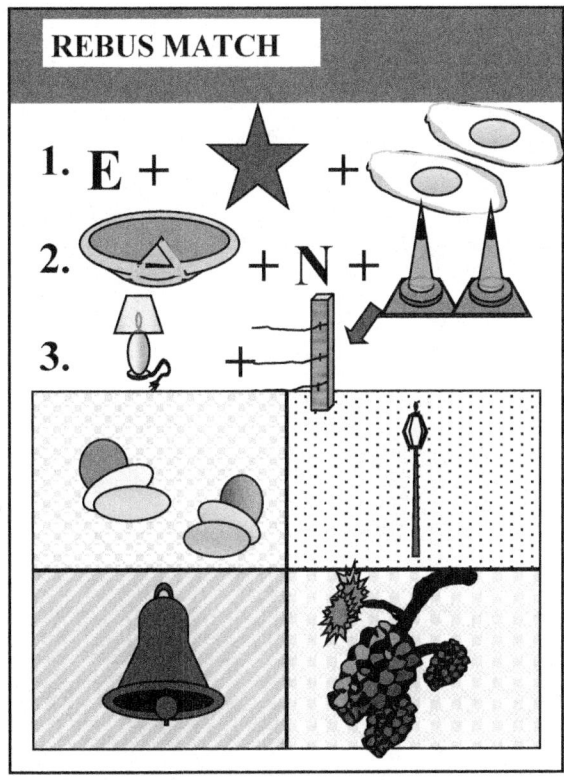

87

REBUS MATCH 2

Directions: Decode the rebus words 1,2 and 3, and match them to their objects to determine the object which does not have a matching rebus.

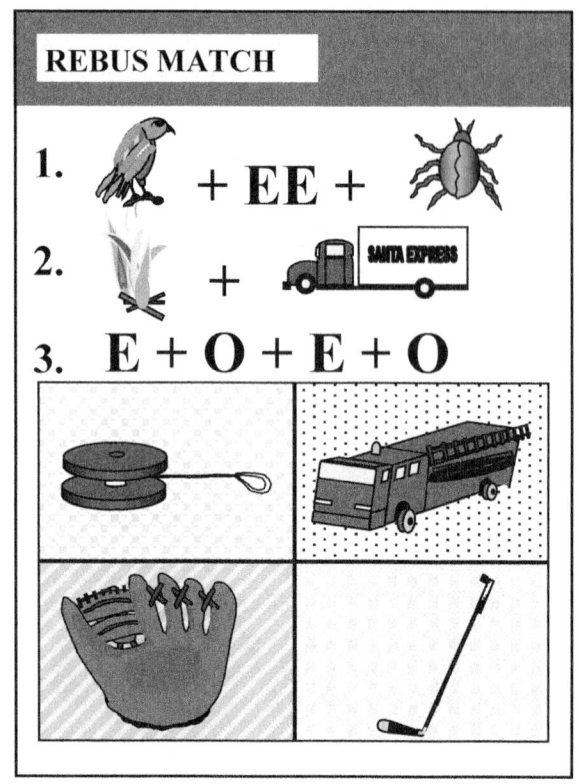

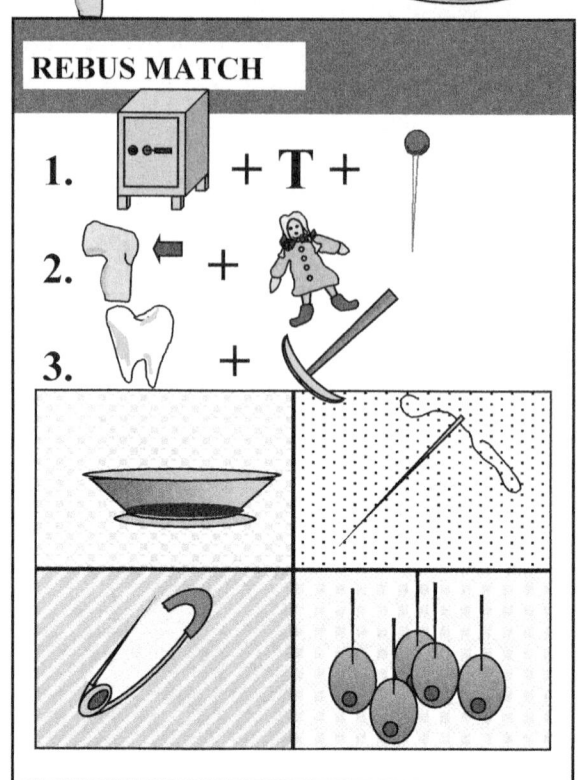

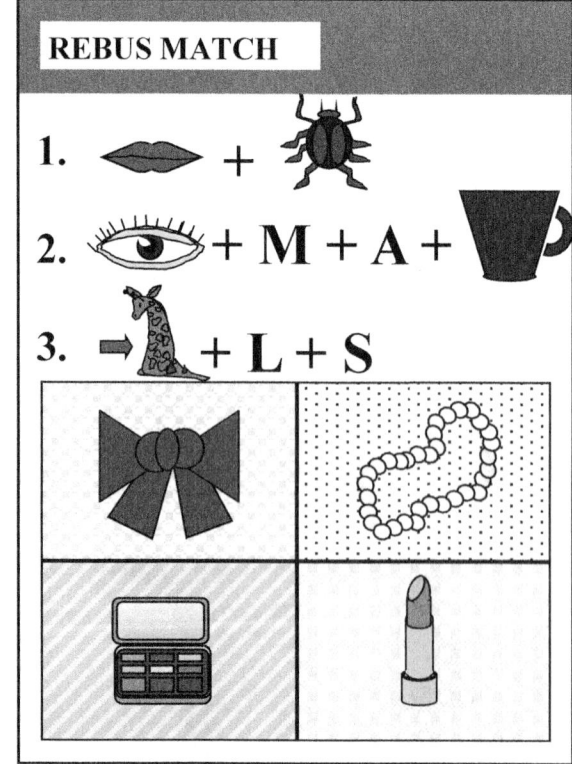

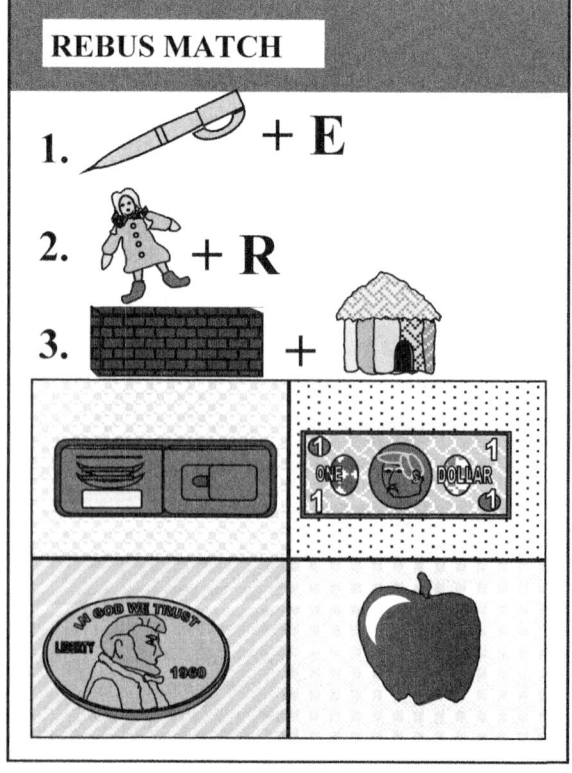

SUBTRACTION

The following activity is more difficult than earlier tasks. The student is required to remove the onset form of the word and pronounce the remaining rhyming ending which will also be a word.

At first, the parent or teacher may pronounce the letter or clusters to be removed and also the object. Then ask the child to say the word that is left when the preceding letters are taken away. The symbol for no ⊘ is used to designate subtraction or removal of a letter or letters.

Eventually, the desired goal is to have the child do this activity with the parent or teacher as an observer who corrects the incorrect guesses (attempts).

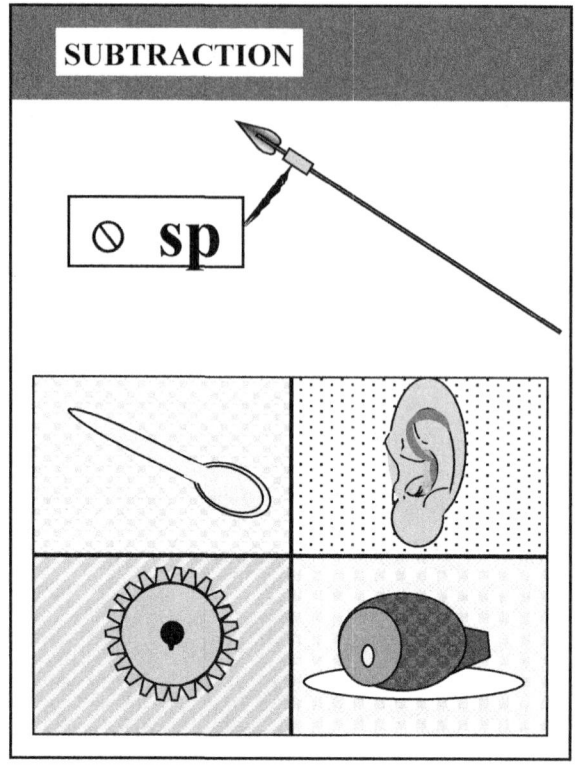

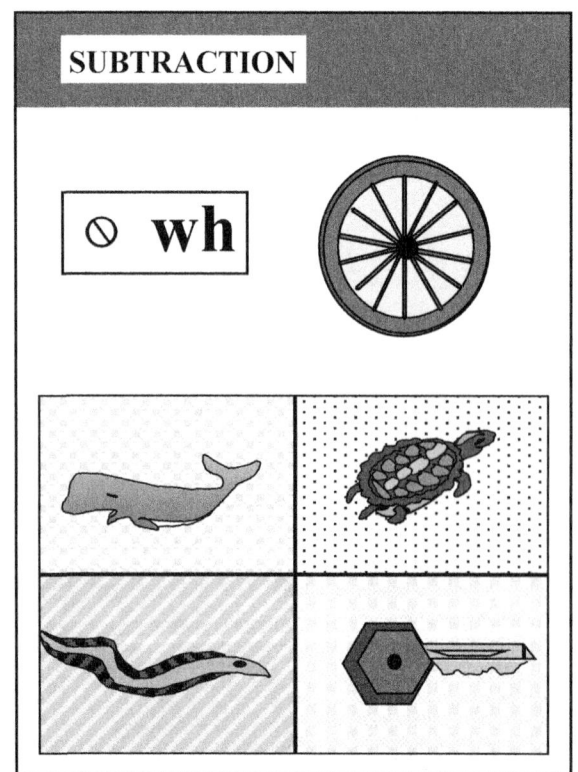

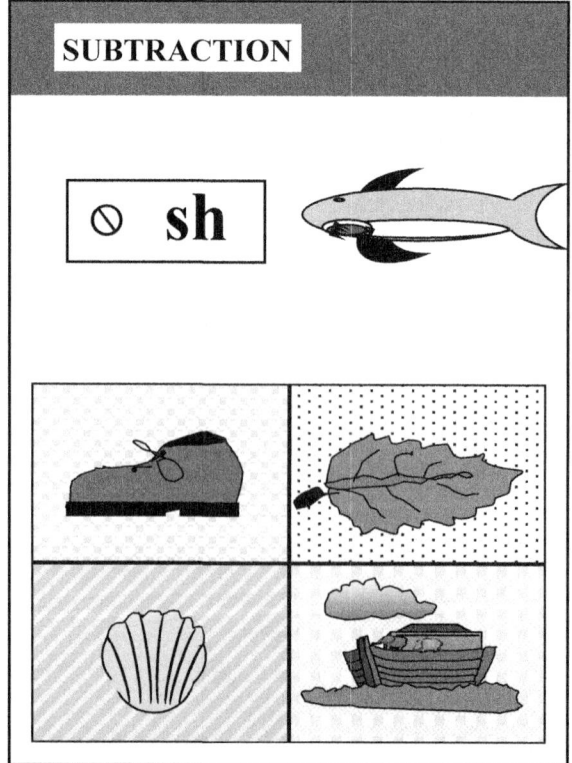

SUBTRACTION

⊘ d

SUBTRACTION

⊘ b

$1.00

SUBTRACTION

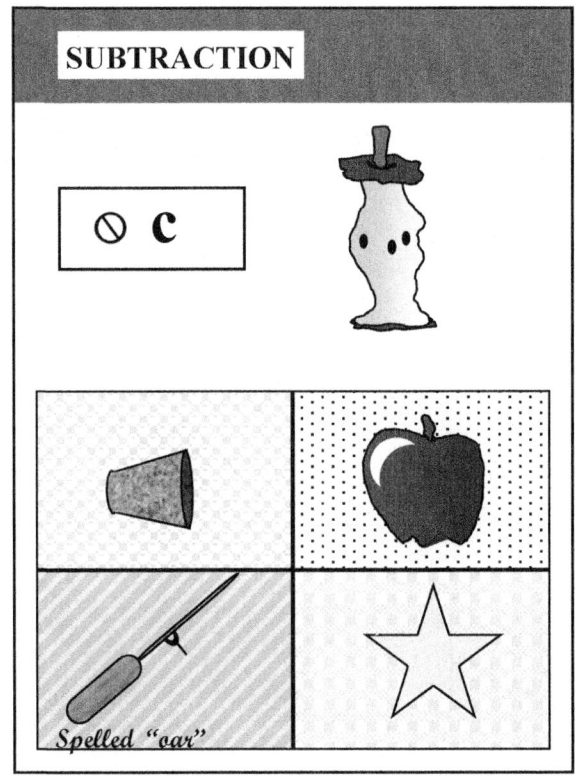

⊘ c

Spelled "oar"

SUBTRACTION

⊘ r

91

Directions: One of the four objects in each section is the answer to subtraction of one or more initial letters from the front of the word.

SUBTRACTION

⊘ c

SUBTRACTION

⊘ f

SUBTRACTION

⊘ g

SUBTRACTION

⊘ l

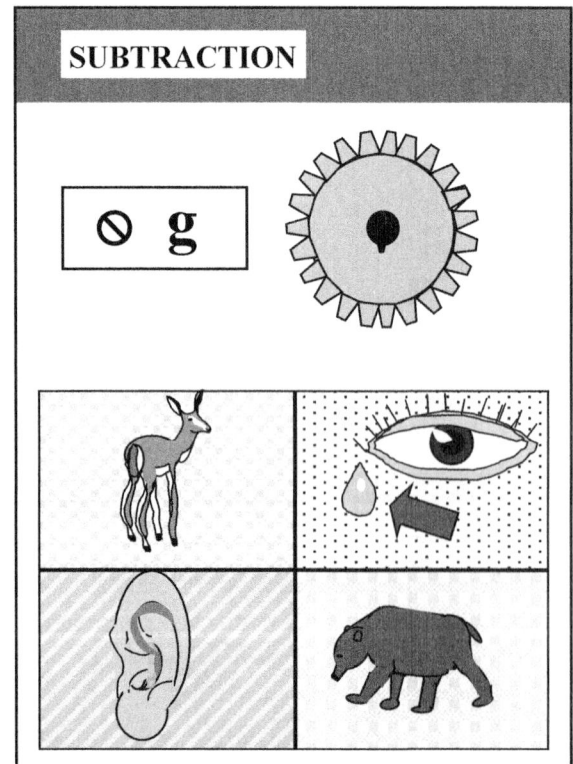

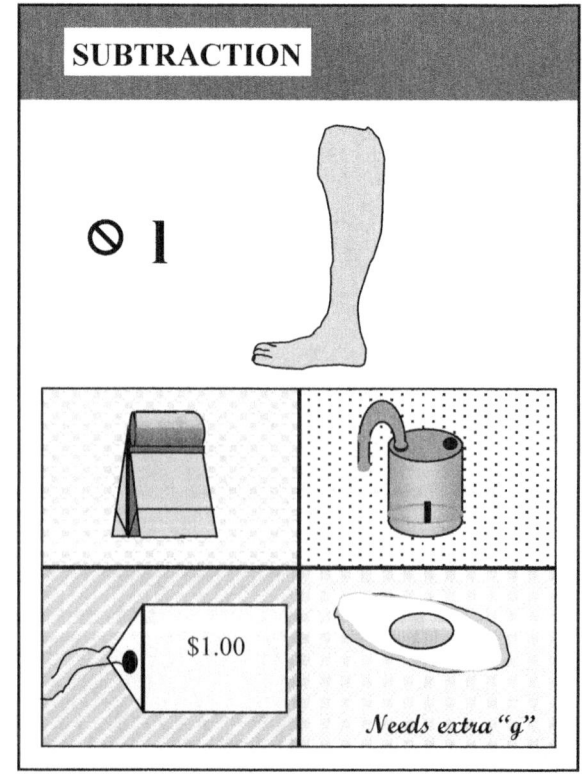

$1.00

Needs extra "g"

92

Directions: One of the four objects in each section is the answer to subtraction of one or more intitial letters from the front of the word.

SUBTRACTION

⊘ h

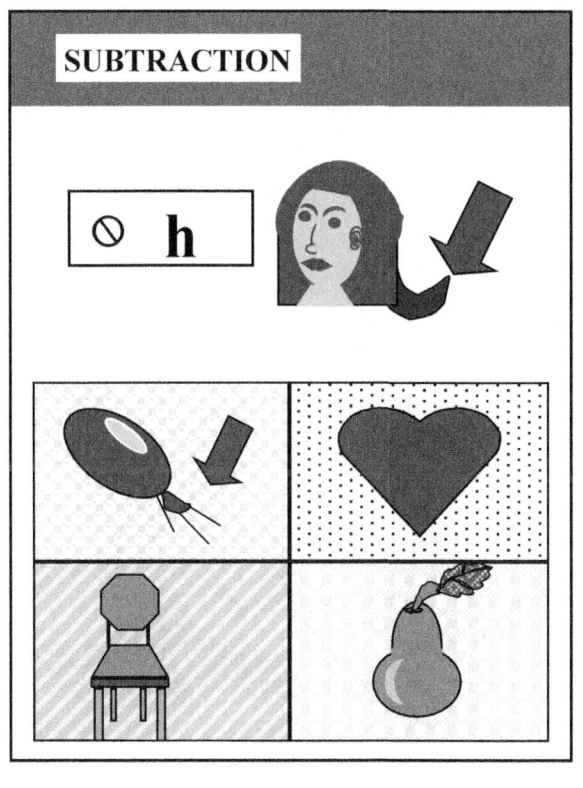

SUBTRACTION

⊘ k

Needs extra "g"

SUBTRACTION

⊘ t

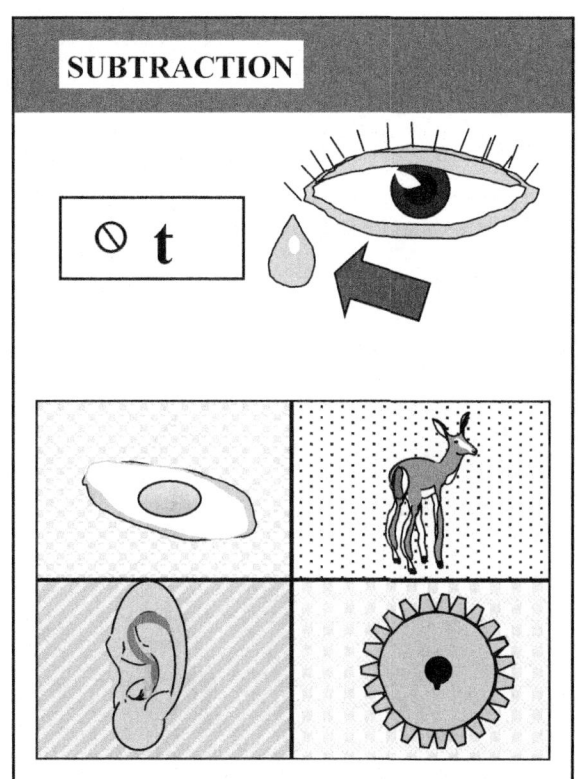

SUBTRACTION

⊘ t

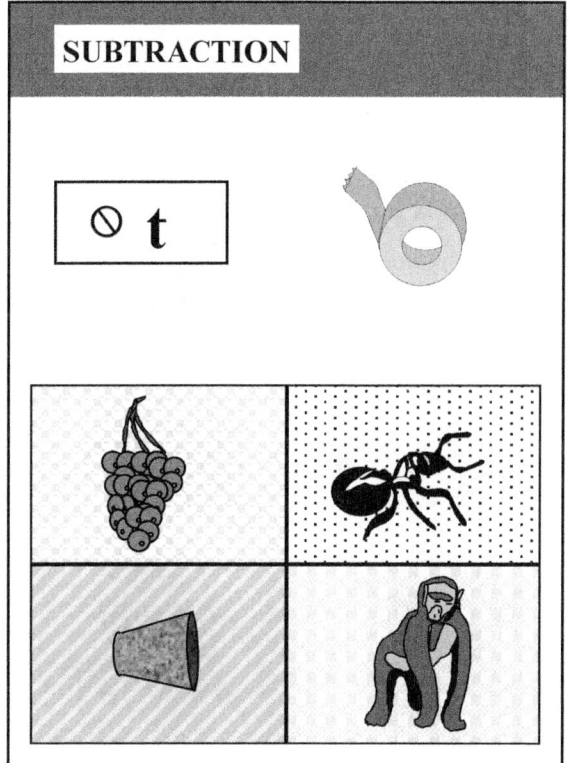

93

SUBTRACTION

SUBTRACTION

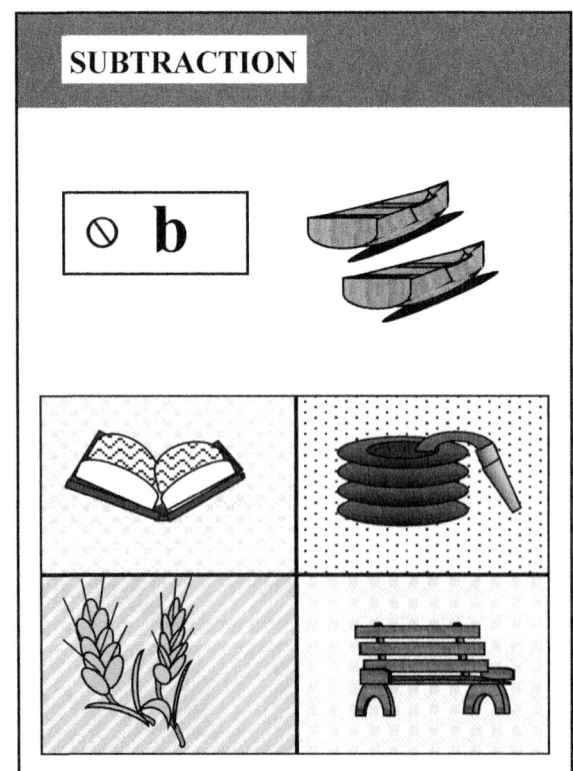

SUBTRACTION

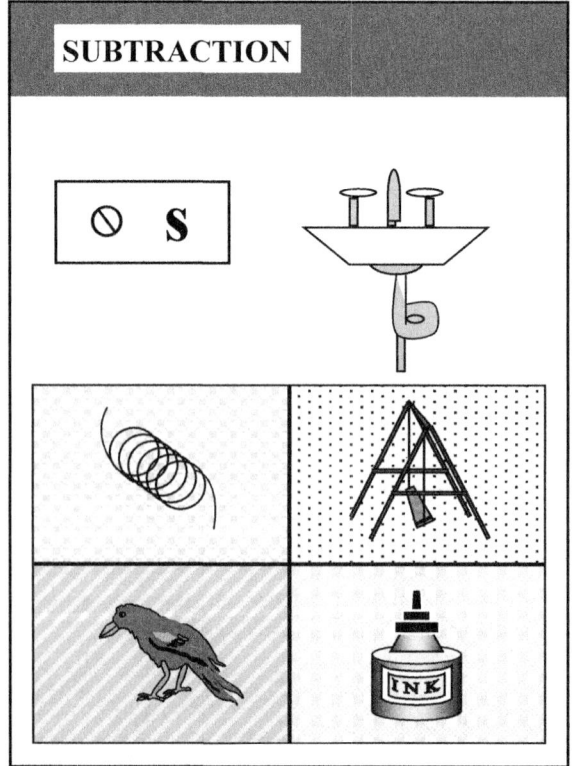

94

SUBTRACTION

⊘ **h**

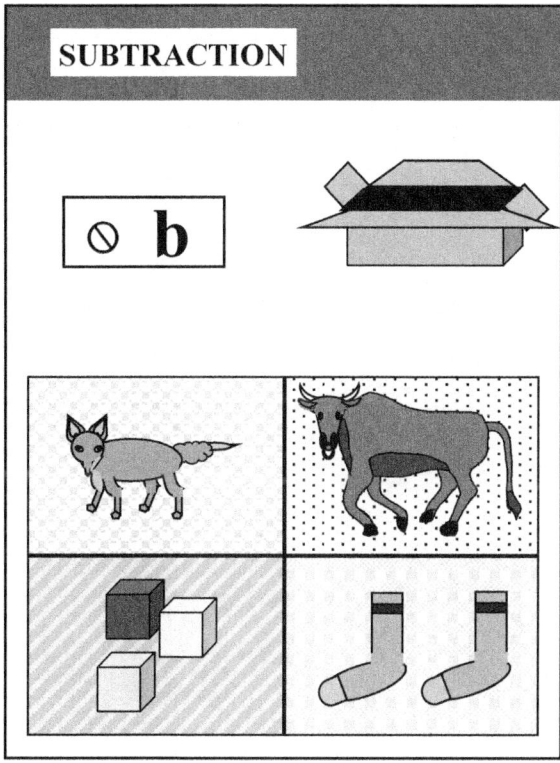

SUBTRACTION

⊘ **b**

SUBTRACTION

⊘ **f**

SUBTRACTION

⊘ **f**

95

SUBTRACTION

⊘ **c**

SUBTRACTION

⊘ **f**

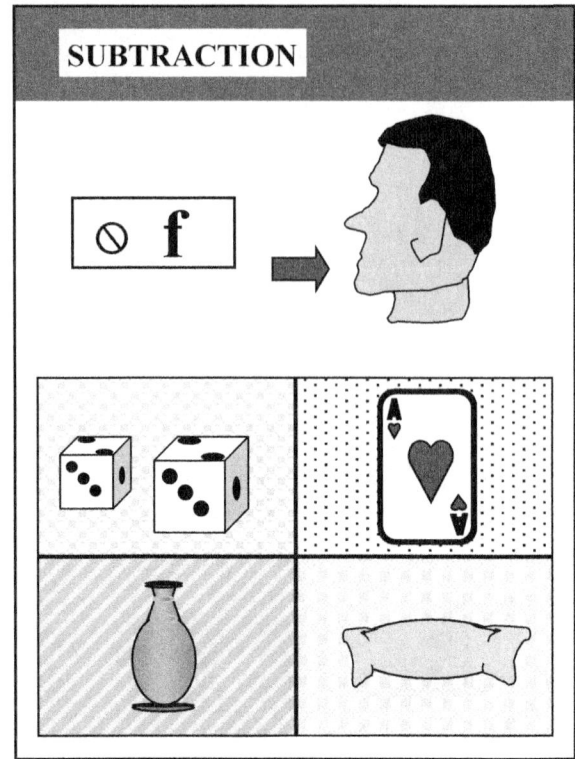

SUBTRACTION

⊘ **g**

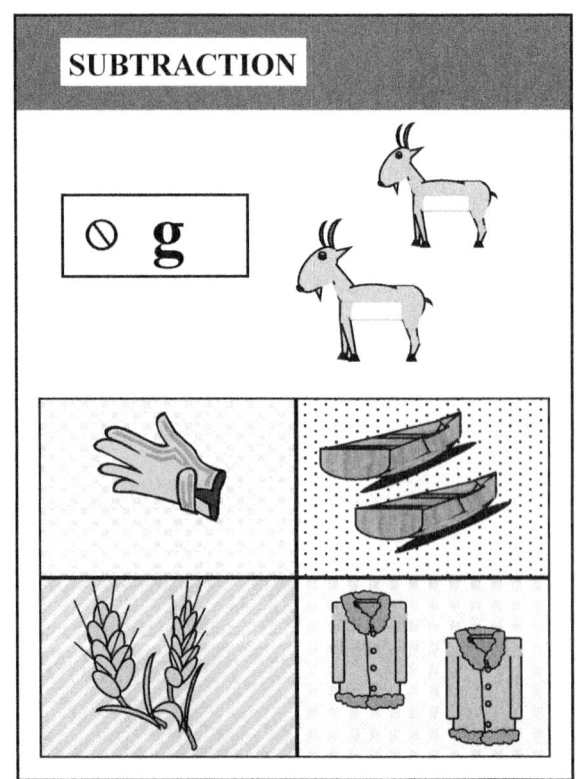

SUBTRACTION

⊘ **p**

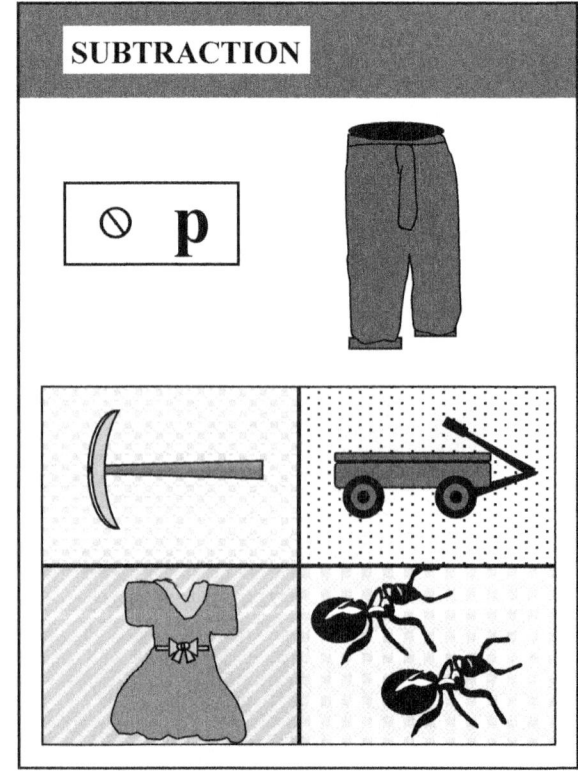

Directions: One of the four objects in each section is the answer to subtraction of one or more intitial letters from the front of the word.

SUBTRACTION

⊘ **t**

Spelled different

SUBTRACTION

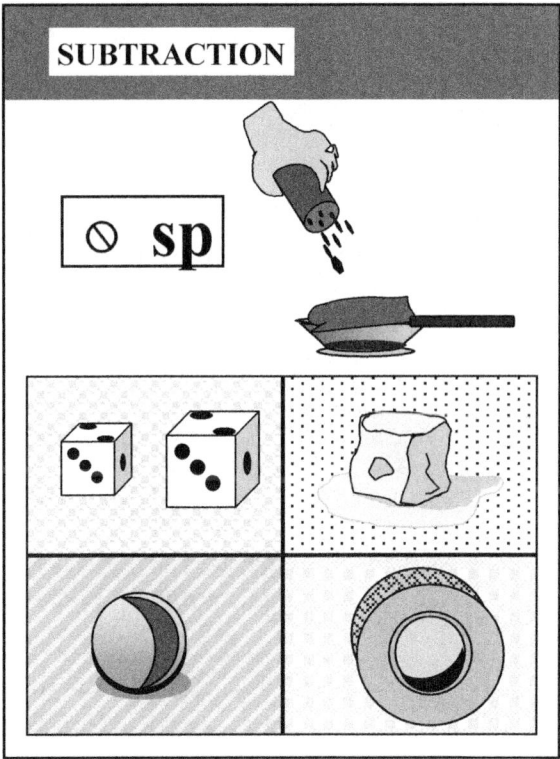

⊘ **sp**

SUBTRACTION

⊘ **s**

Spelled different

SUBTRACTION

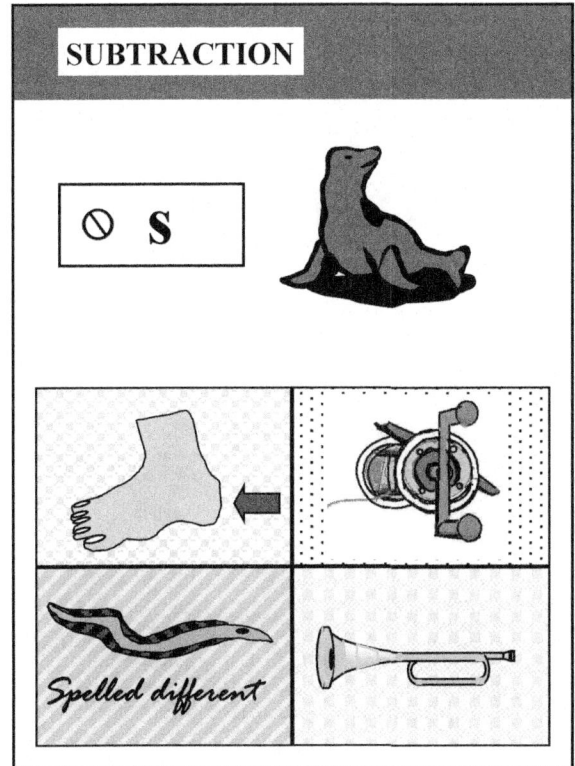

⊘ **d**

Spelled different

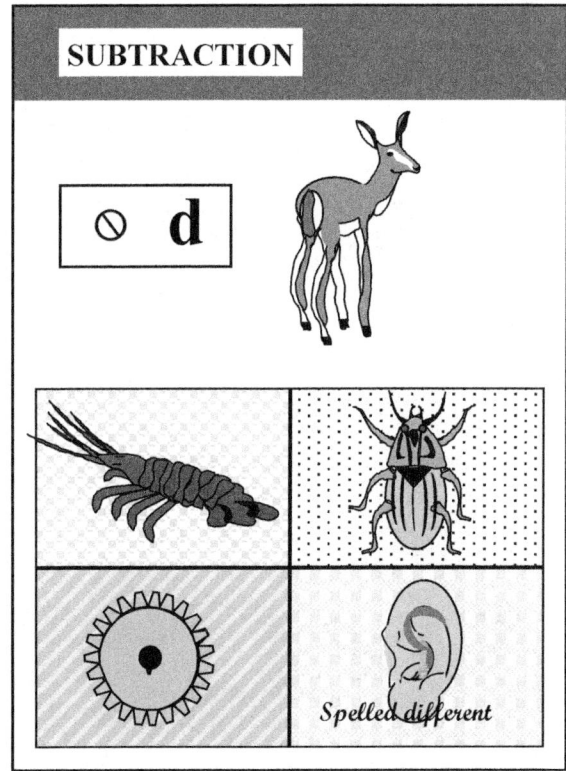

SUBTRACTION

⊘ **pl**

SUBTRACTION

⊘ **sh**

SUBTRACTION

⊘ **ch**

SUBTRACTION

⊘ **sh**

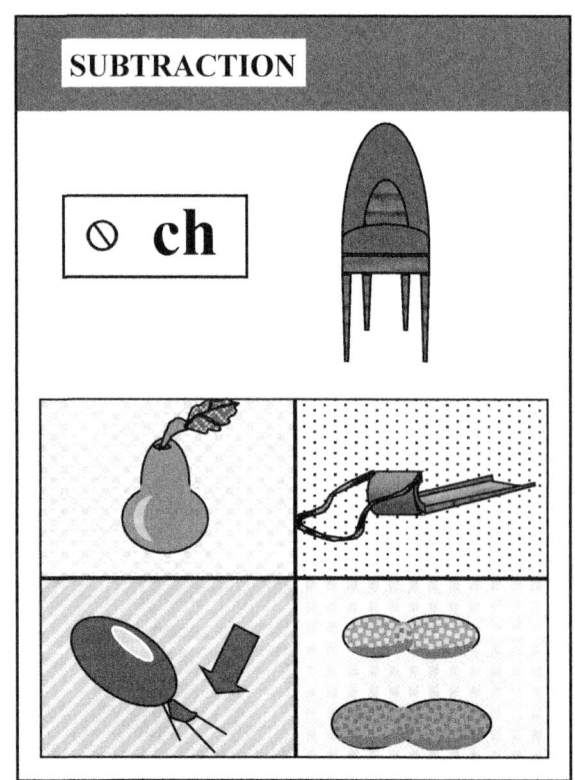

98

SUBTRACTION

⊘ c

SUBTRACTION

⊘ sp

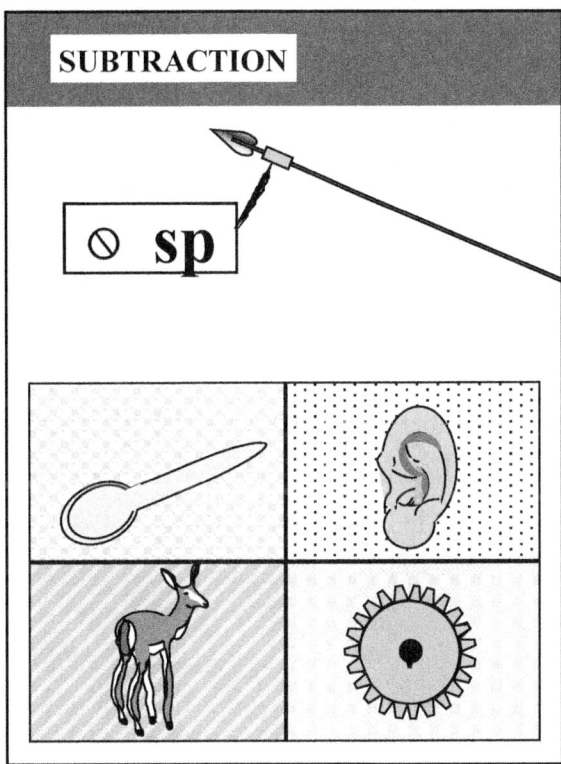

SUBTRACTION

⊘ wh

SUBTRACTION

⊘ sp

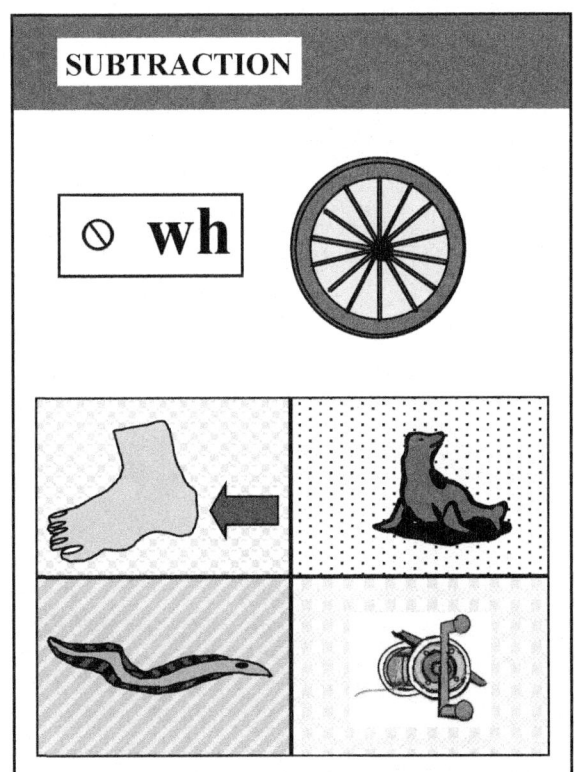

SUBSTITUTION

The following activities require the student to substitute or exchange one letter or set of letters for others. The parent or teacher may wish to help the child to begin. Pronounce the object following the letters and then tell him/her to substitute orally one letter or set of letters for the other. The symbol for **greater than** > is used to show the direction the one letter or letter set is moving to be exchanged or substituted for the other. In time, the child will become more proficient in doing this activity and eventually be able to perform the tasks with minimal supervision with the parent or teacher available just for the purpose of hinting or correcting.

SUBSTITUTION

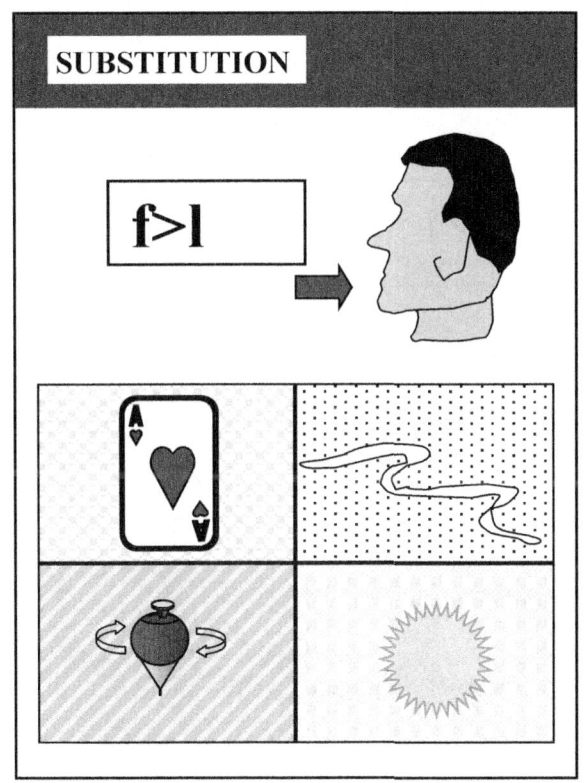

SUBSTITUTION

SUBSTITUTION

SUBSTITUTION

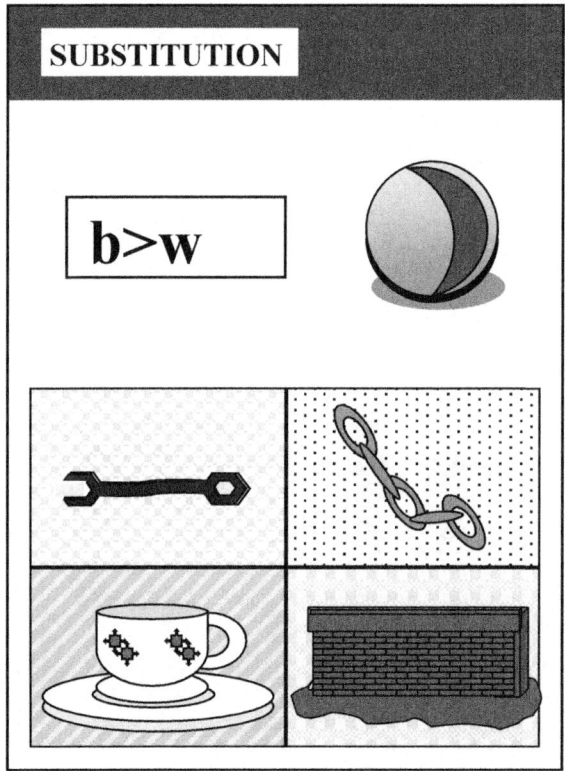

101

Directions: One of the four objects in each section is the answer to substituting one intitial letter for another.

SUBSTITUTION

b>w

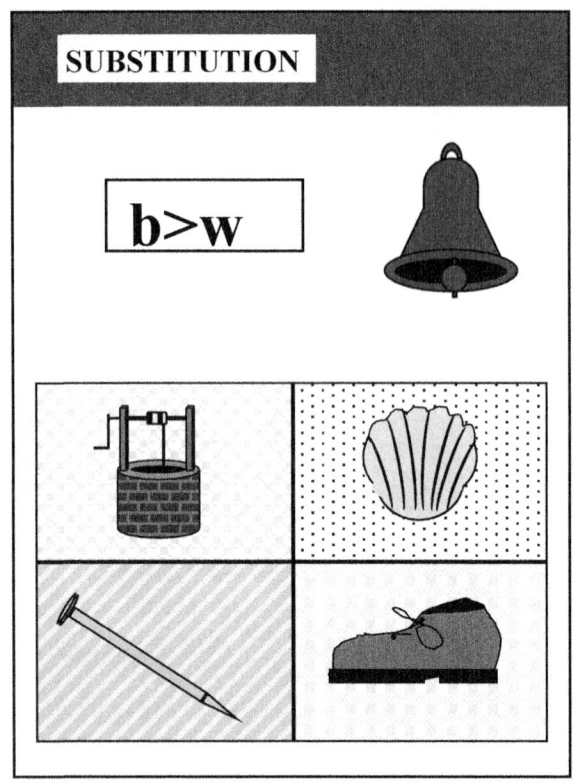

SUBSTITUTION

g>t

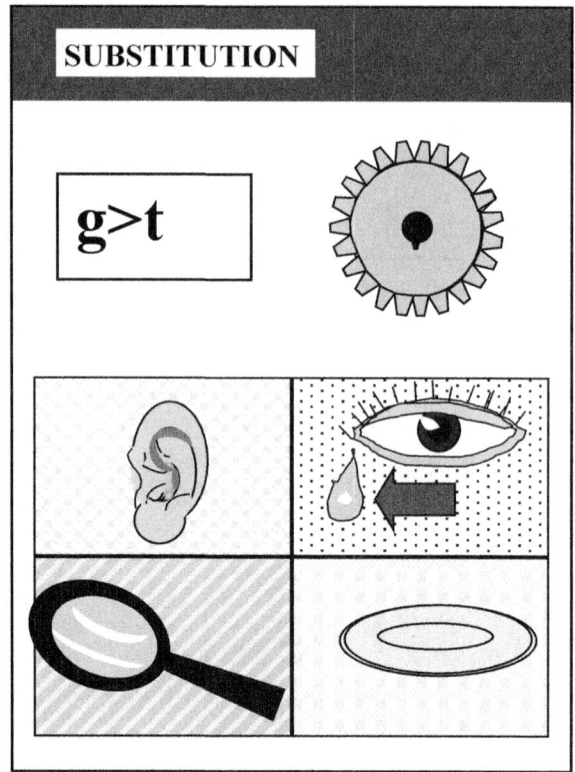

SUBSTITUTION

p>h

SUBSTITUTION

m>j

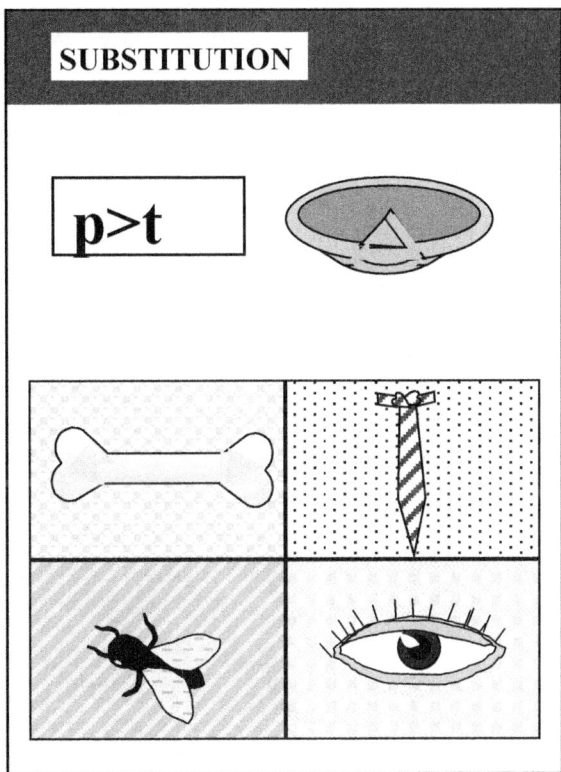

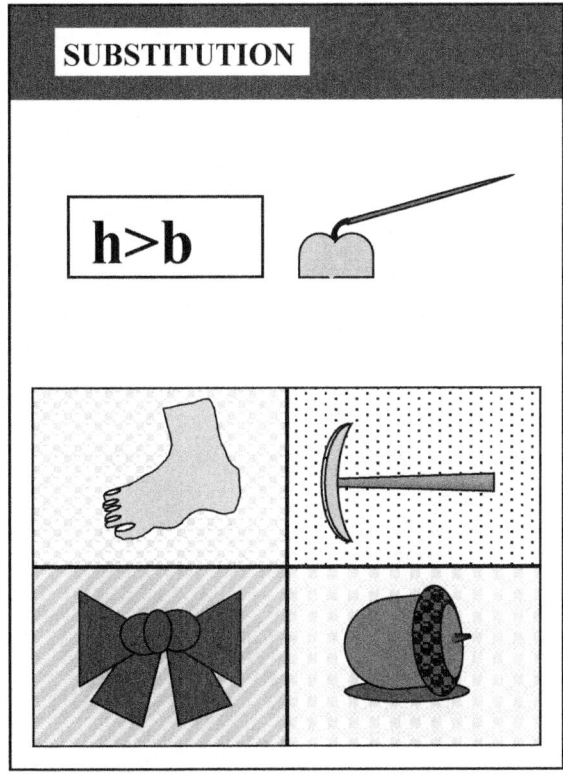

103

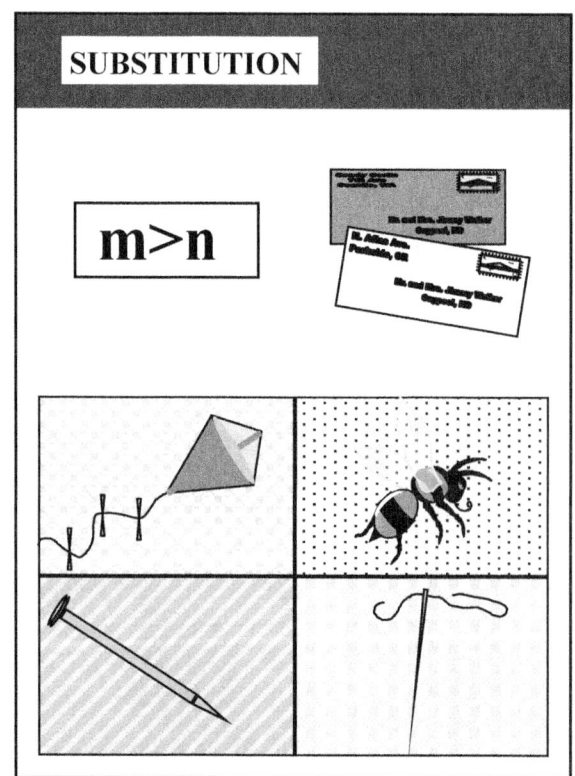

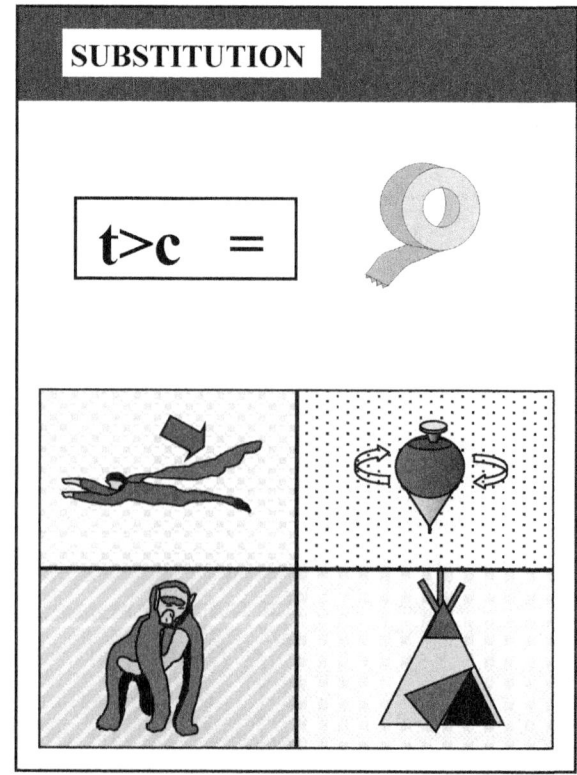

104

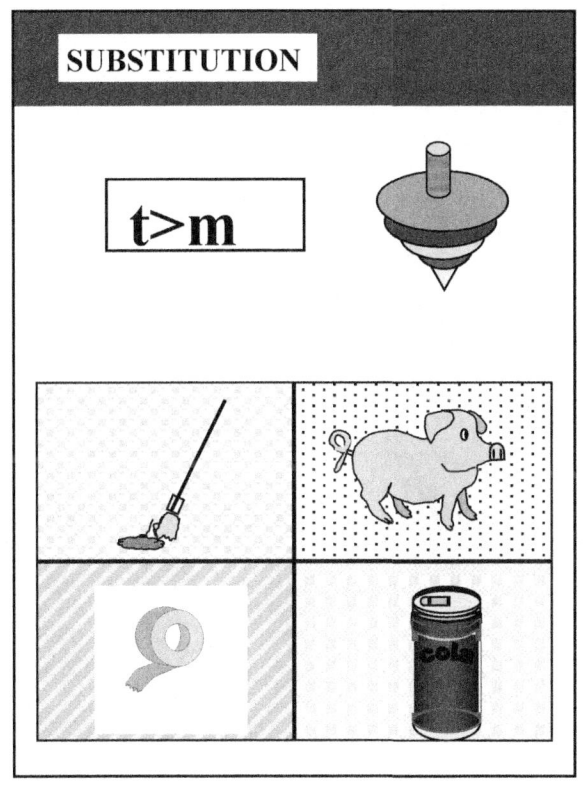

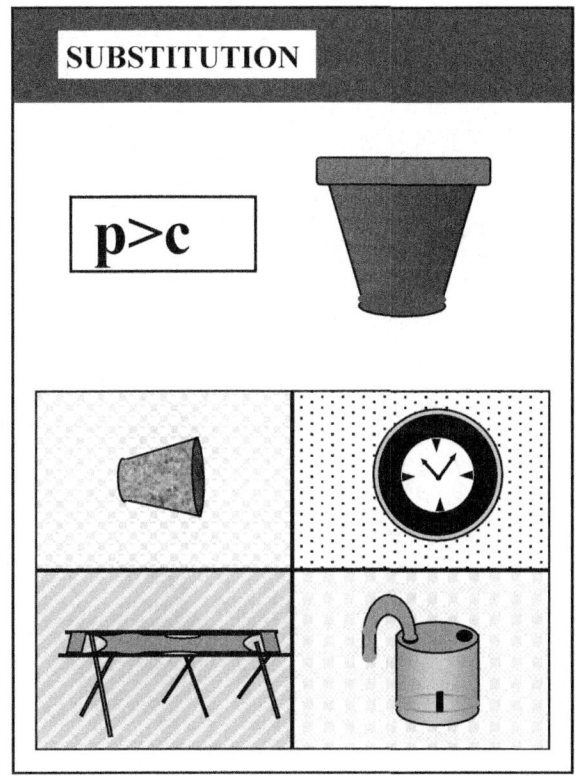

105

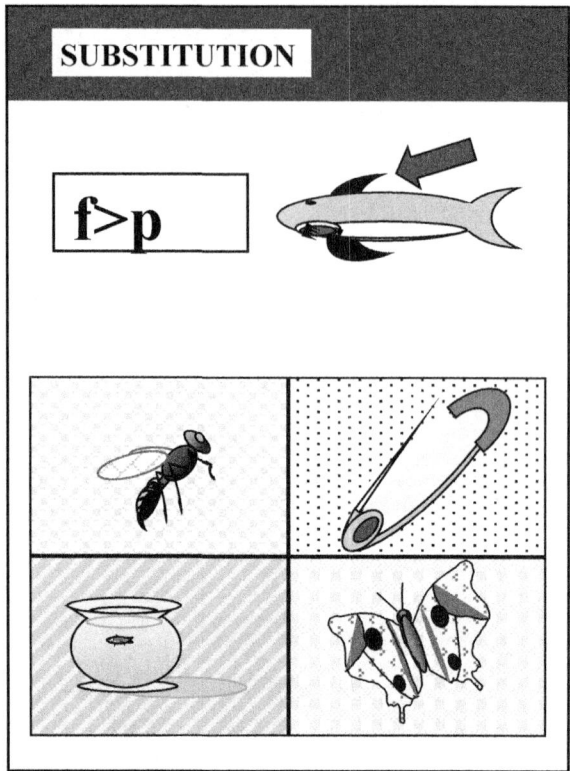

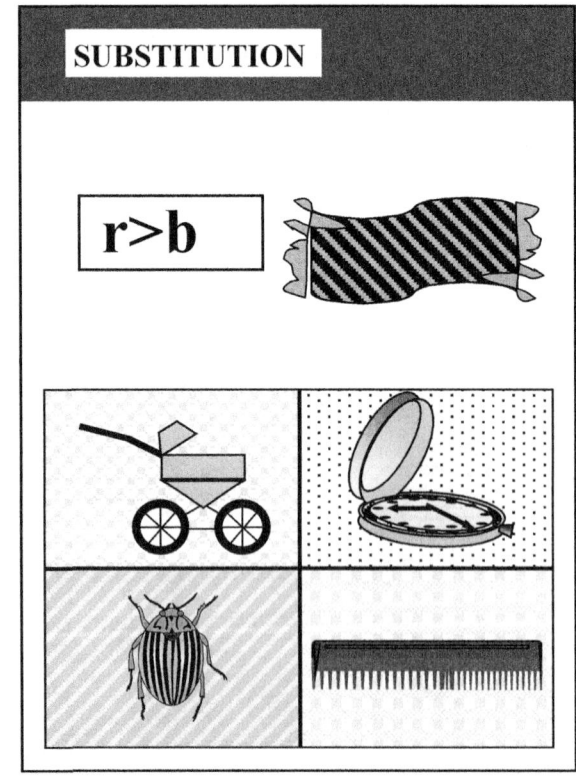

106

Directions: One of the four objects in each section is the answer to substituting one intitial letter for another.

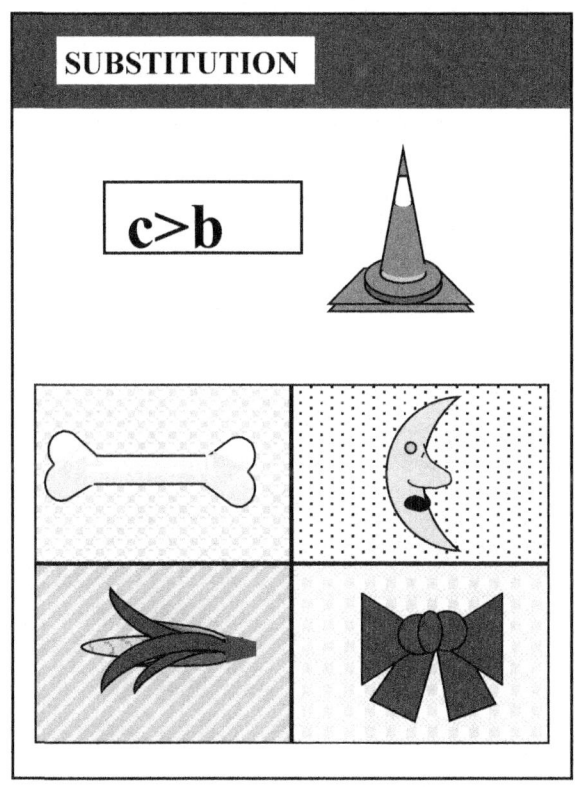

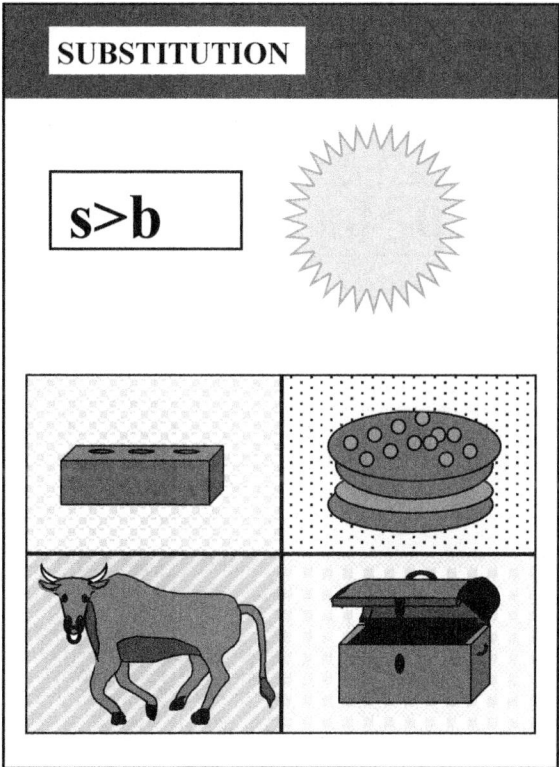

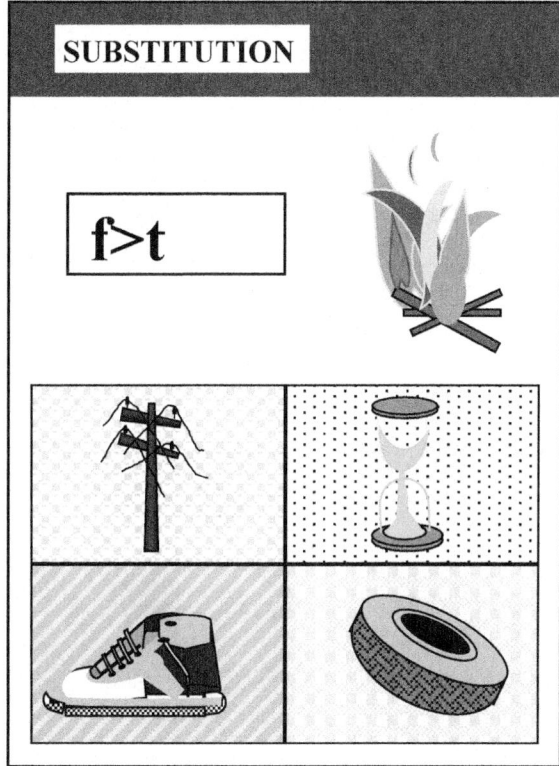

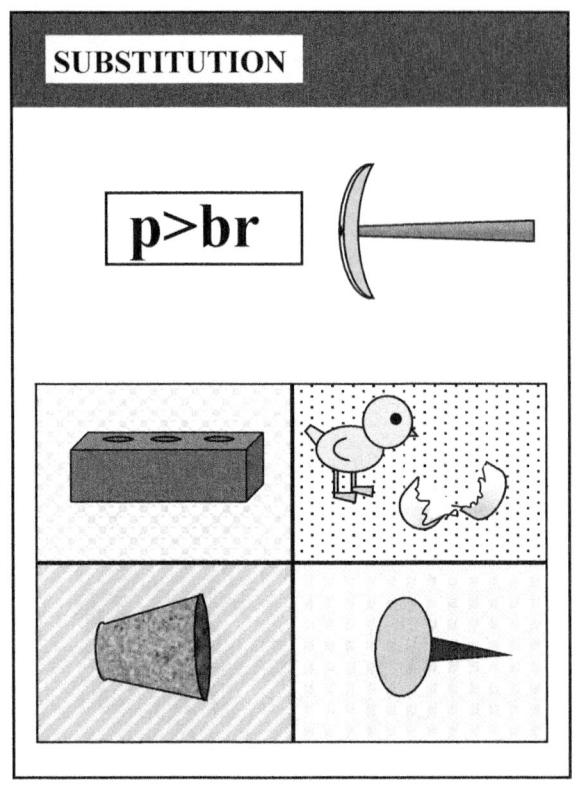

SUBSTITUTION

p>br

SUBSTITUTION

p>w

SUBSTITUTION

d>h

SUBSTITUTION

p>w

108

Directions: One of the four objects in each section is the answer to substituting one intitial letter for another.

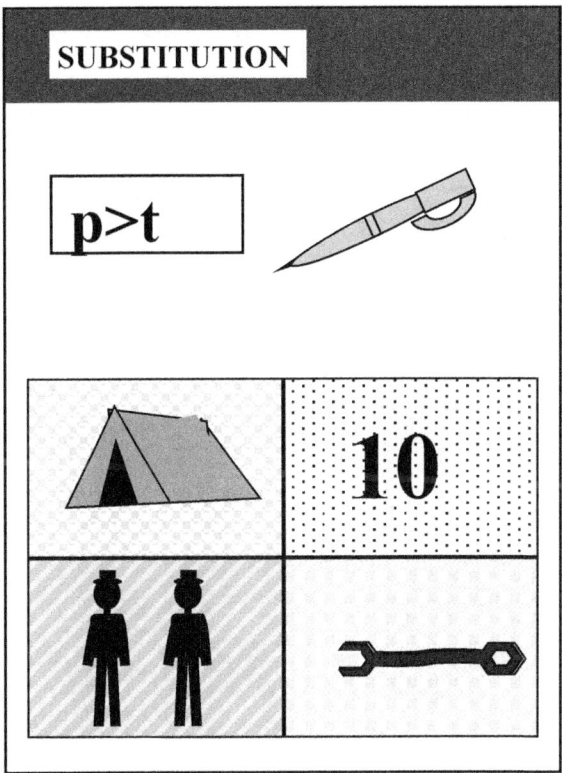

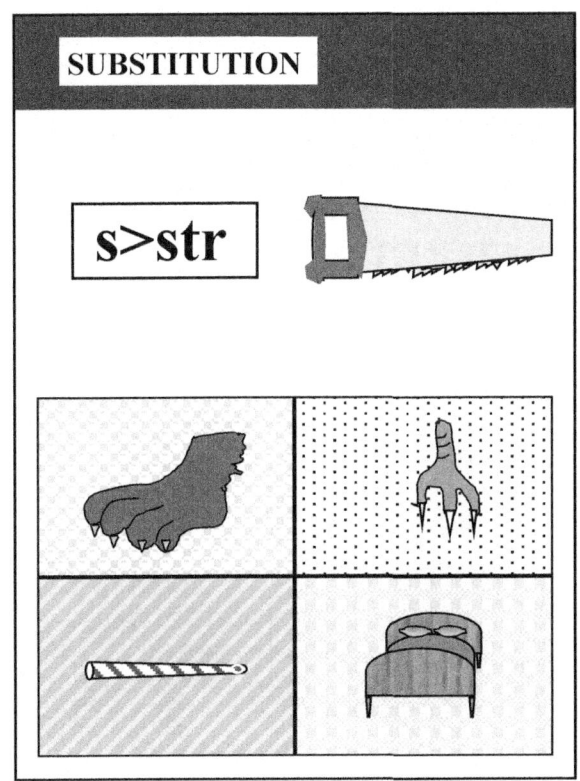

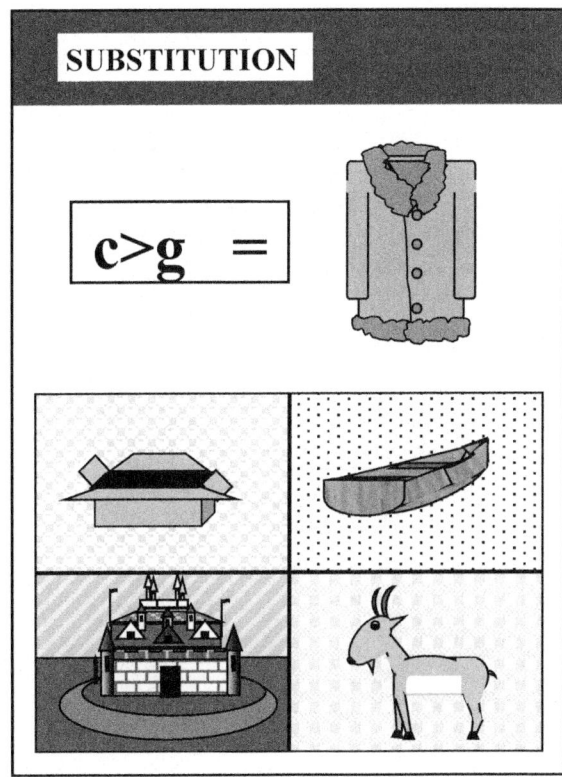

109

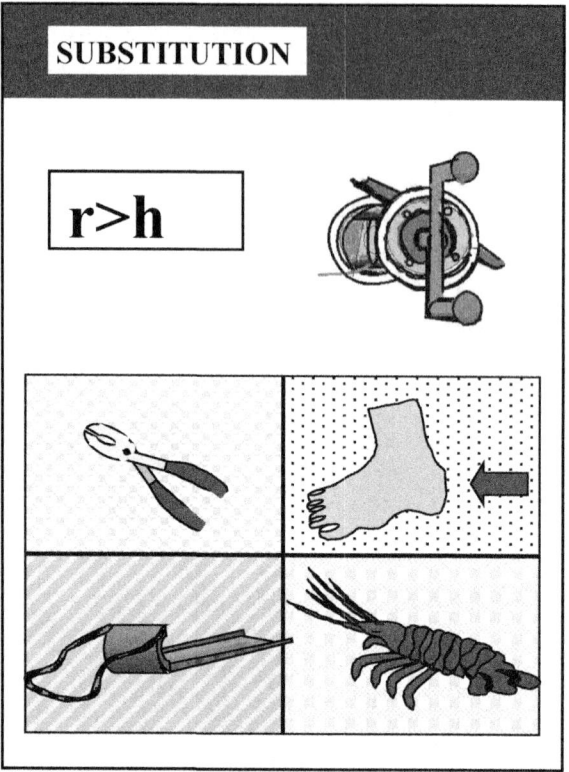

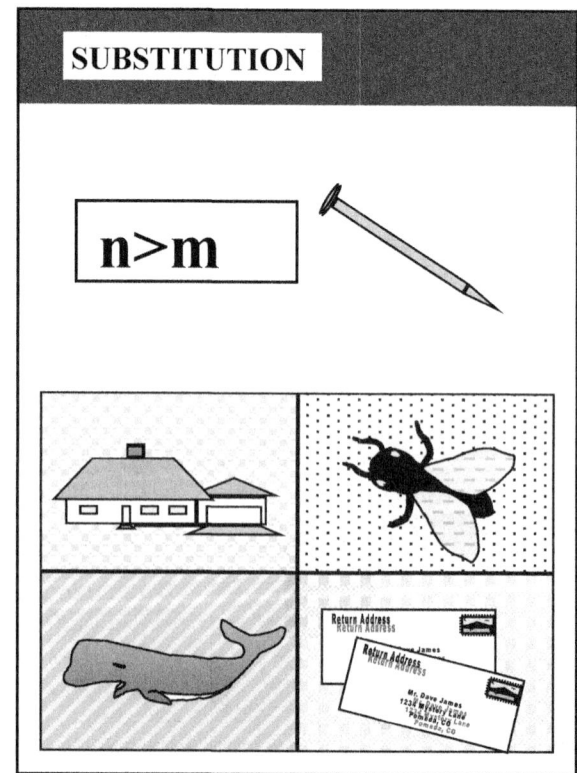

110

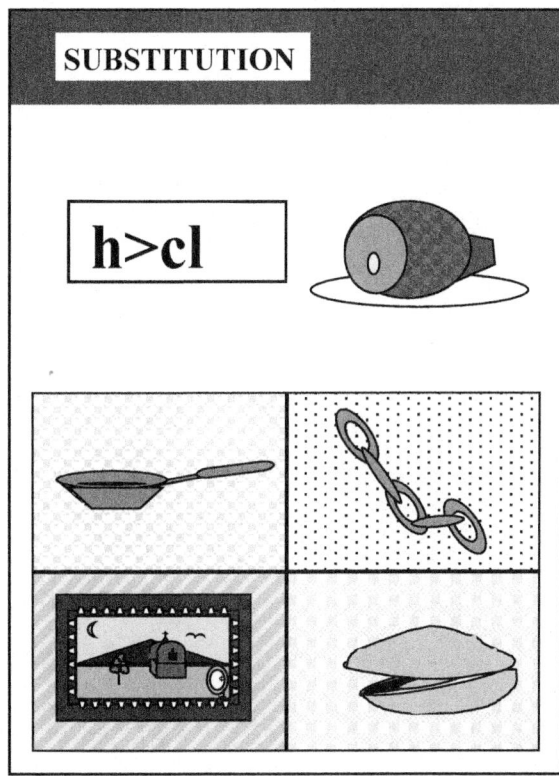

111

SUBSTITUTION

SUBSTITUTION

SUBSTITUTION

SUBSTITUTION

112

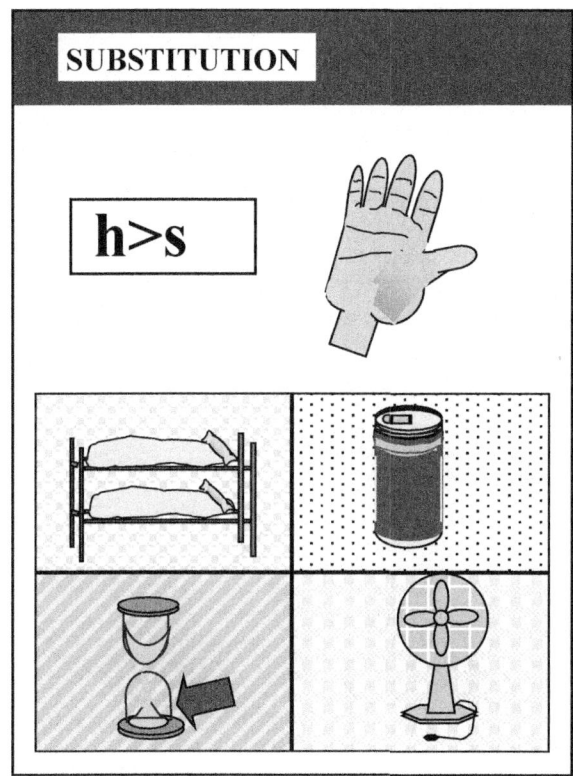

113

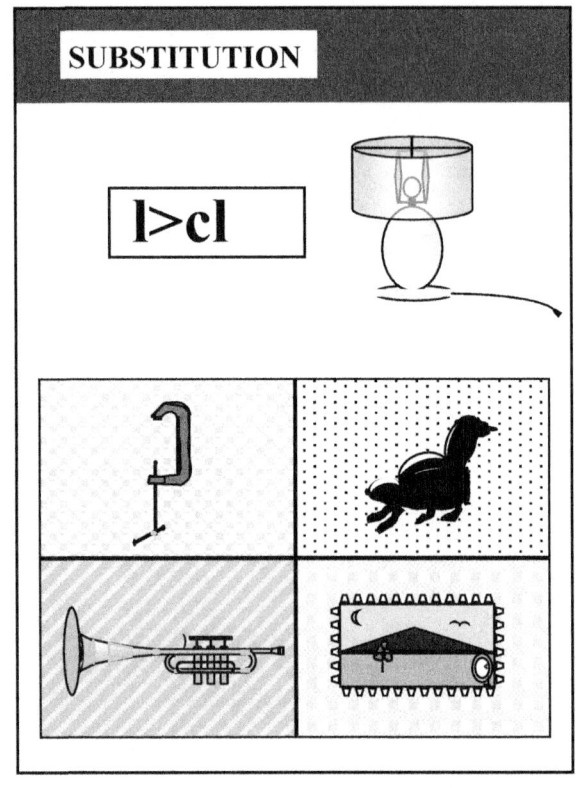

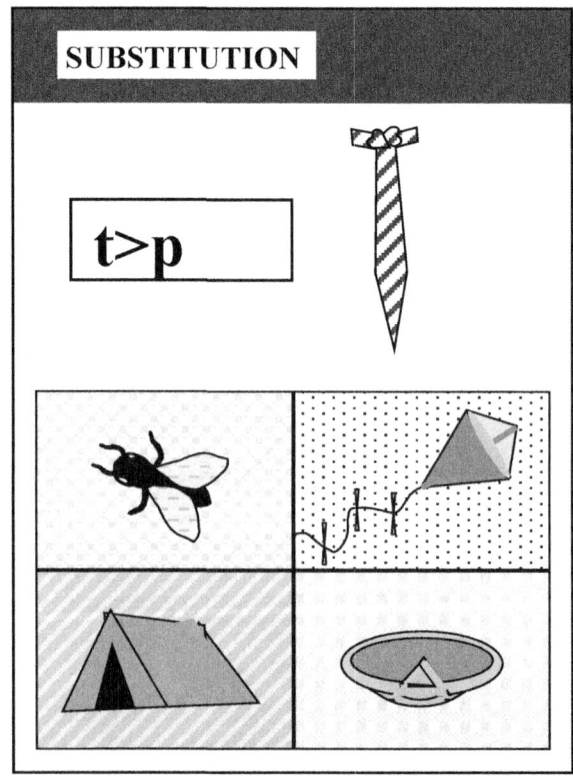

114

SUBSTITUTION

j>c

SUBSTITUTION

n>h

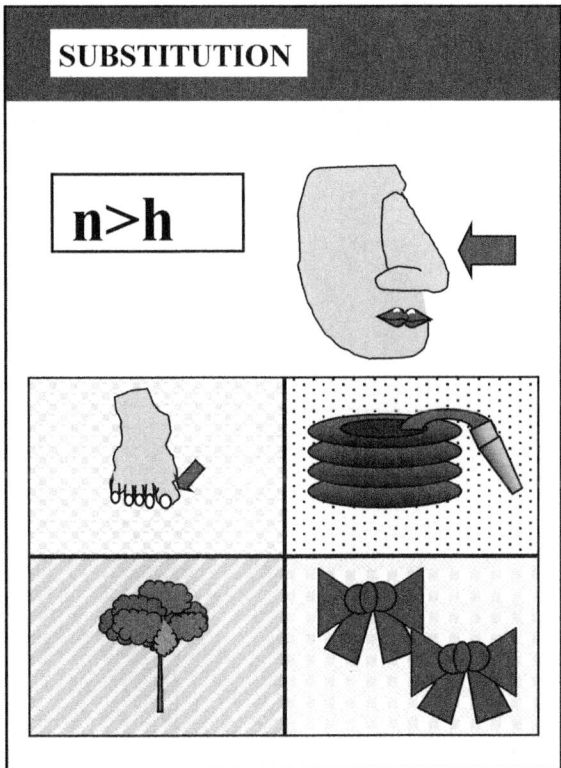

SUBSTITUTION

c>g

SUBSTITUTION

b>w

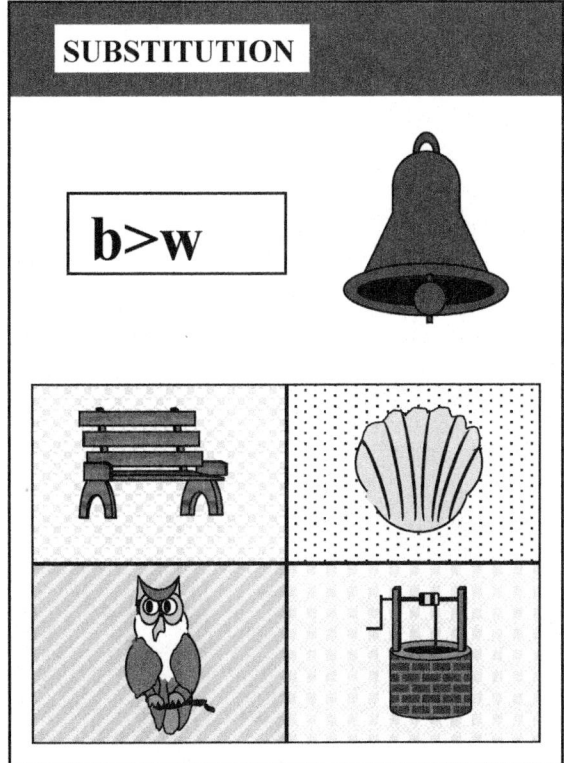

115

MIXED FORMULAE

In this section, you will need to decode the various combined forms of syllables or sound units such as addition, subtraction and substitution as in the previous sections. Also the asterisk (*) will be used to indicate the "uh" sound as found at the end of the word "Santa".

The parent or teacher will need to assist the student to become acquainted with how to decode the rebus words. In time, he/she will become more proficient, and eventually will be able to decode the words without much assistance.

Directions: Decode the rebus and match it to the correct object in the section below the rebus.

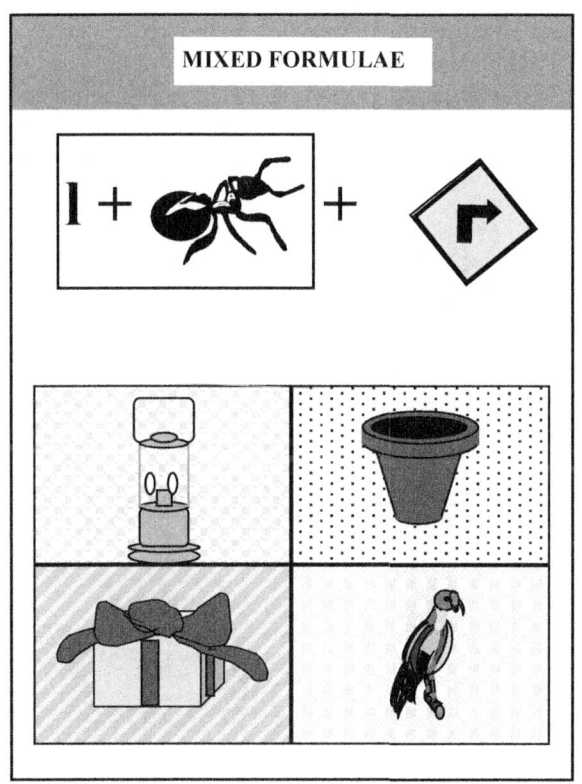

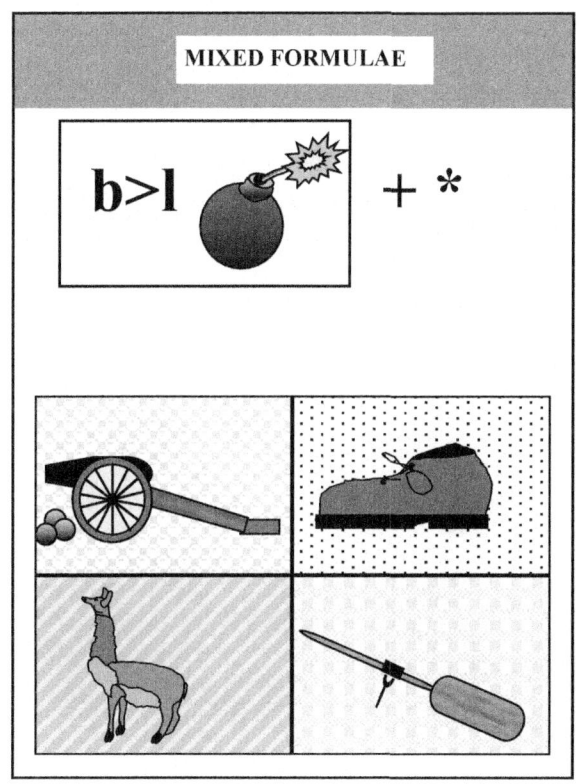

117

Directions: Decode the rebus and match it to the correct object in the section below the rebus.

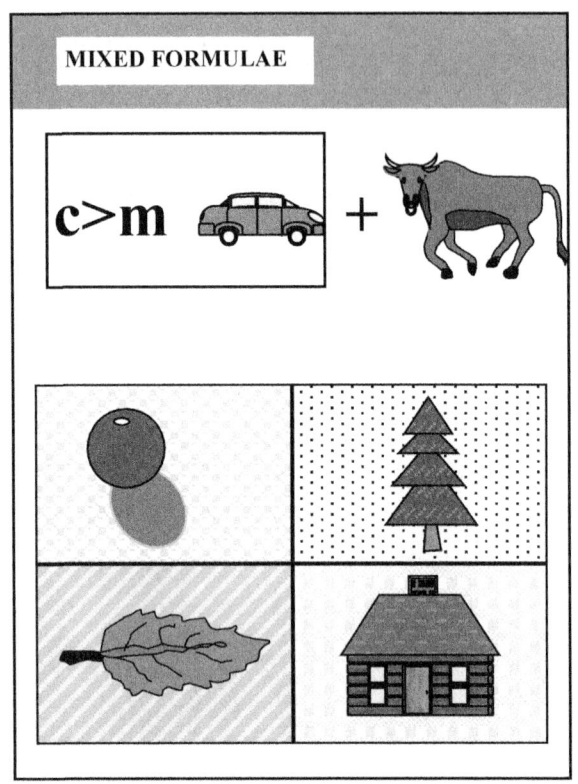

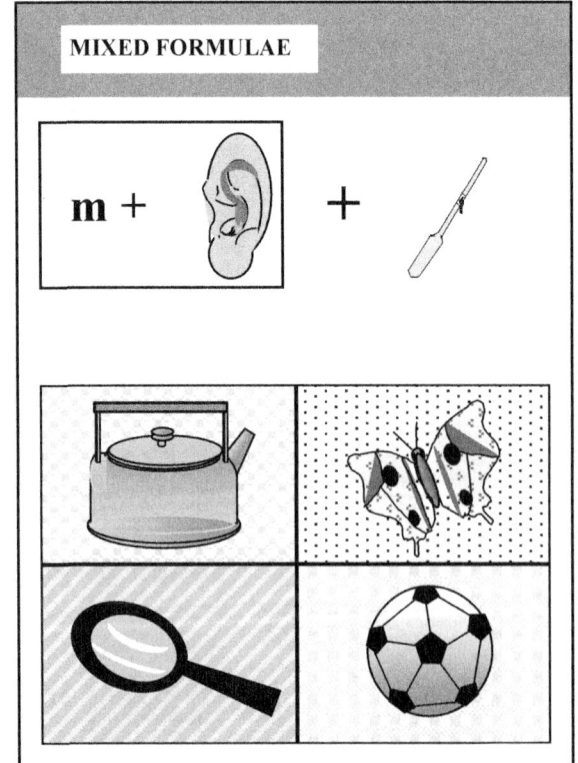

118

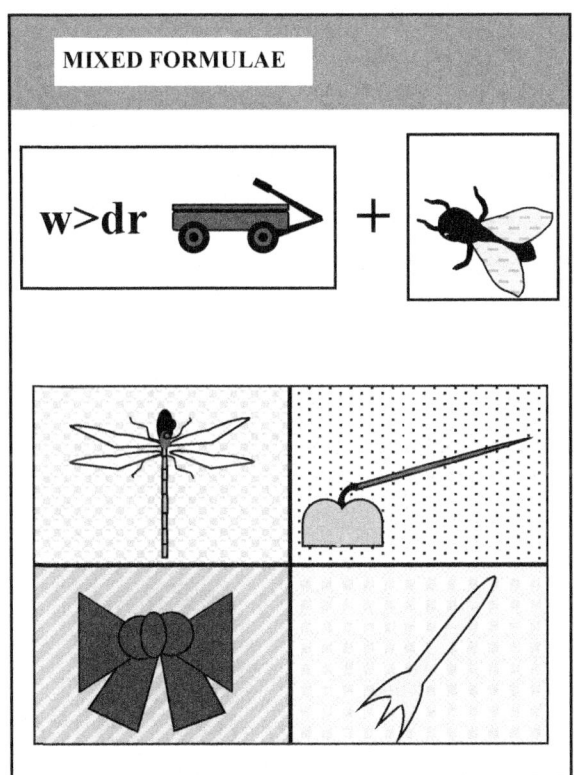

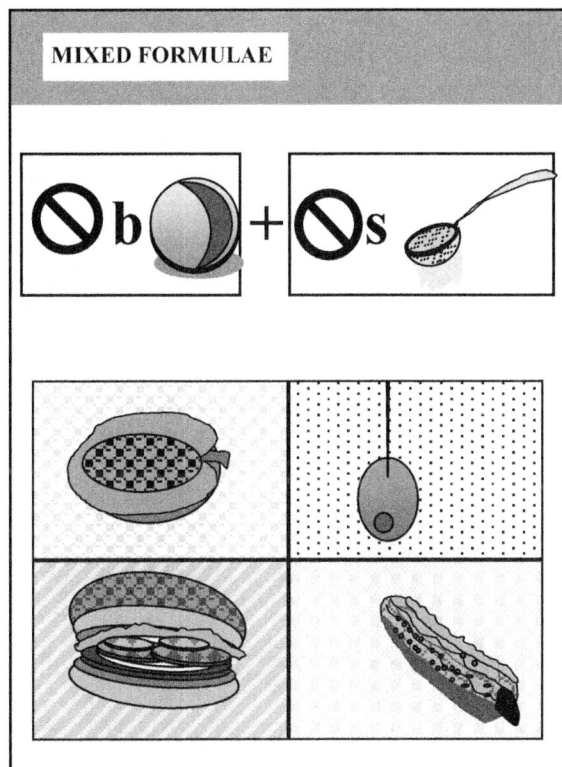

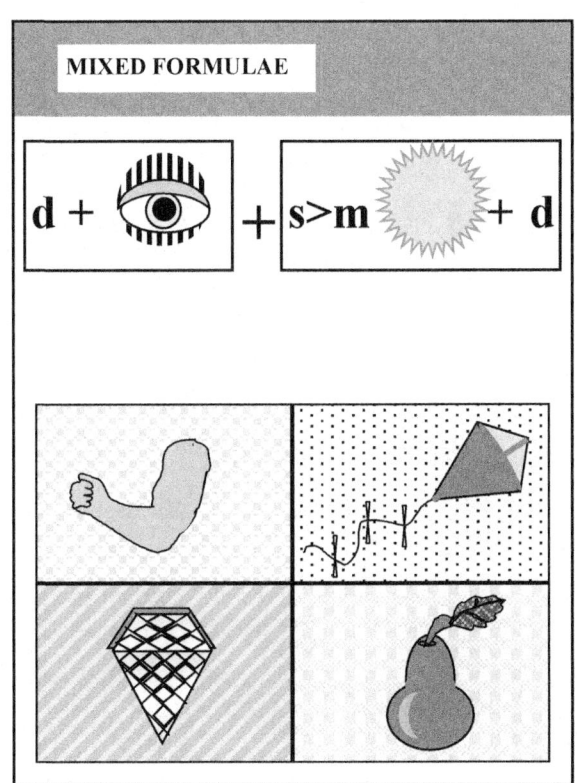

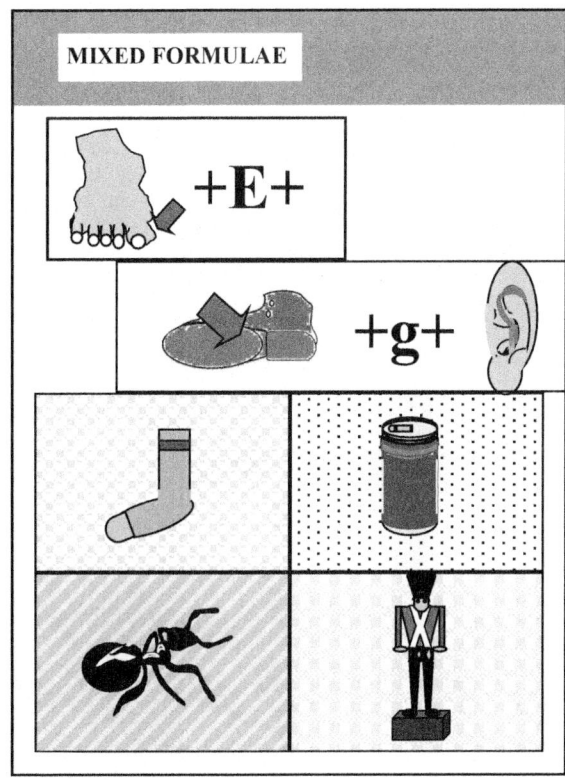

119

Directions: Decode the rebus and match it to the correct object in the section below the rebus.

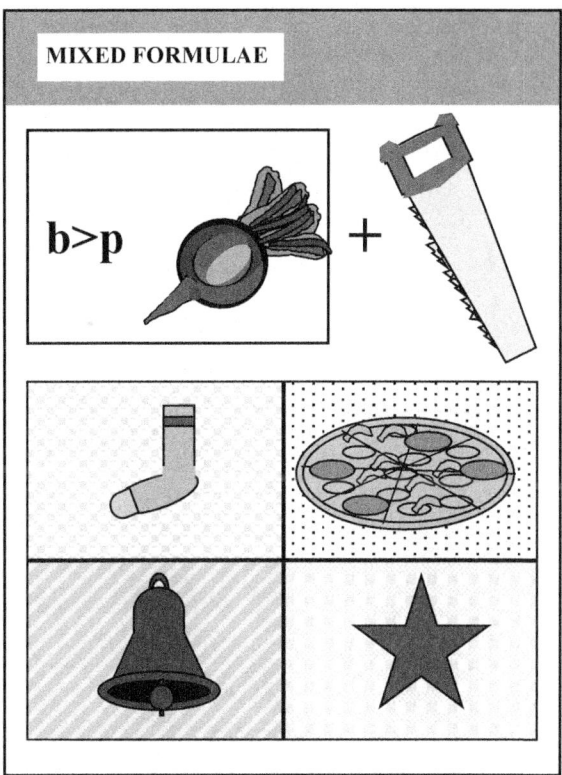

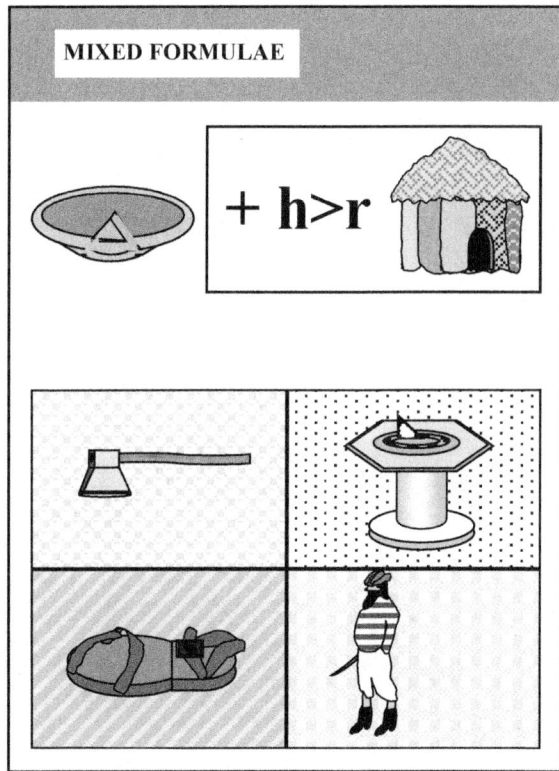

121

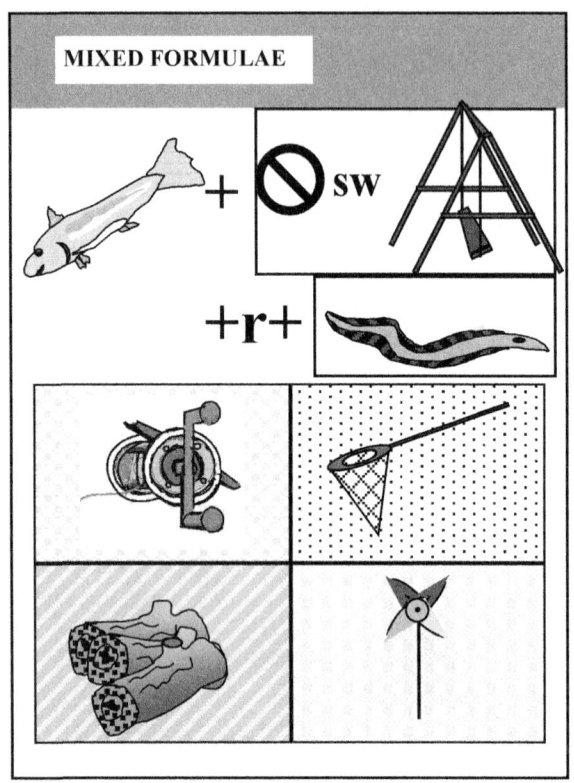

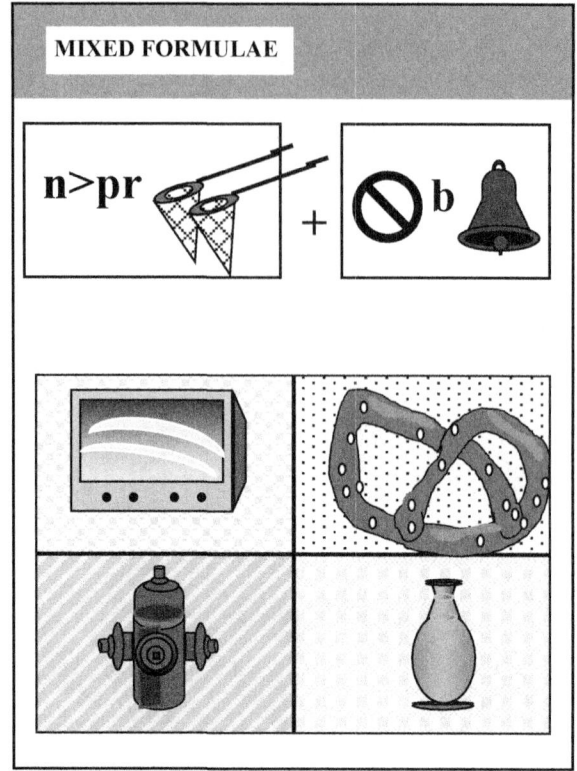

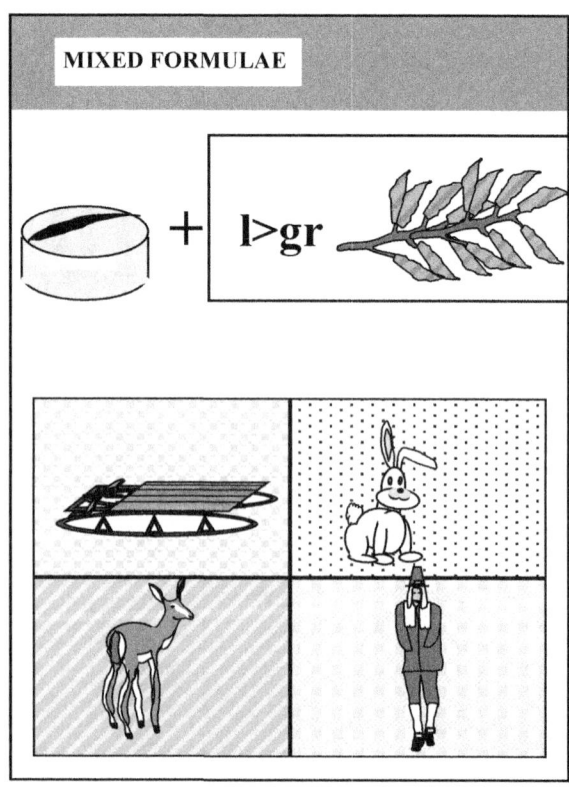

122

Directions: Decode the rebus and match it to the correct object in the section below the rebus.

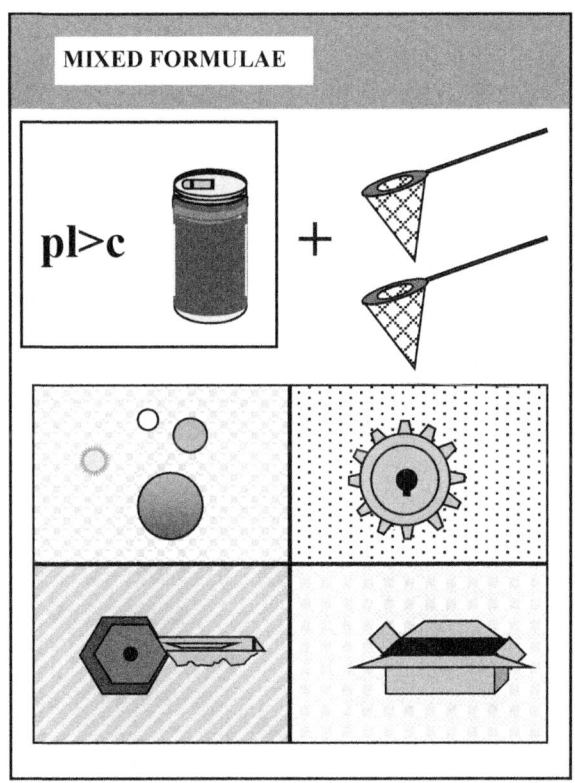

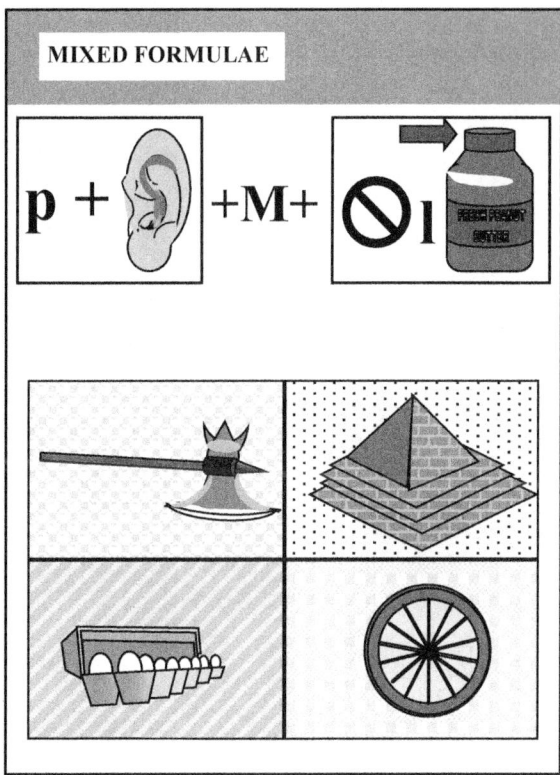

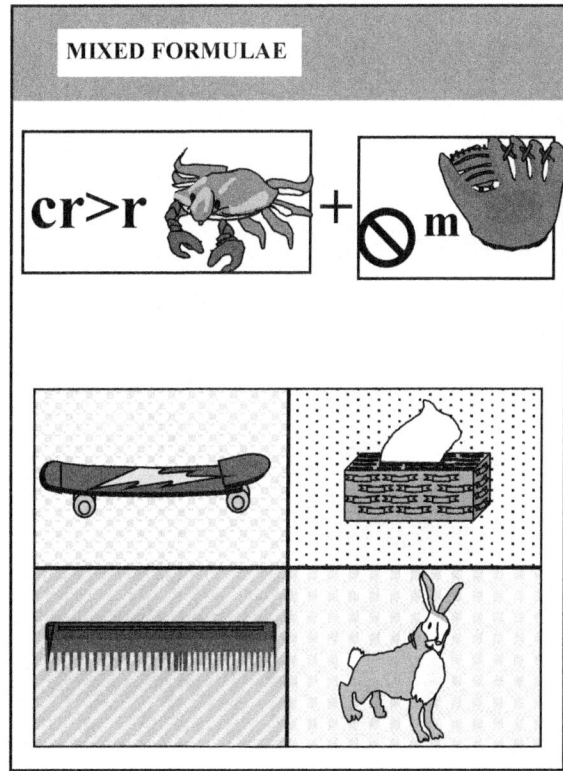

Directions: Decode the rebus and match it to the correct object in the section below the rebus.

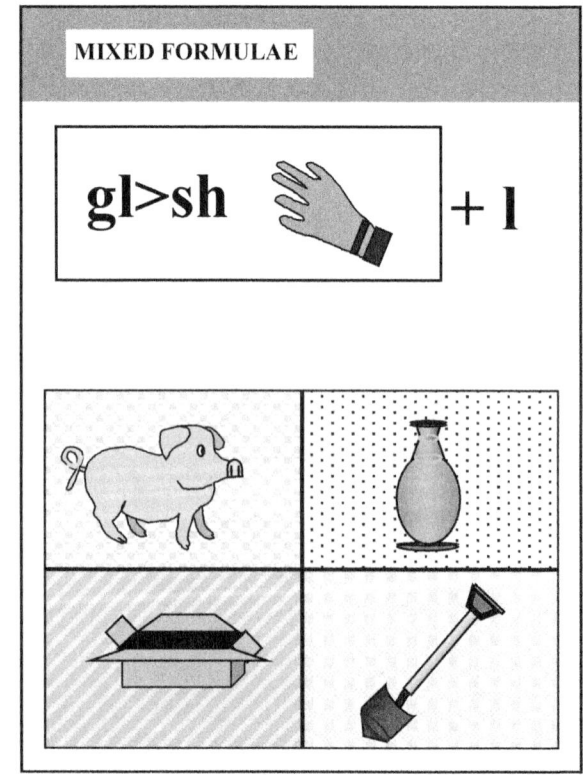

Directions: Decode the rebus and match it to the correct object in the section below the rebus.

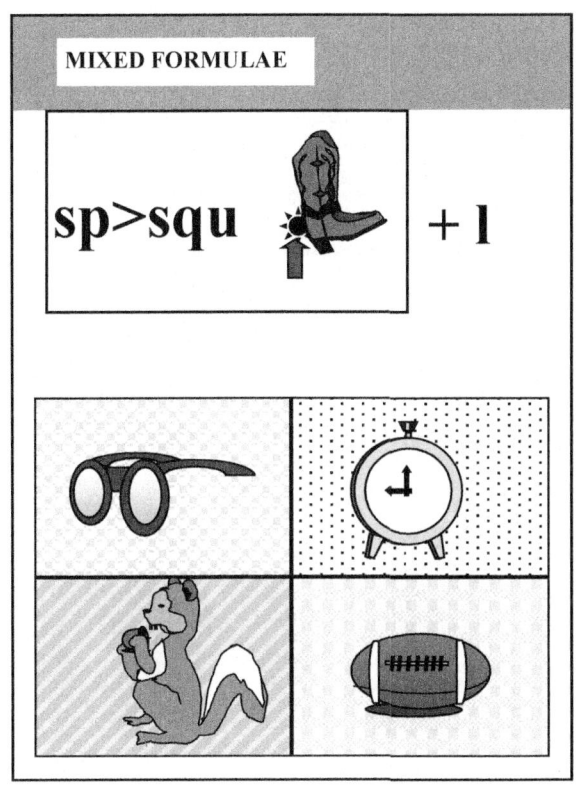

125

Directions: Decode the rebus and match it to the correct object in the section below the rebus.

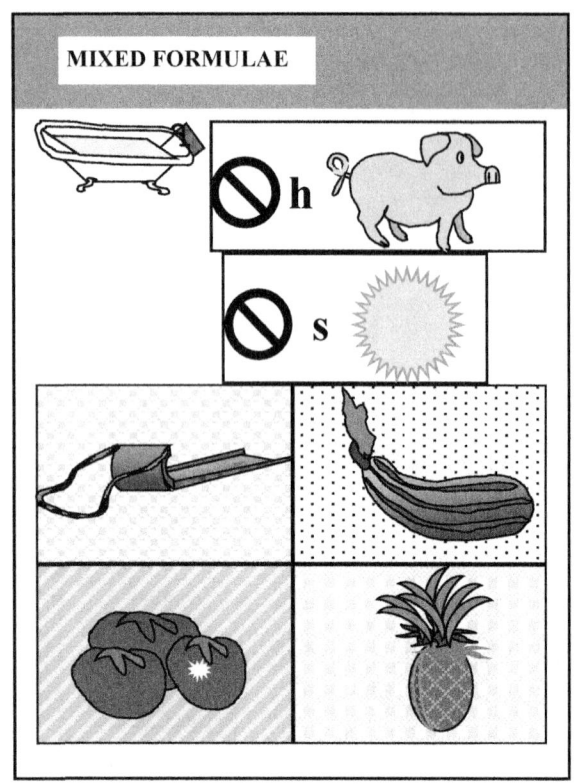

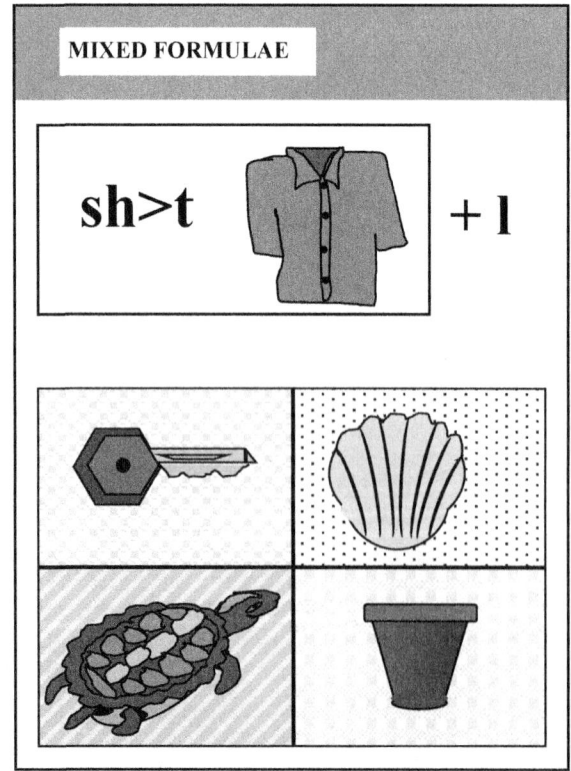

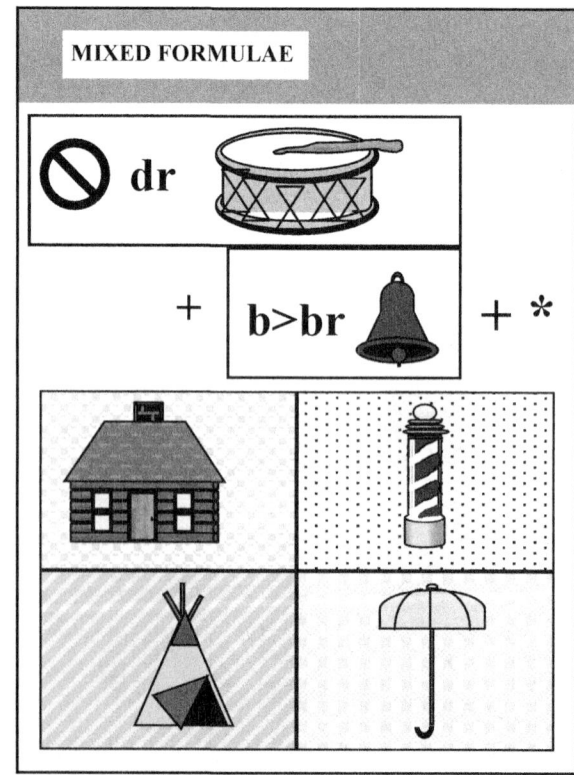

CODED STORIES

The following section presents short stories to be read by the student. Below the lines of words appear the coded symbols that represent each word similar to the rebuses from the preceding chapter of mixed formulae. The parent or teacher may choose to place an index card over the rebus clues to hide them to see if the child is able to read without the clues. When the reader becomes stumped, the adult may slip down the card to reveal the coded clue.

Eventually, the child should be able to do this activity by himself. Finally, the child may try to read the stories without clues from the pages at the back of the section.

HOW TO USE THIS SECTION

In order to decode (unlock) words, the reader must first know the sounds each letter and letter cluster makes when it appears in text — both upper and lower case. Then the reader must sound these letters from left to right, top to bottom, in sound "units" or syllables as single- or polysyllabic words.

For example, for the single syllable word "doll", the reader sounds the onset letter "d" as "duh" and attaches it to the rime (ending) " oll" (pronounced **AWL**) to form the sound.

Using the formulae which appear in the framed in boxes, the reader moves along decoding each word until the entire sentence has been revealed.

"This symbol is used to denote a **SIGHT WORD**, a common word which is used often, such as **THE** and **WAS.**

FOUR BASIC RULES FOR DECODING REBUS FORMULAE

1. **ADDITION** — (+) the **plus symbol** joins words and word parts together to form a coded word.
Example: b + @ equals the word **bat.**
　　　　Compounds — joined together form the compound word **doghouse.** 🐕 + 🏠

2. **ASTERISK** —(*) this symbol stands for the hard "uh" sound. example: 🍳 + d* stands for the word **panda.** 🥫 +*+d* would mean **Canada.**

3. **SUBSTITUTION** — (>) the letter or letters are substituted one for the other — the first letter or letters replace the letter after the arrow. Example: f > c 🚗 equals the word **far.**

Also , the substitution will sometimes follow the rebus syllable or word.
For example: 🚗 t > r would mean **cat.**

4. **SUBTRACTION** — (⊘) the **NO** symbol before a letter or cluster means that the given letter is to be removed from the word represented by the picture which follows.

For example: ⊘ c 🐈 would mean the word **cat** becomes **at.**

HINT: The adult working with a child may help by pronouncing the word part or by coaxing the child to blend the word parts. Also, teach the child how to employ the formulae in decoding.

As the child gains fluency or proficiency at decoding, use an index card to cover the coded formulae to see whether the child is able to read without the coded clues. However, when the child struggles with a word, slip the card down to reveal the coded word and then back up when the word is decoded.

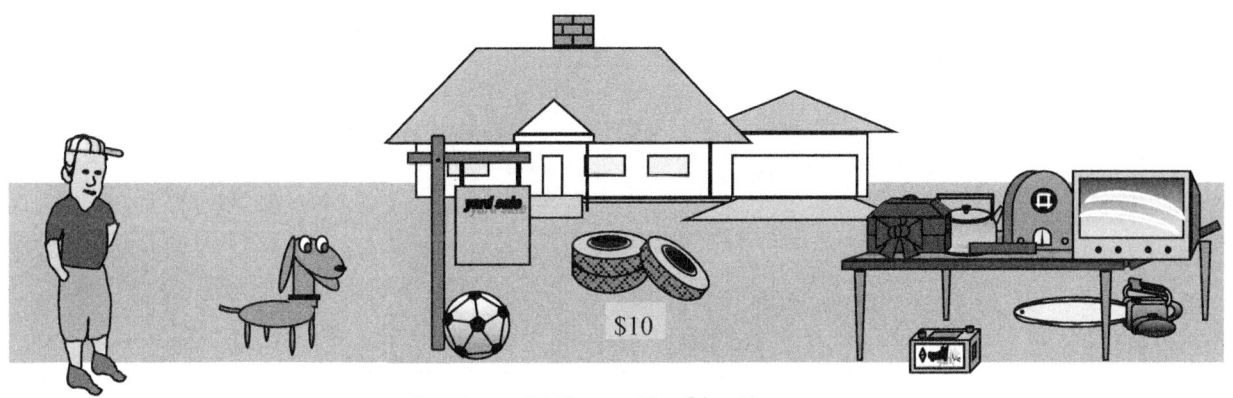

The Yard Sale

Jack is at the back of the house.

A yard sale is taking place.

A stack of tires is for sale for ten

dollars.

Chocolate candy is on the table.

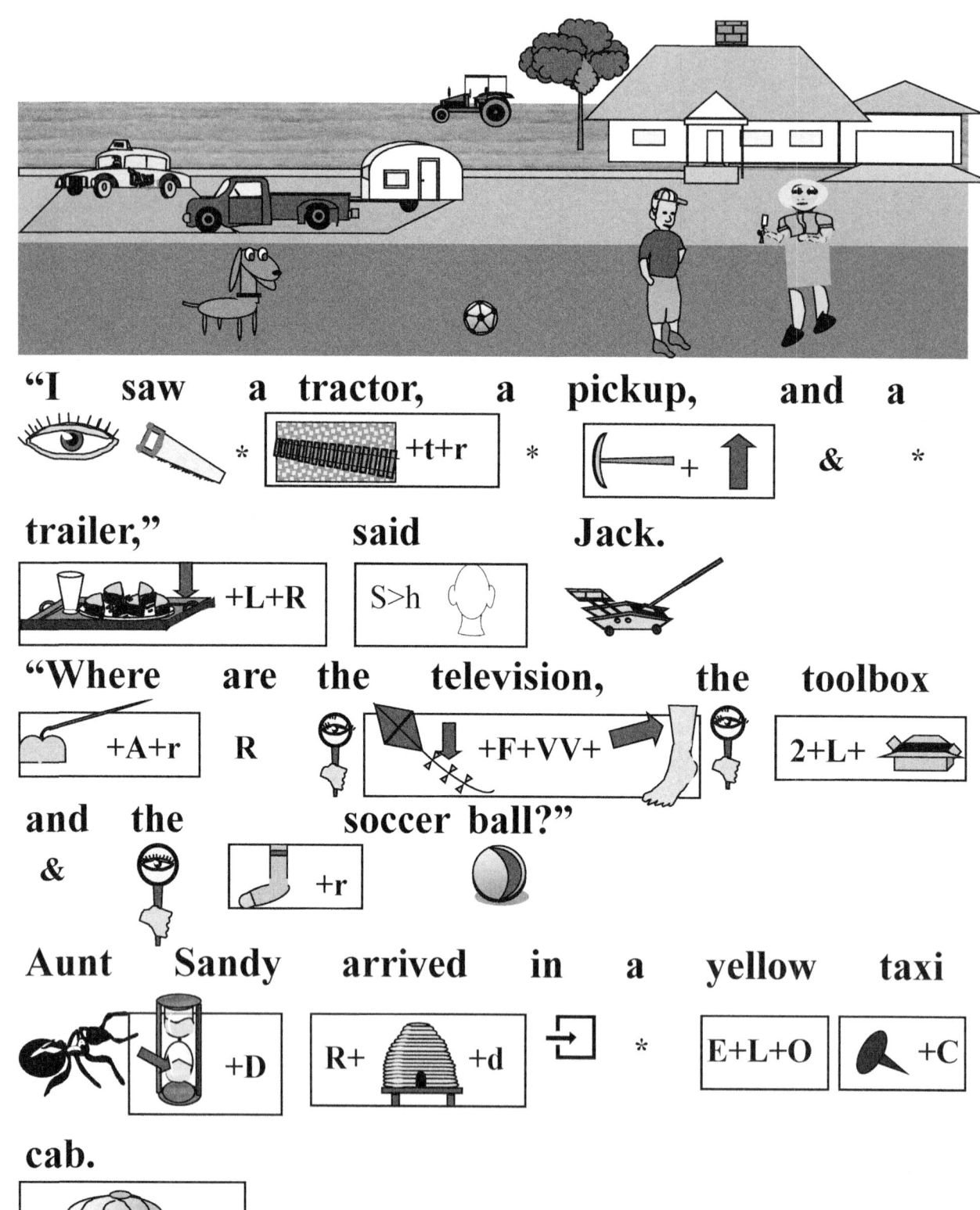

"I saw a tractor, a pickup, and a

trailer," said Jack.

"Where are the television, the toolbox

and the soccer ball?"

Aunt Sandy arrived in a yellow taxi

cab.

Aunt   Sandy   handed   five   dollars   to

+D   [hand] + [head]   5   [doll] +RR   2

the   driver.

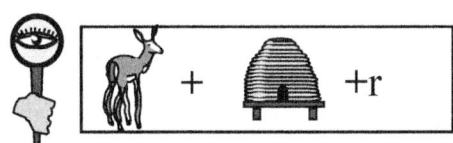

[deer] + [beehive] +r

The   driver   drove   away.

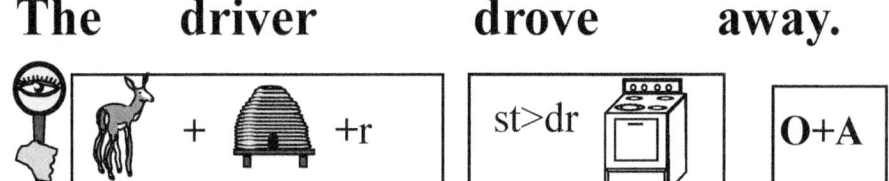

[deer] + [beehive] +r   st>dr [stove]   O+A

Sandy   saw   many   things   for   sale.

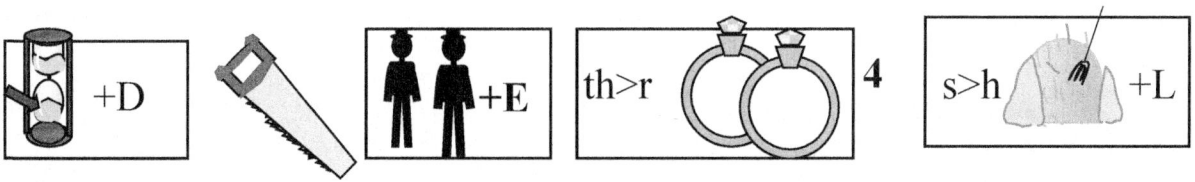

+D   [saw]   [men] +E   th>r [rings] 4   s>h [shirt] +L

131

Jack said, "I see you located our sale.

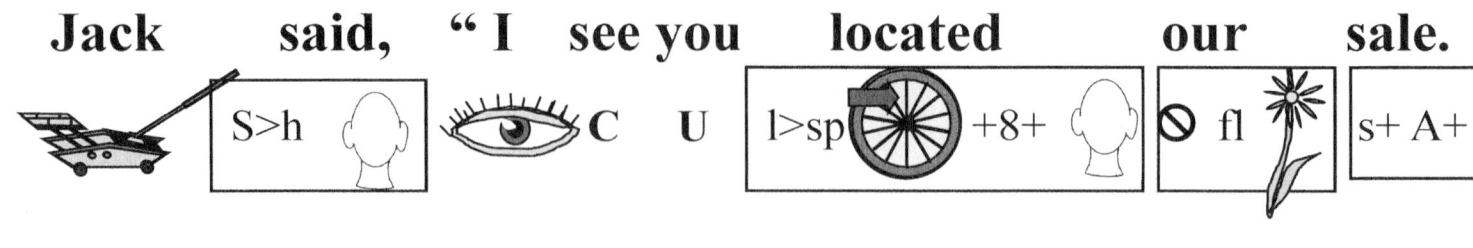

Do you see anything you wish to buy?"

Aunt Sandy said, "I would like to buy

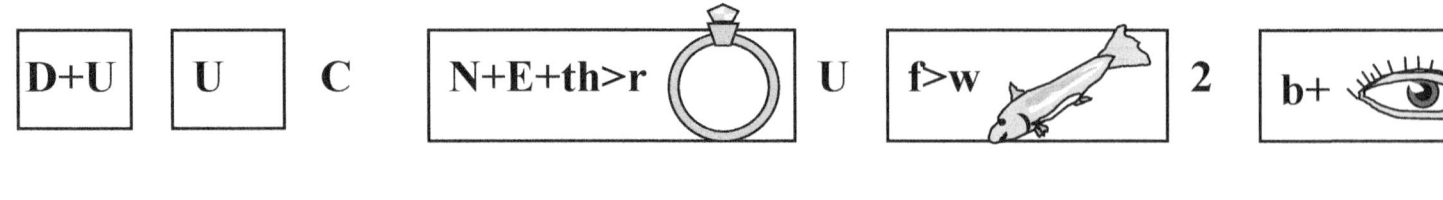

the bicycle."

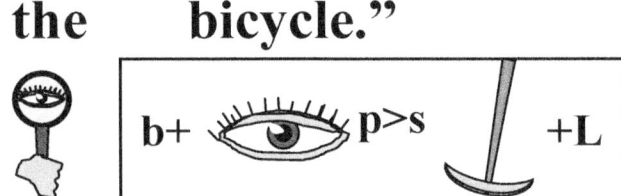

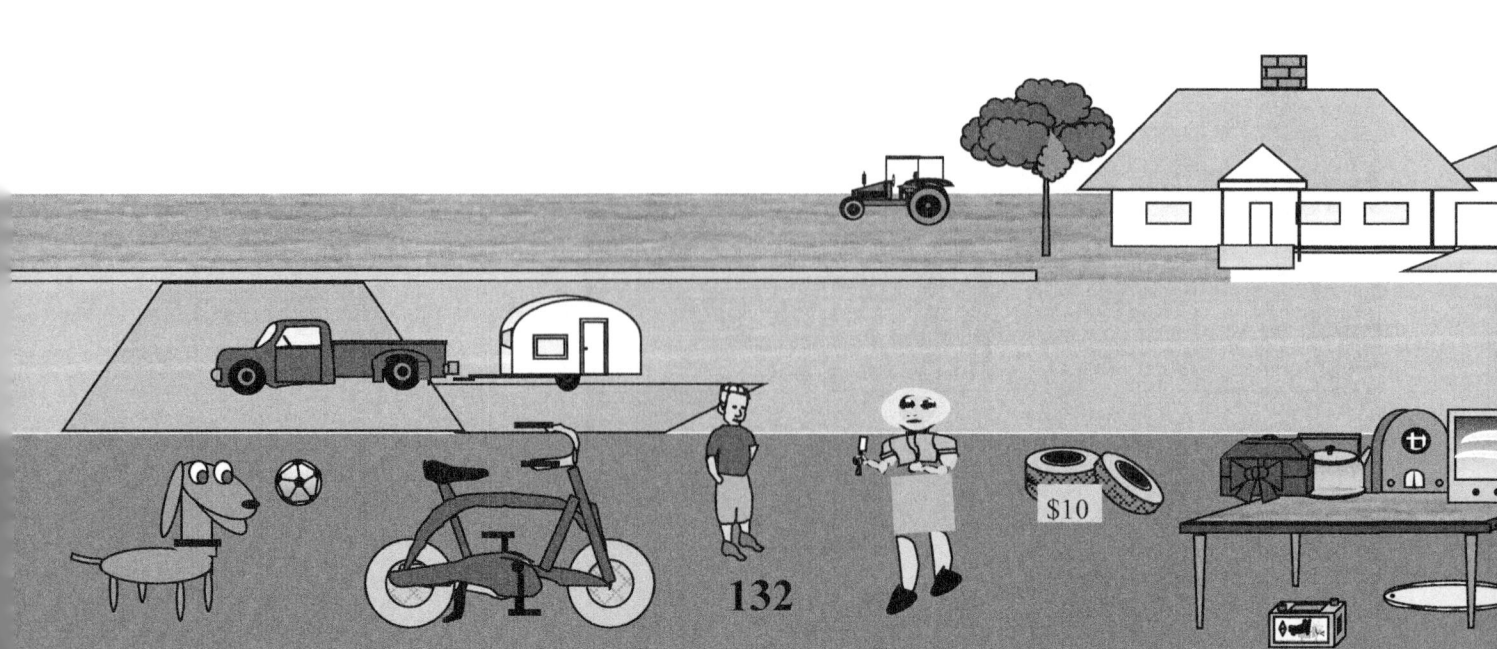

132

Aunt   Sandy   examined   a   toboggan,

  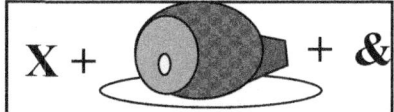 *

a   tennis   racket,   a   wagon,   and   a

* 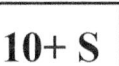  * 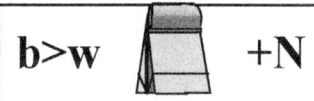 **&** *

tackle   box.

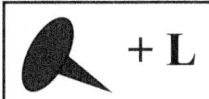 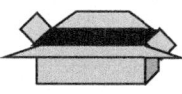

Jack   turned   and   saw   Grandpa

  **&**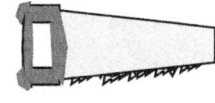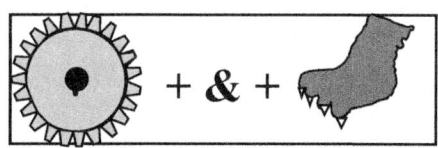

standing   on   the   porch.

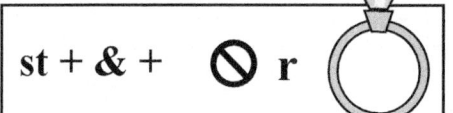   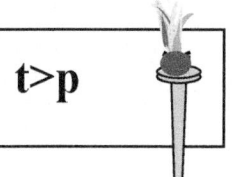

Aunt   Sandy   said   that   she   did

not   wish   to   buy   the   battery.

She   paid   Grandpa   for   the   bicycle.

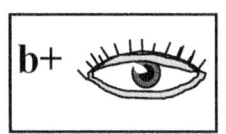  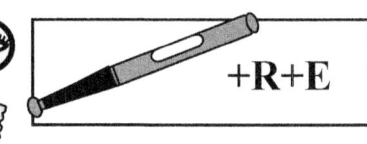

Then   they   went   into   the   house.

 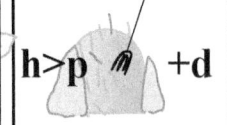 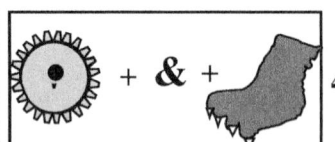 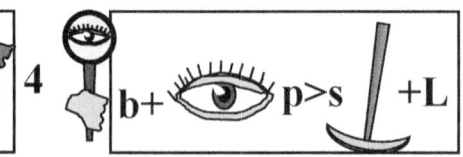

 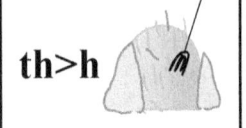 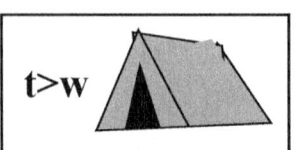 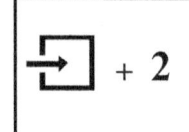 

Treasure on the Island

Captain   Crook   and   many   pirates

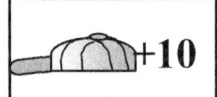  &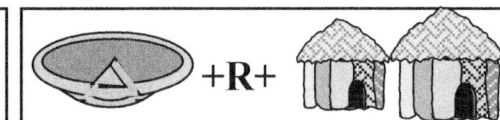

landed   on   goat   island.

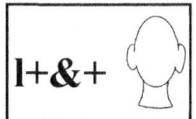  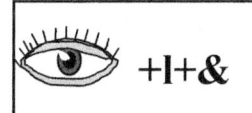

The   Captain   looked   at   a   map.   An   X

 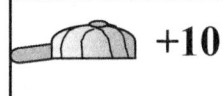  @ *  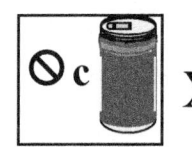 X

marked   the   buried   treasure.

  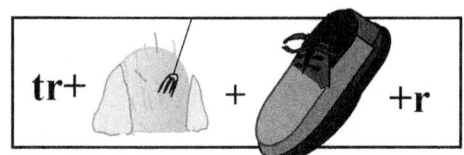

The **men** **walked** **through** **the** **jungle.**

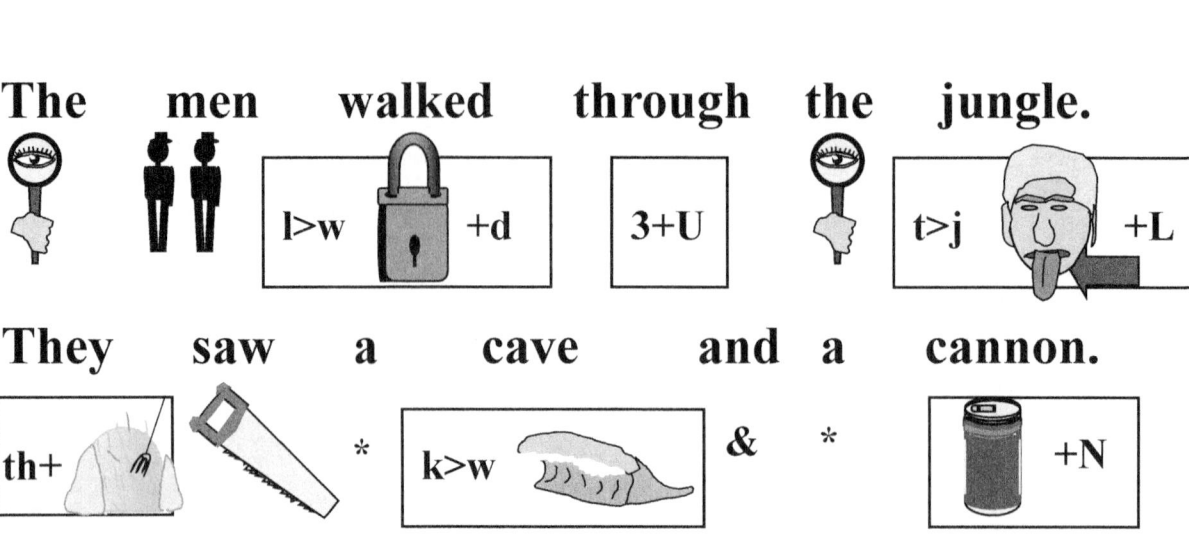

They **saw** **a** **cave** **and** **a** **cannon.**

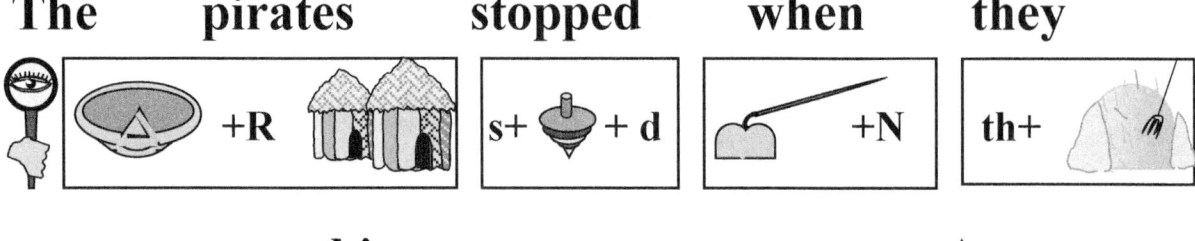

The **pirates** **stopped** **when** **they**

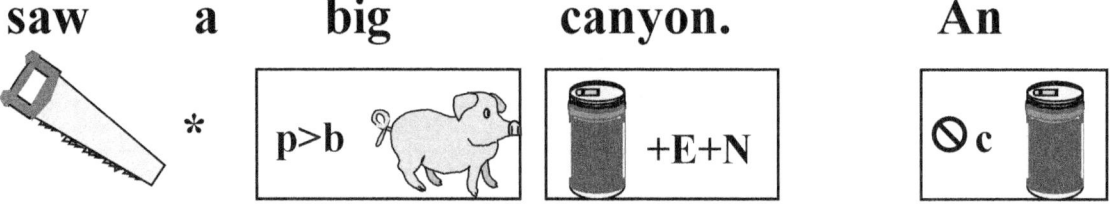

saw **a** **big** **canyon.** **An**

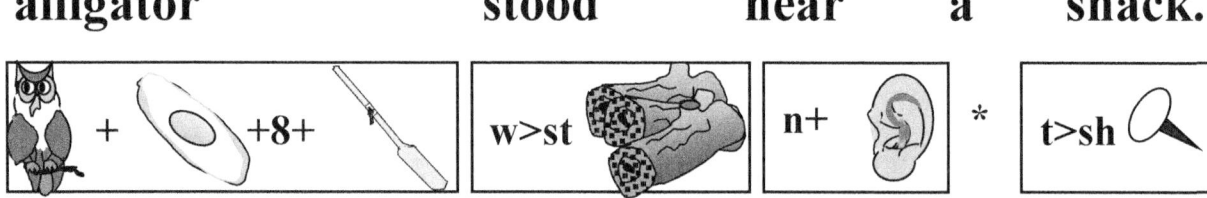

alligator **stood** **near** **a** **shack.**

Night **was** **coming** **and** **the** **men**

| k>n | | dr>c 🥁 ⊘r 💍 | & | | |

set **up** **camp.**

| s>n | ⬆ | l>c |

They **built** **a** **fire** **and** **cooked** **fish.**

| th+ | ⬇ +t | * | | & | b>c 📖 +t | |

The **pirates** **crawled** **into** **their**

| | +R+ | b>cr +d | ⊡ + 2 | th+ ⬇ |

beds **for** **the** **night.**

| | 4 | | k>n |

The next day, the men began

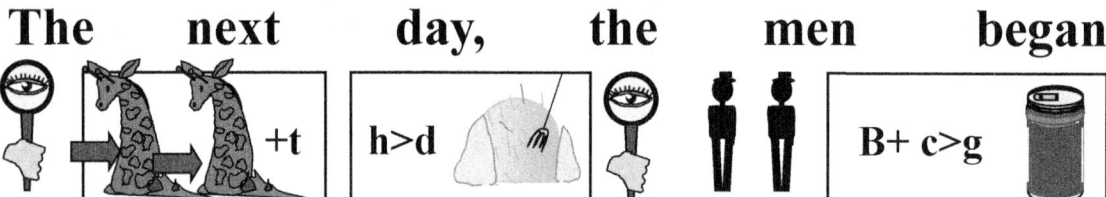

to look for the treasure again.

  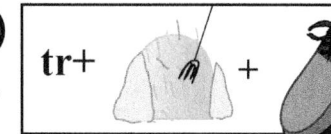 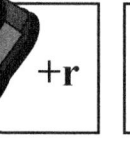 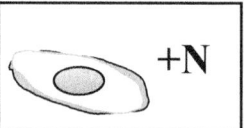

They found the three leaf palm

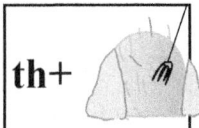   3

tree and began to dig.

 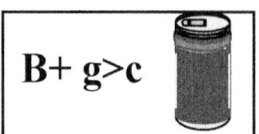 

138

The   **pirates**   **loaded**   **the**   **treasure**

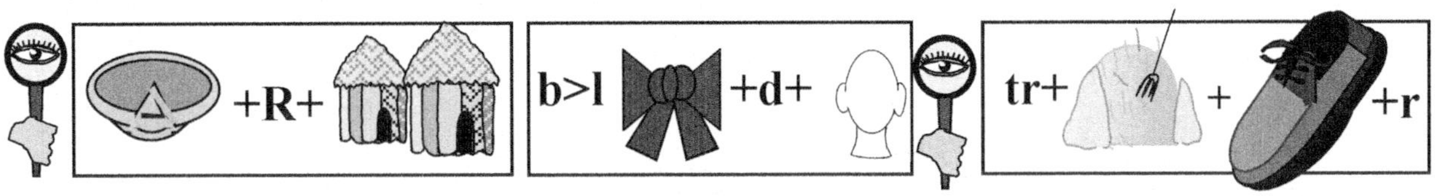

+R+   b>l +d+   tr+ + +r

onto   **the**   **boat.**

⊘ p +2

They   **began**   **to**   **row**   **to**   **the**   **ship.**

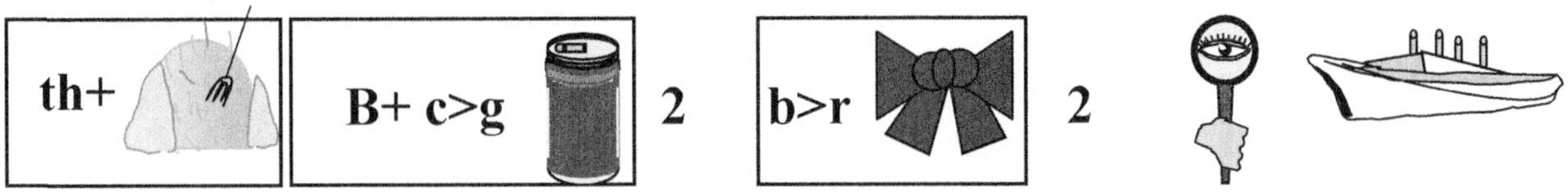

th+   B+ c>g   2   b>r   2

The   **men**   **hauled**   **the**   **chest**   **on**   **board.**

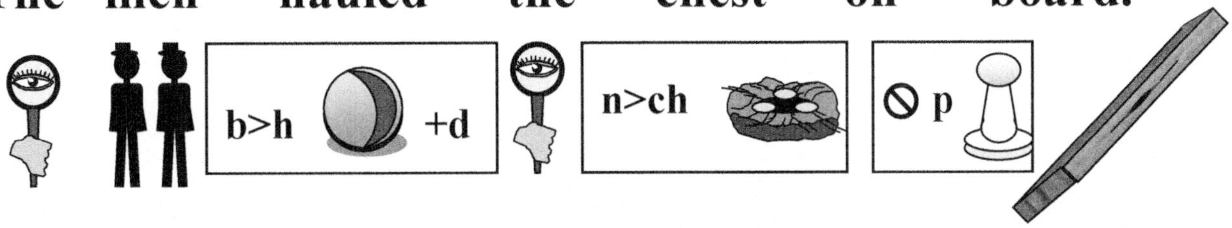

b>h +d   n>ch   ⊘ p

Captain **Crook** **ordered** **the** **men**

to **their** **places.**

2

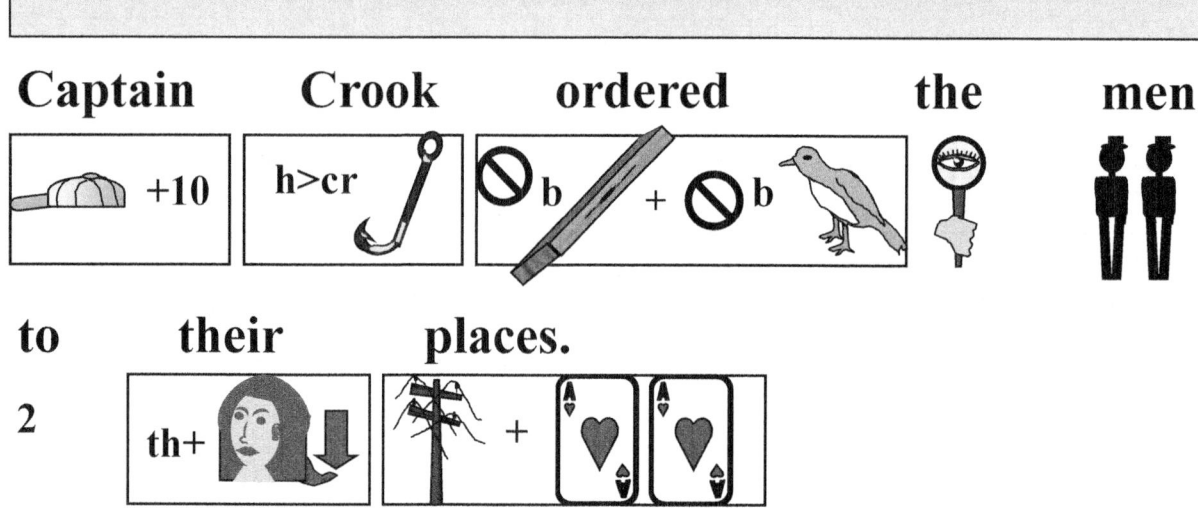

The **sails** **caught** **the** **wind.**

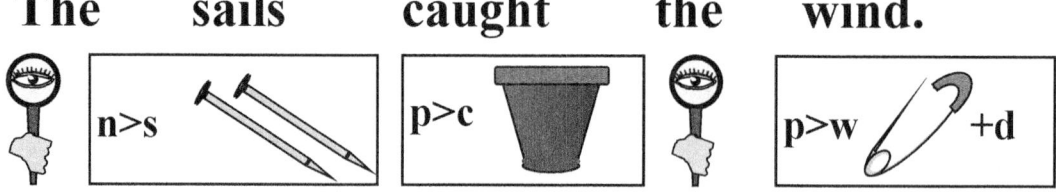

The **ship** **sailed** **for** **England.**

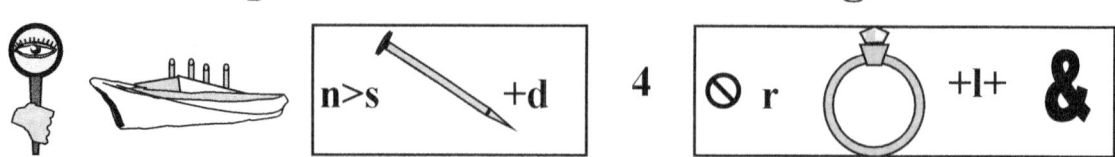

At the Zoo

Many   **different**   **animals**   **are**

at   **the**   **zoo.**   **Billy**   **and**   **Tony**

went   **to see**   **them.**   **They**   **walked**

the   **trail.**

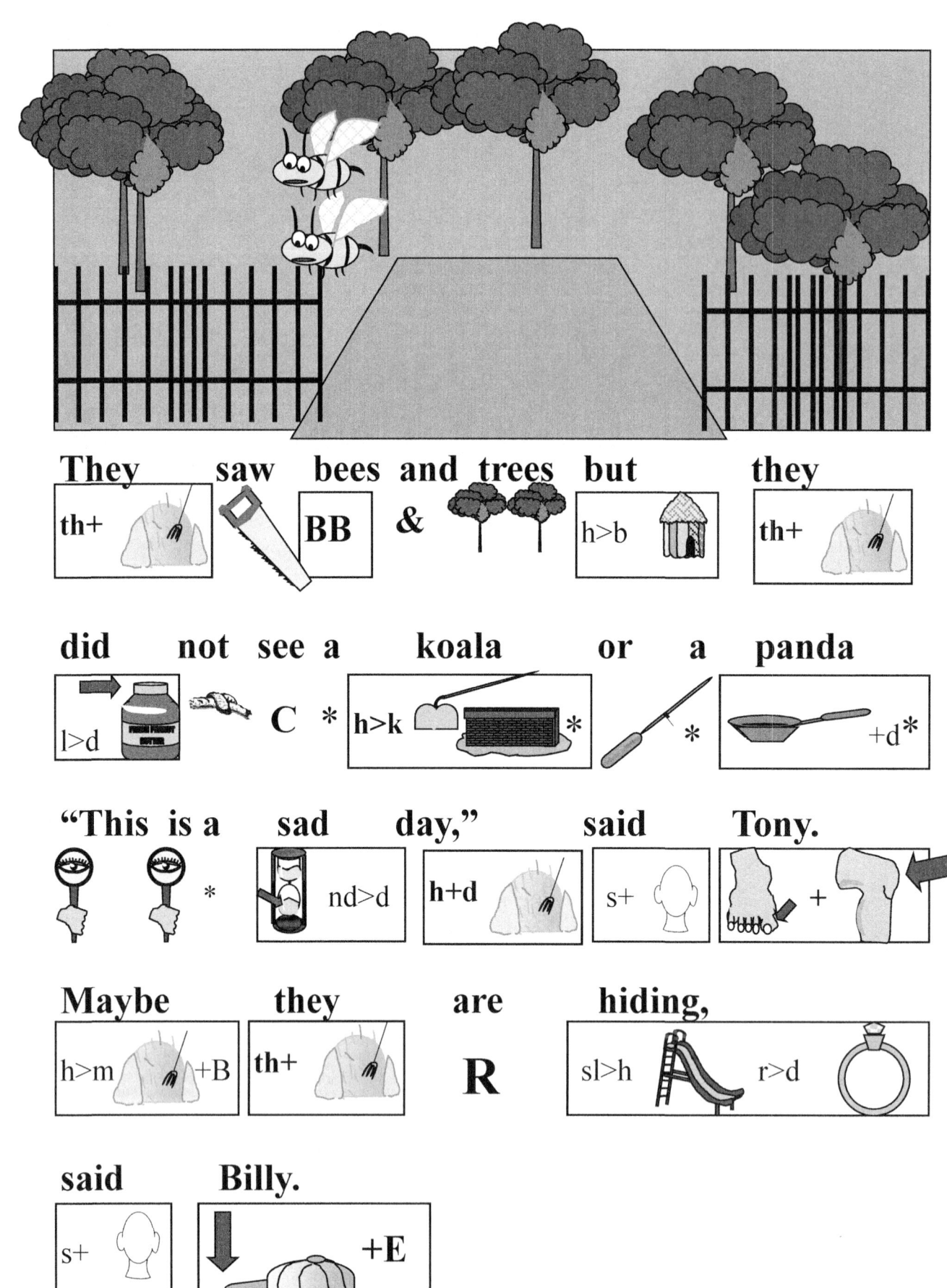

They saw bees and trees but they

did not see a koala or a panda

"This is a sad day," said Tony.

Maybe they are hiding,

said Billy.

142

"I can not see the animals," said

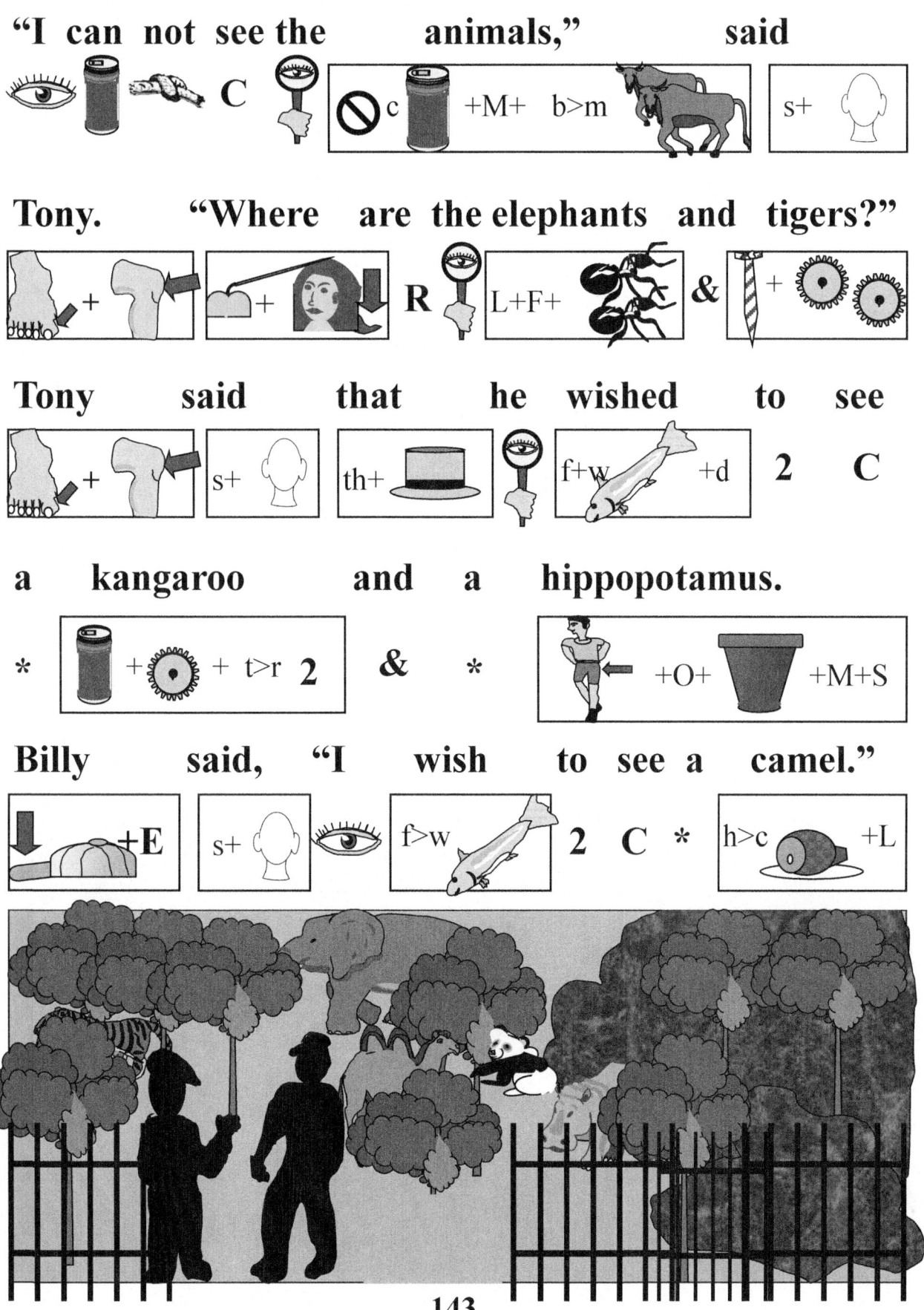

Tony. "Where are the elephants and tigers?"

Tony said that he wished to see

a kangaroo and a hippopotamus.

Billy said, "I wish to see a camel."

143

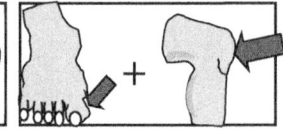

"We should go home," said Tony.

 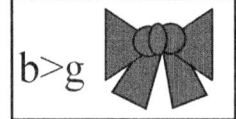 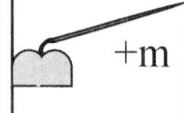 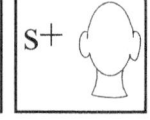 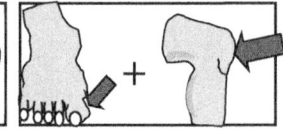

"We have not seen any animals."

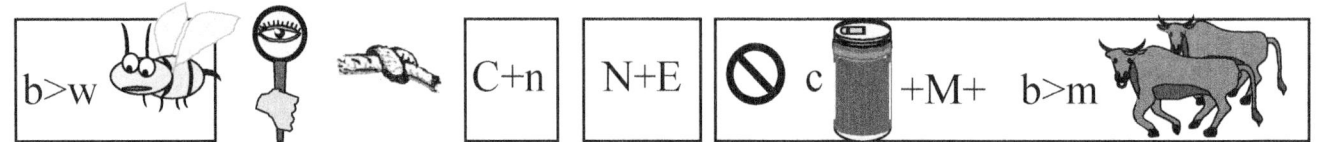

"I agree." said Billy.

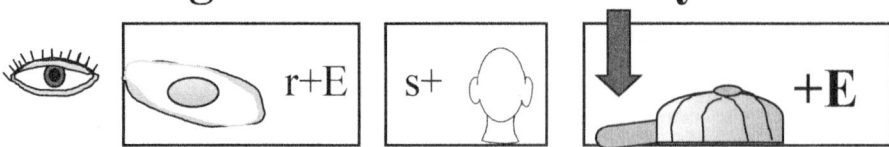

The two boys went home slowly.

 2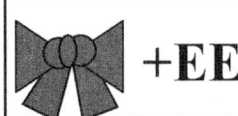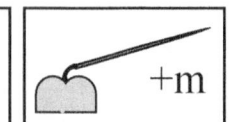

The Camping Trip

Barney   bought   a   green   canvas   tent   so

that   he   could   go   camping   and   fishing

with his   companion   Corky.   The   boys   saw

two   brown   bears   eating   huckleberries.

Corky   and   Barney   set   up   the   tent,

put   down   the   sleeping   bags,   and

started   for   the   lake.

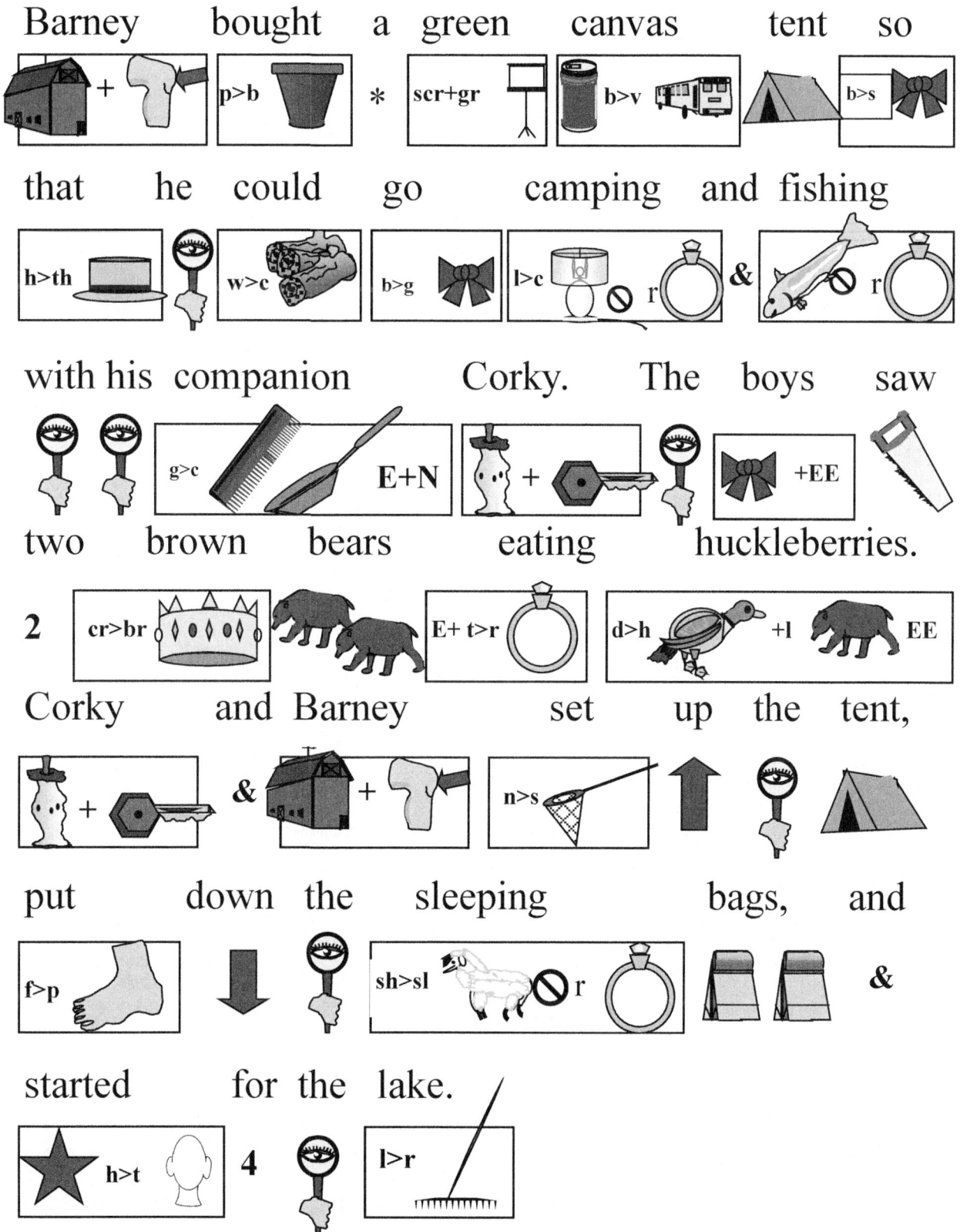

145

Clouds began to rise in the sky and

rain began to fall. They ran to

their tent. They sat in the tent

watching the rain for a couple hours.

Then the sun came out. They took

fishing poles and headed for the lake.

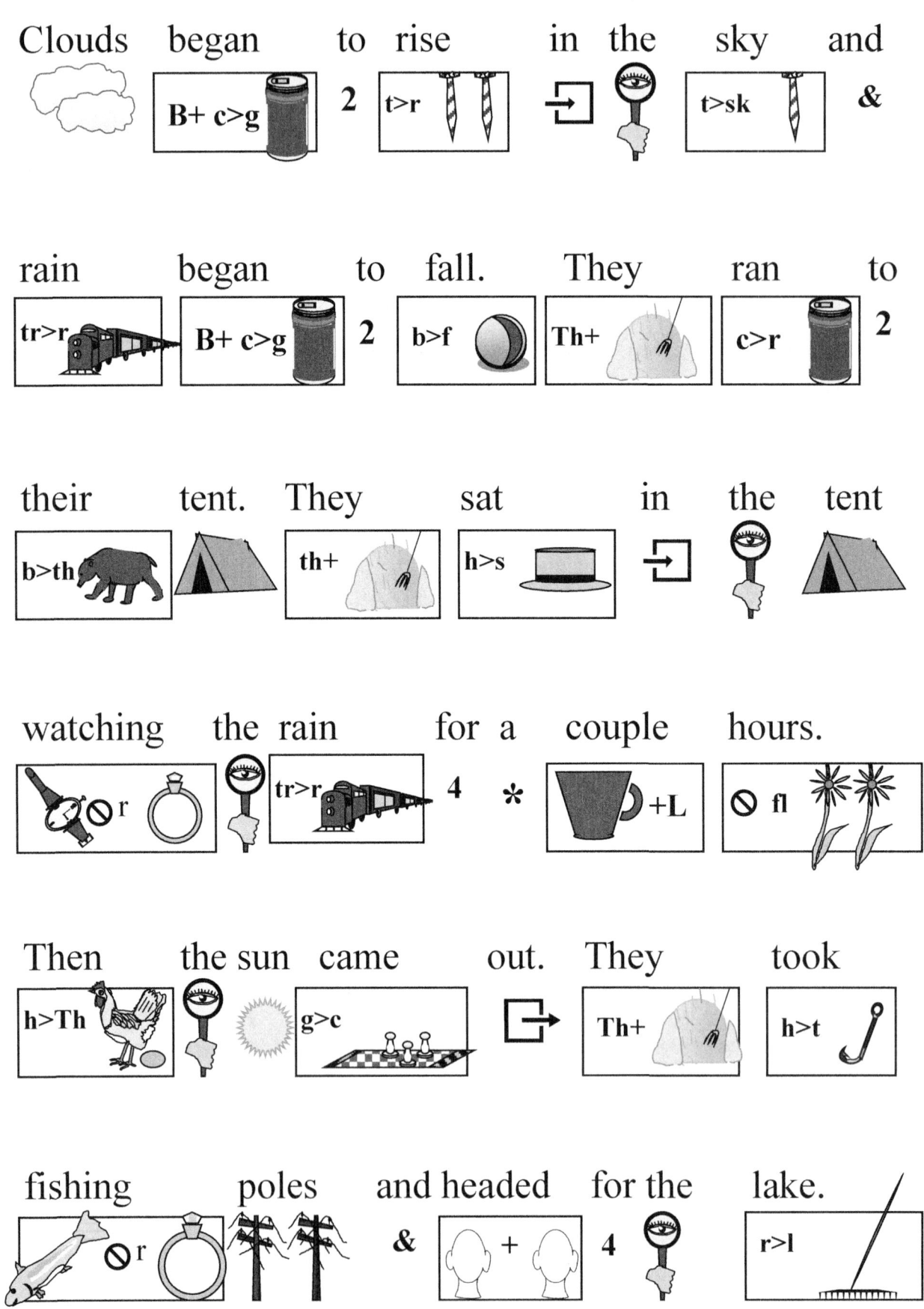

146

The Yard Sale

Jack is at the side of the house. A yard sale is taking place. A stack of tires is for sale for ten dollars. Chocolate candy is on the table.

"I saw a tractor, a pickup, and a trailer," said Jack. "Where are the television, the toolbox and the soccer ball?"

Aunt Sandy arrived in a yellow taxi cab. Aunt Sandy handed five dollars to the driver. The driver drove away. Sandy saw many things for sale.

Jack said, " I see you located our sale. Do you see anything you wish to buy?"

Aunt Sandy said, "I would like to buy the bicycle." Aunt Sandy examined a toboggan, a tennis racket, a wagon, and a tackle box.

Jack turned and saw Grandpa standing on the porch.

Aunt Sandy said that she did not want to buy the battery. She paid Grandpa for the bicycle. Then they went into the house.

Treasure on the Island

Captain Crook and many pirates landed on goat island. The Captain looked at a map. An X marked the buried treasure. The men walked through the jungle. They saw a cave and a cannon. The pirates stopped when they saw a big canyon. An alligator stood near a shack. Night was coming and the men set up camp. They built a fire and cooked fish. The pirates crawled into their beds for the night.

The next day, the men began to look for the treasure again. They found the three leaf palm tree and   began to dig.

The pirates loaded the treasure onto the boat. They began to row to the ship. The men hauled the chest on board.

Captain Crook ordered the men to their places. The sails caught the wind. The ship sailed for England.

At the Zoo

Many different animals are at the zoo. Billy and Tony went there to see them. They walked the trail. They saw bees and trees but they did not see a koala or a panda.

"This is a sad day," said Tony.

"Maybe they are hiding," said Billy.

"I can not see the animals." said Tony. "Where are the elephants and tigers?"

Tony said that he wished to see a kangaroo and a hippopotamus.

Billy said, "I wish to see a camel."

"We should go home," said Tony. "We have not seen any animals."

"I agree." said Billy.

The two boys went home slowly.

The Camping Trip

Barney bought a green canvas tent so that he could go camping and fishing with his companion Corky. The boys saw two brown bears eating huckleberries. Corky and Barney set up the tent, put down the sleeping bags, and started for the lake.
Clouds began to rise in the sky and rain began to fall. They ran to their tent. They sat in the tent watching the rain for a couple hours. Then the sun came out. They took fishing poles and headed for the lake.

REBUS PHRASES

The parent or teacher may wish to wait until later to have children do the following activities. They contain common expressions or familiar phrases that are more difficult than in previous sections. They are designed to be challenging as well as fun, so you may have a child try them from time to time. These rebuses help a child to reinforce recognition of syllables, to learn to connect parts that may not be complete syllables (as in blending), and to determine which syllables or sound units are to be accented in order to aid in the solving of these common familiar phrases. The rebus phrases reinforce the left-to-right, top-to-bottom eye-movement necessary in the reading process, as well, demonstrating that reading involves comprehending words in sequence as well as decoding of words.

Answers to the phrases appear upside-down at the lower right hand corner of each page.

Directions: Decode the rebus phrases, left to right, as you would a sentence.
Sample phrase: 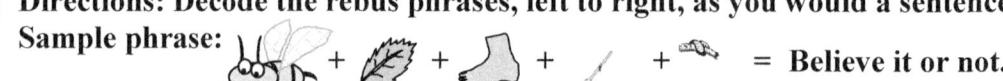 = Believe it or not.

phrase 1

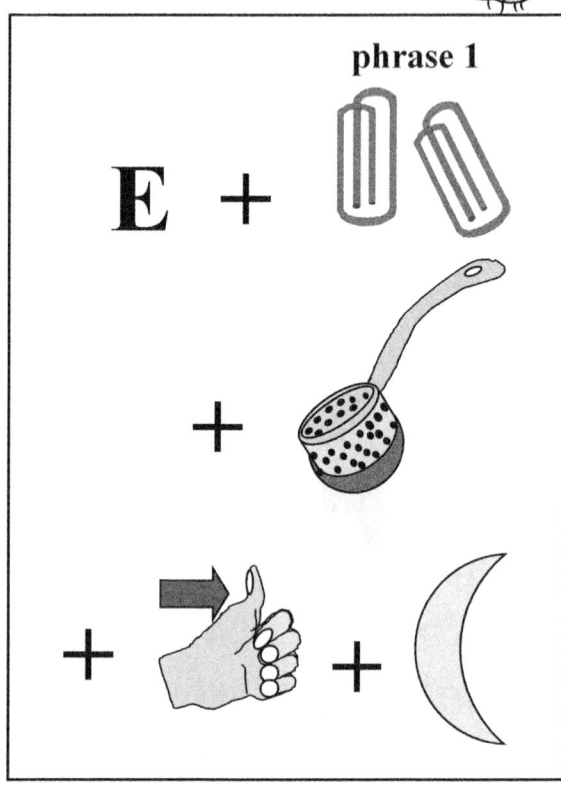

phrase 2

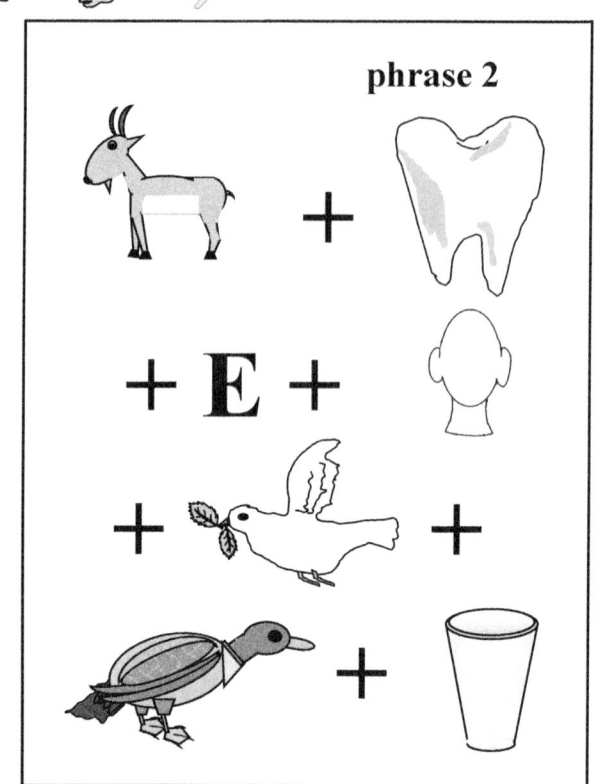

phrase 3

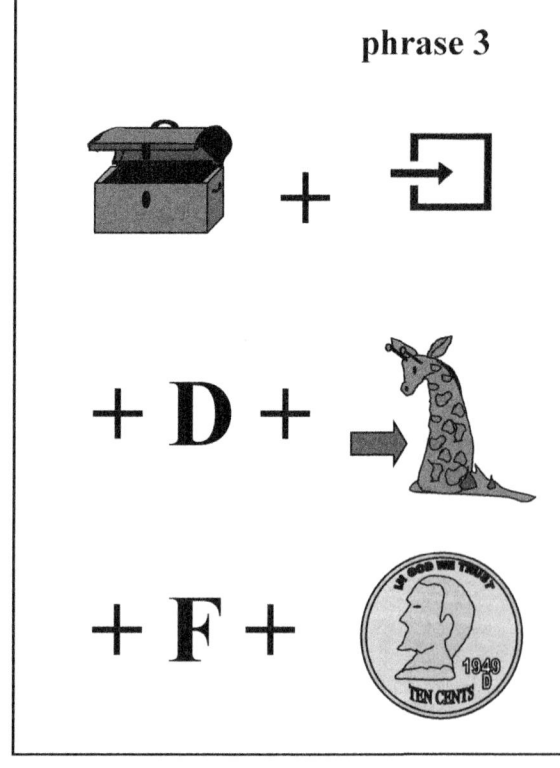

phrase 4

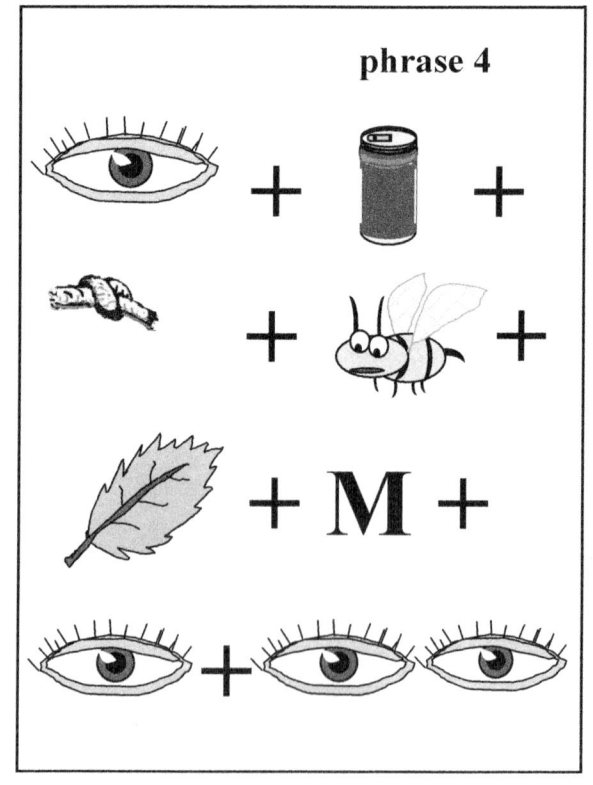

ANSWERS : cannot believe my eyes
3. Just in the nick of time 4. I
1. Eclipse of the moon 2. Go to the head of the class

phrase 1

phrase 2

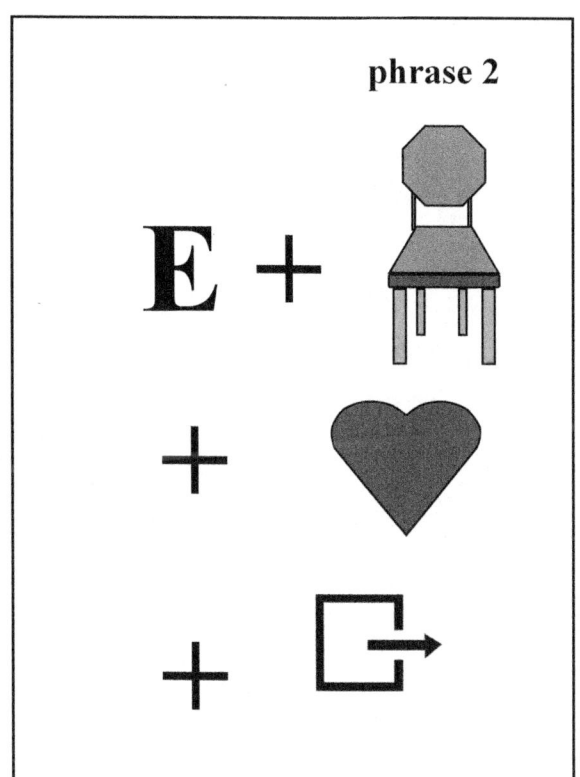

phrase 3

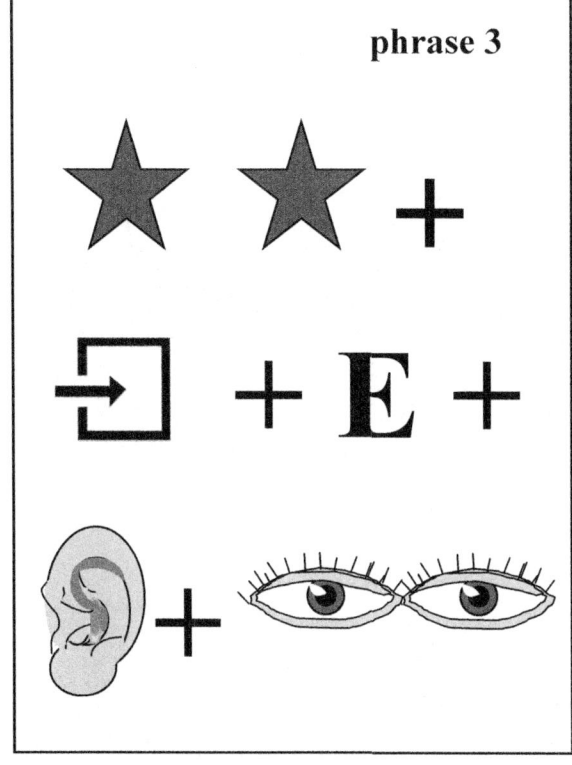

phrase 4

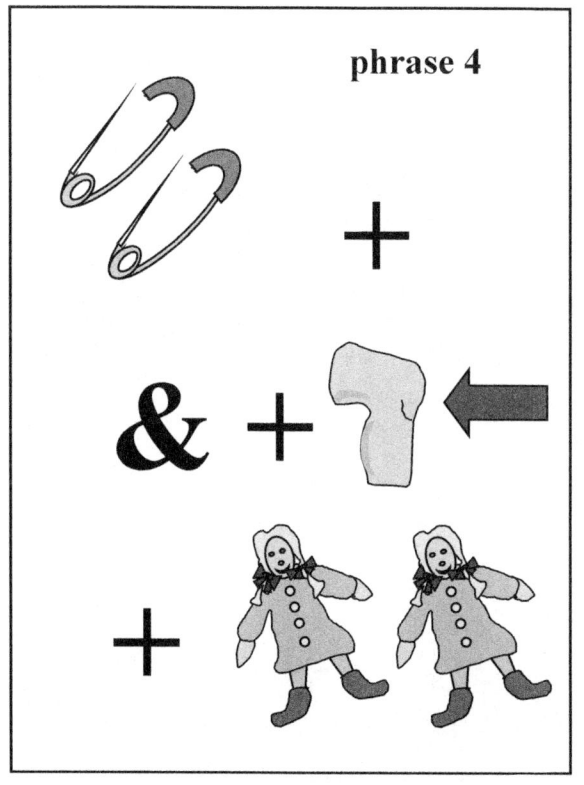

153

ANSWERS :

1. Crazy like a fox 2. Eat your heart out 3. Stars in
your eyes 4. Pins and needles

REBUS PHRASES

Directions: Decode the rebus phrases, left to right, as you would a sentence.

Sample phrase: 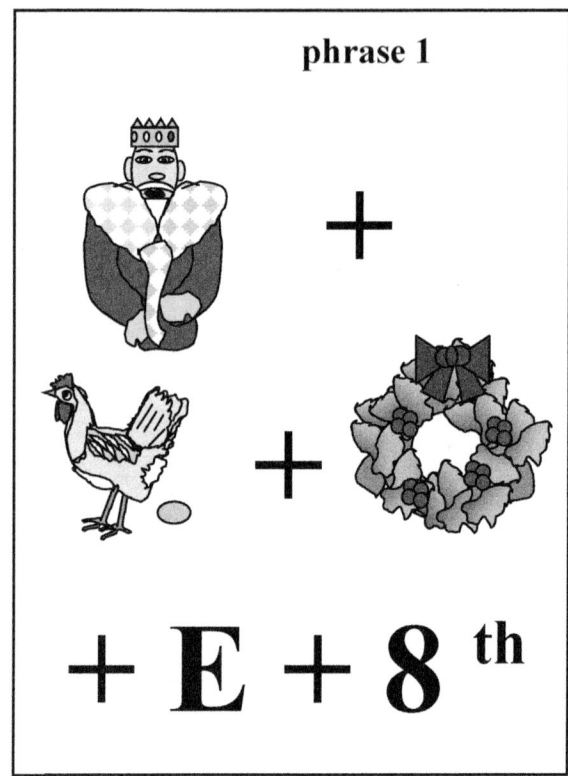 = Believe it or not.

phrase 1

phrase 2

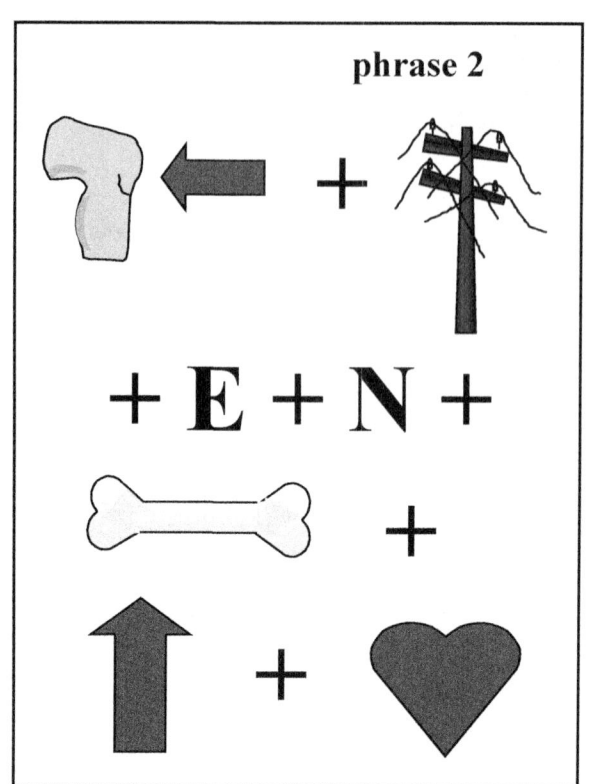

phrase 3

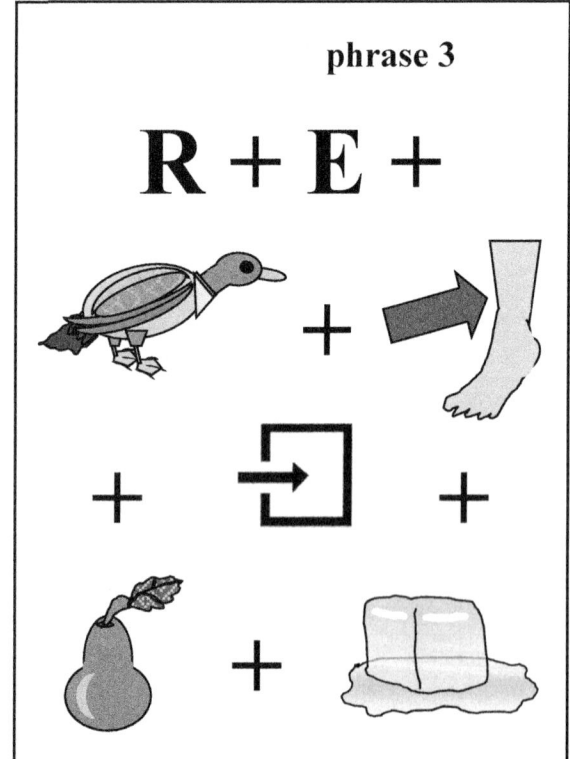

phrase 4

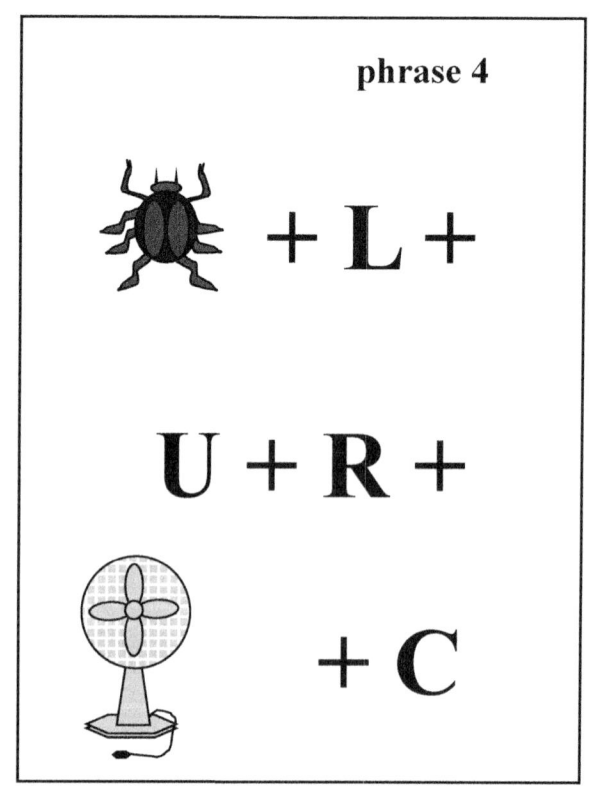

ANSWERS :
1. King Henry the Eighth 2. Napoleon Bonaparte 3. A reduction in price 4. Tickle your fancy

REBUS PHRASES

Directions: Decode the rebus phrases, left to right, as you would a sentence.
Sample phrase: 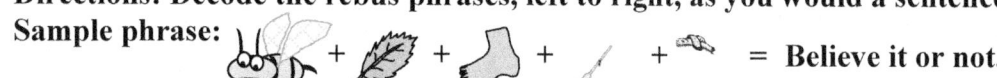 = Believe it or not.

phrase 1

phrase 2

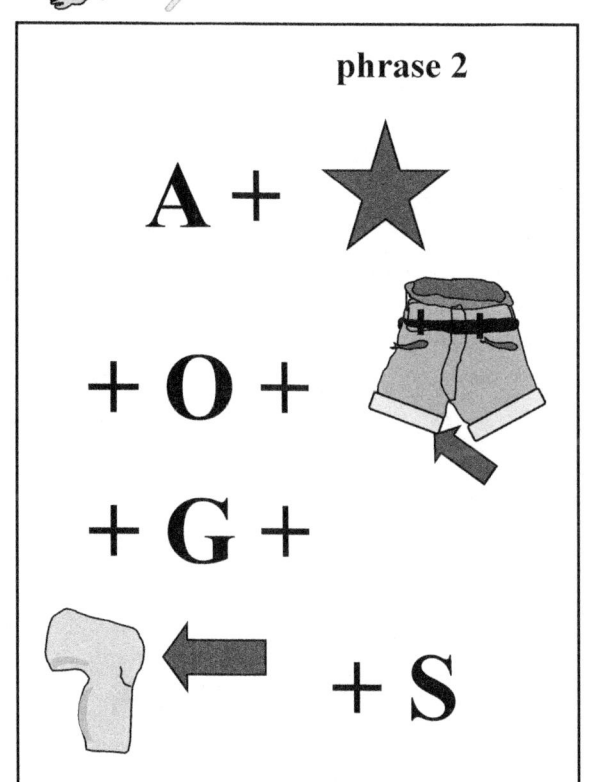

phrase 3

phrase 4

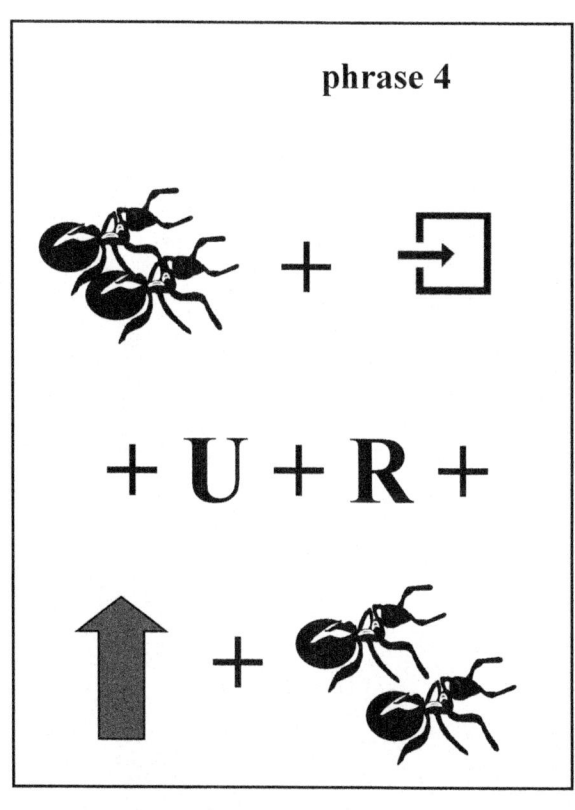

REBUS PHRASES

Directions: Decode the rebus phrases, left to right, as you would a sentence.
Sample phrase: 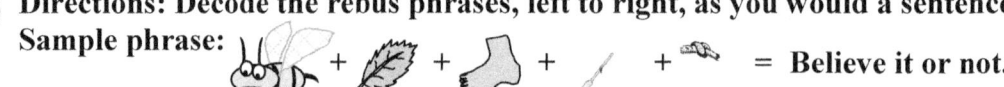 = Believe it or not.

phrase 1

phrase 2

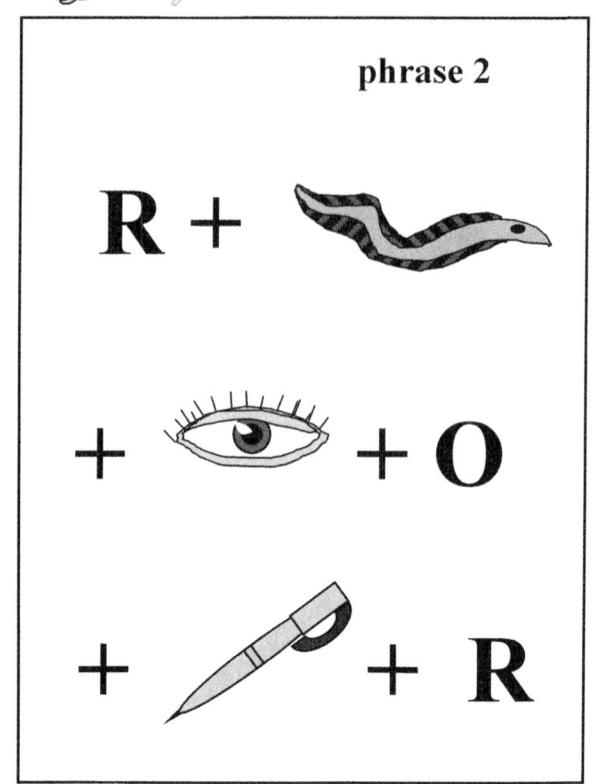

phrase 3

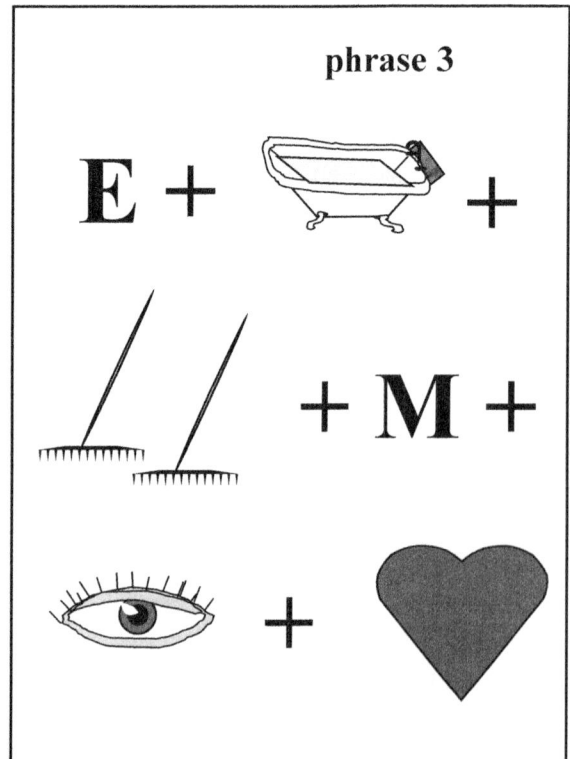

phrase 4

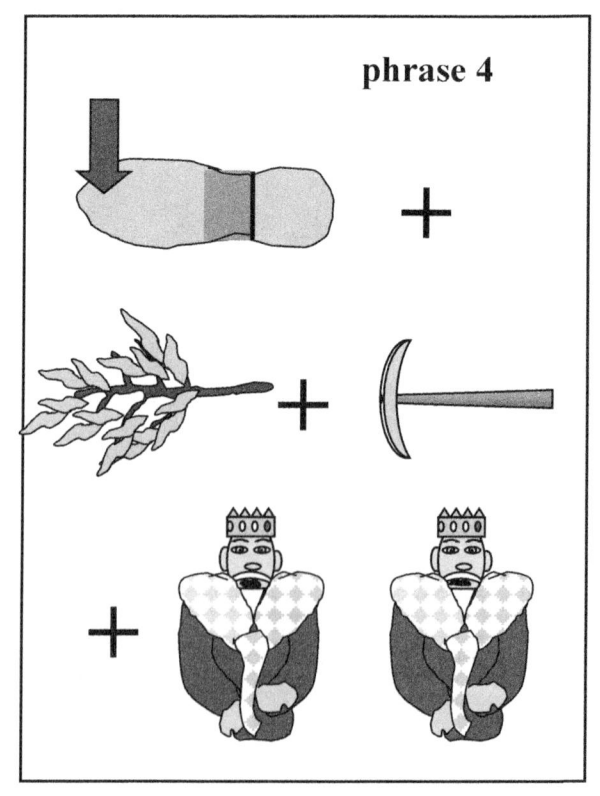

REBUS PHRASES

Directions: Decode the rebus phrases, left to right, as you would a sentence.
Sample phrase:  = Believe it or not.

---

phrase 1

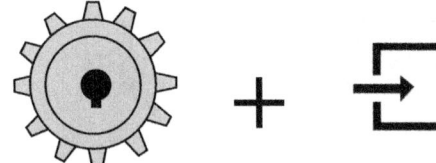

+ **&** +

---

phrase 2

+ E + S +

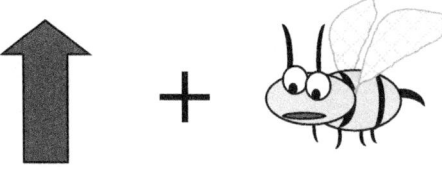

---

phrase 3

+ H +

---

phrase 4

C +

+ 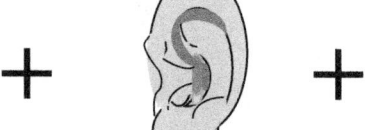 **+**

4 +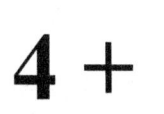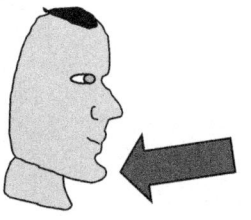

ANSWERS :

4. Seek your fortune

1. Grin and bear it 2. Busy as a bee 3. Not a chance

REBUS PHRASES

Directions: Decode the rebus phrases, left to right, as you would a sentence.
Sample phrase:  = Believe it or not.

phrase 1

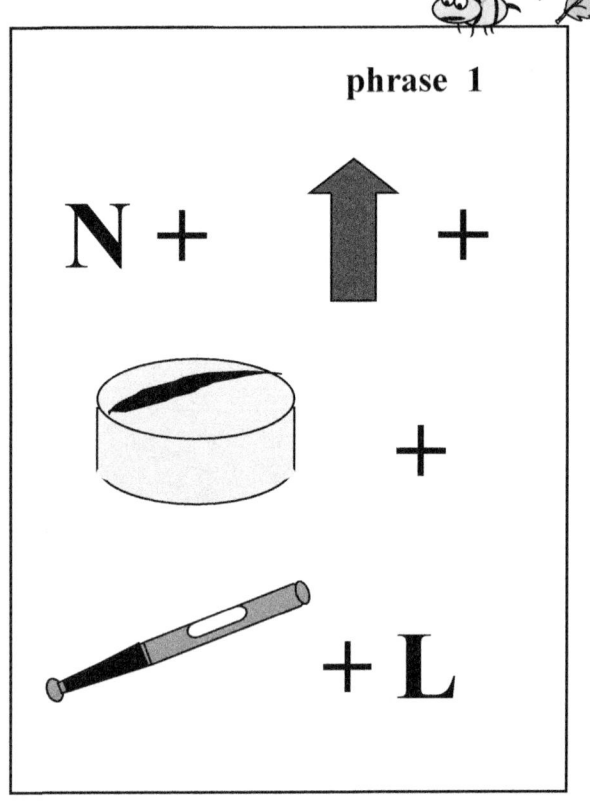

N + ↑ +

+

+ L

phrase 2

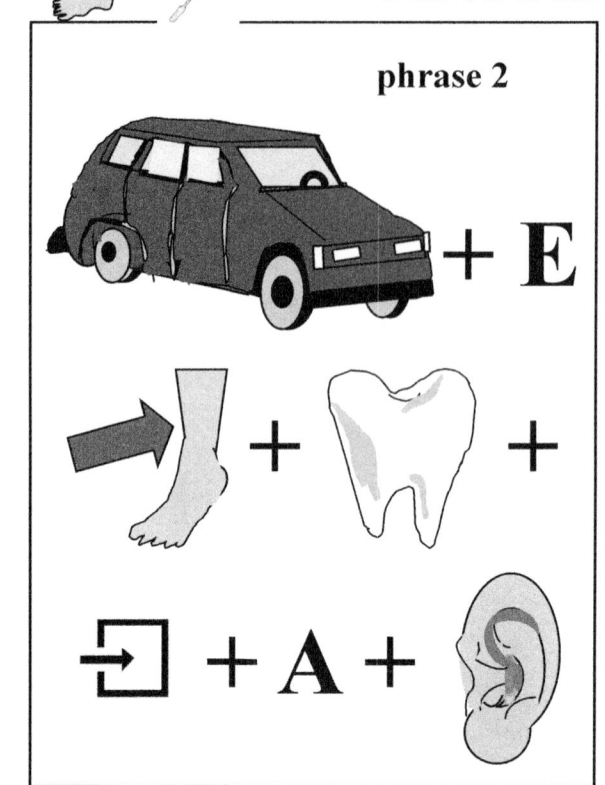

+ E

+ +

+ A +

phrase 3

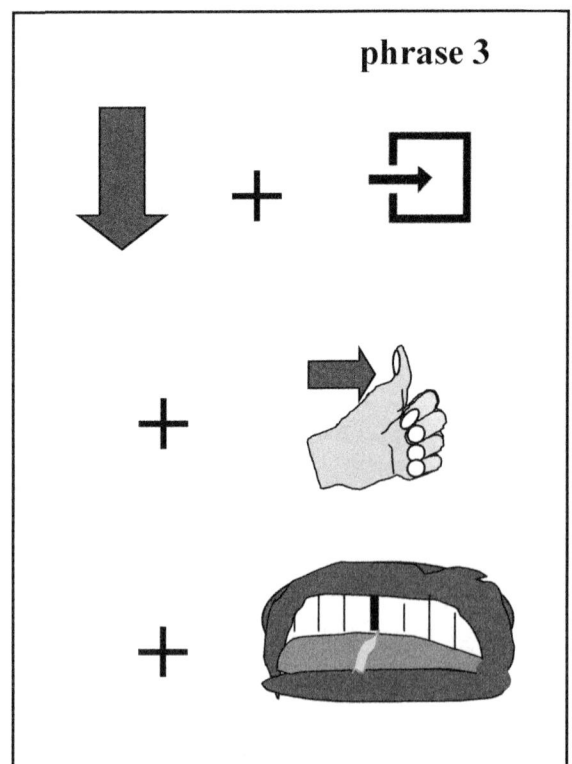

↓ +

+

+

phrase 4

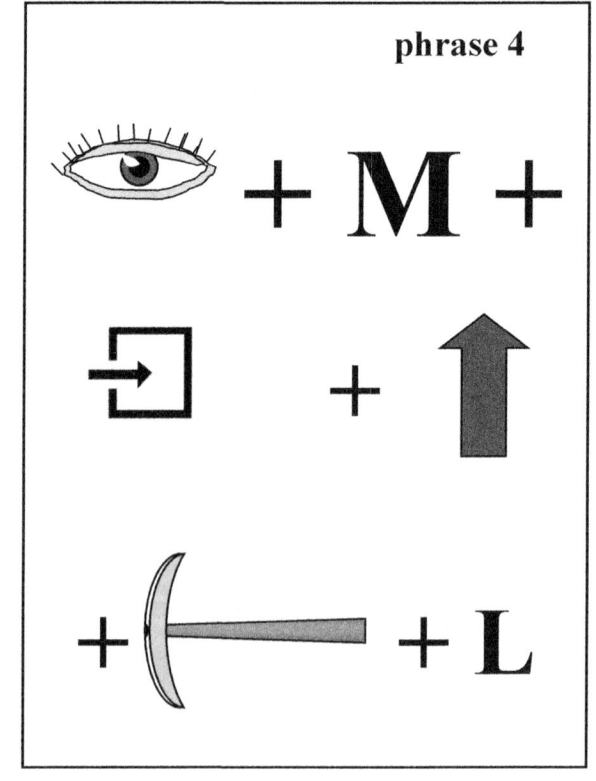

+ M +

+ ↑

+ + L

158

Directions: Decode the rebus phrases, left to right, as you would a sentence.
Sample phrase: 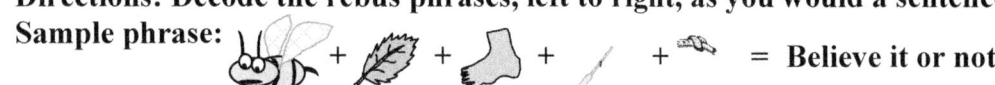 = Believe it or not.

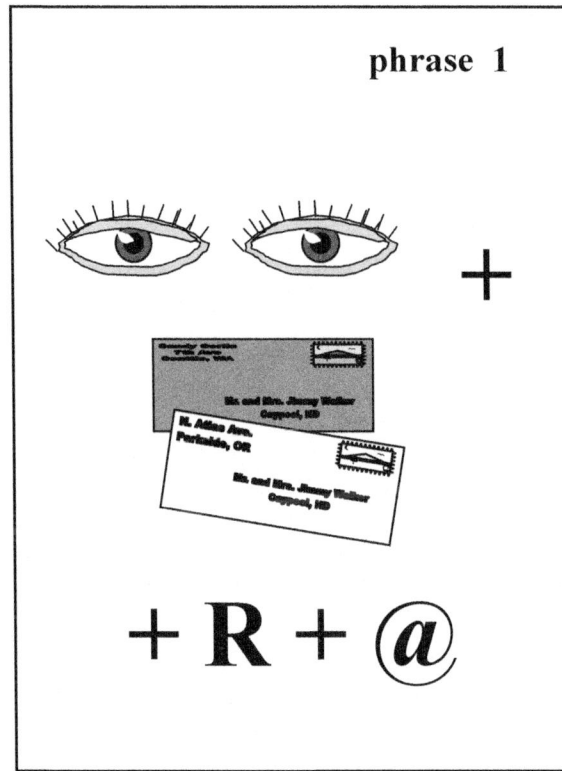

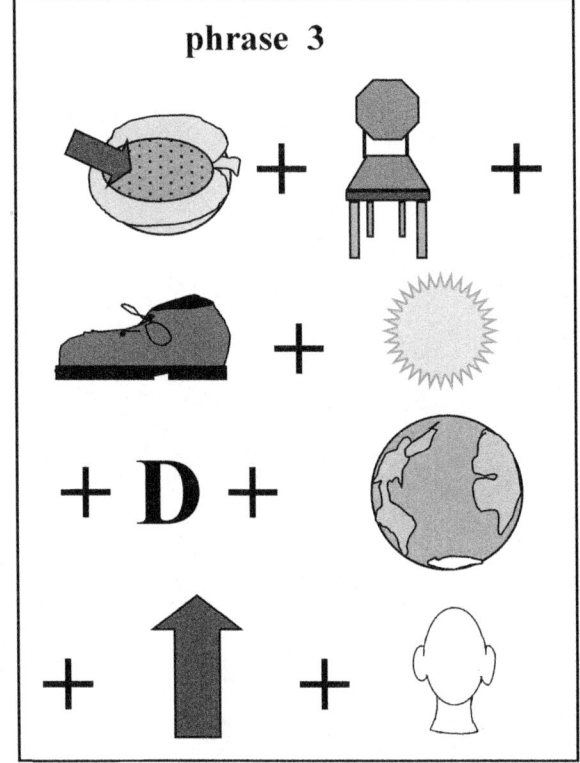

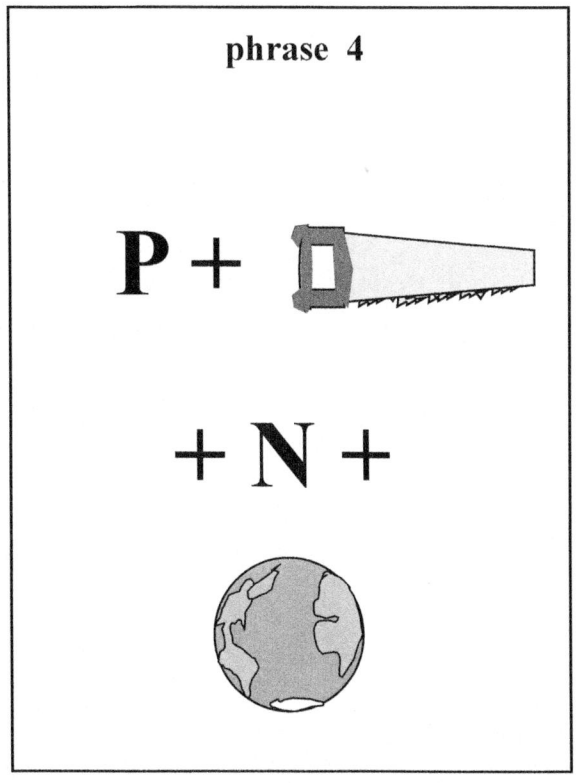

ANSWERS :

1. I smell a rat 2. No spring chicken 3. Put your shoes under the bed 4. Peace on earth

REBUS PHRASES

Directions: Decode the rebus phrases, left to right, as you would a sentence.
Sample phrase:  = Believe it or not.

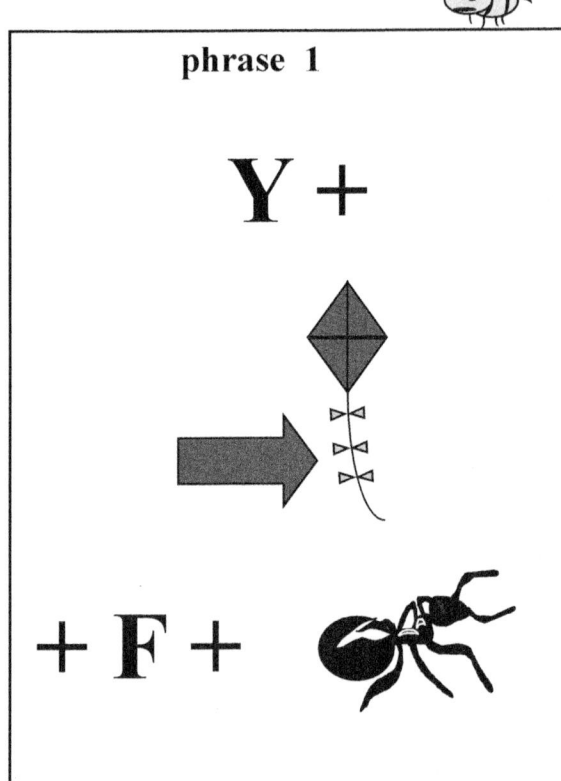

phrase 1

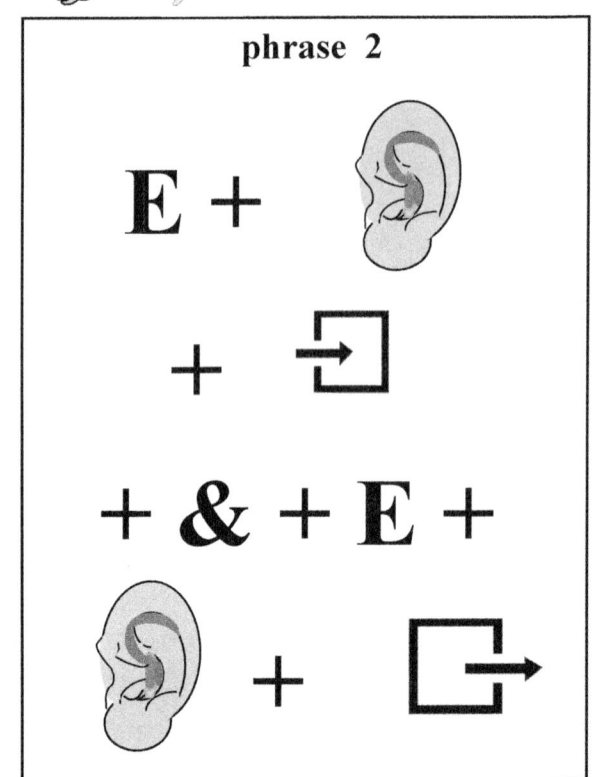

phrase 2

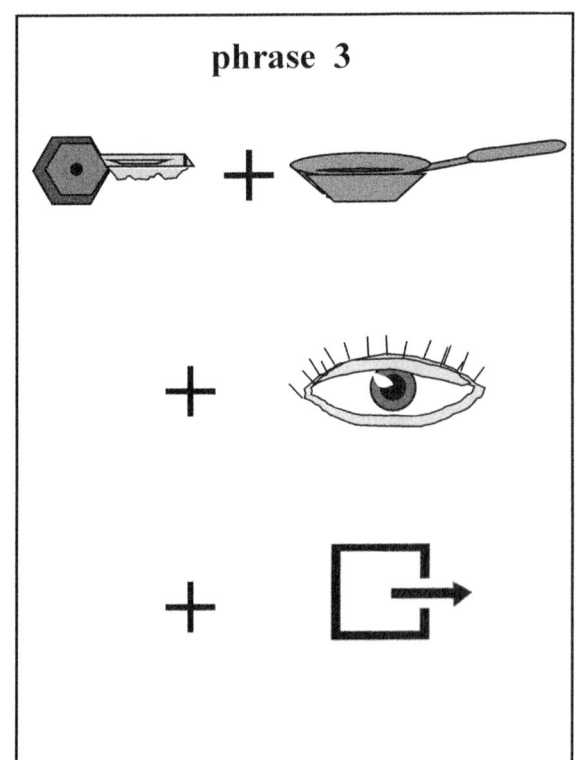

phrase 3

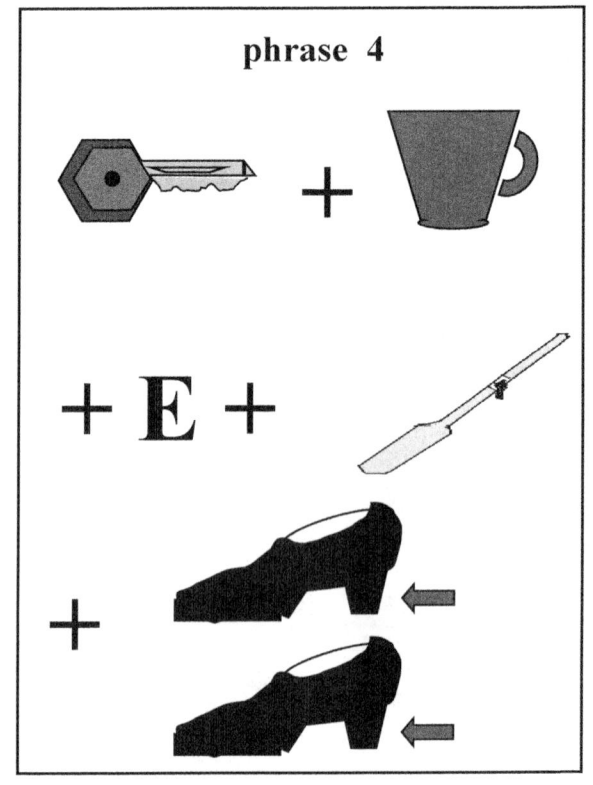

phrase 4

160

REBUS PHRASES

Directions: Decode the rebus phrases, left to right, as you would a sentence.
Sample phrase: 🐝 + 🍃 + 🦶 + ✒ + 🪶 = Believe it or not.

phrase 1

phrase 2

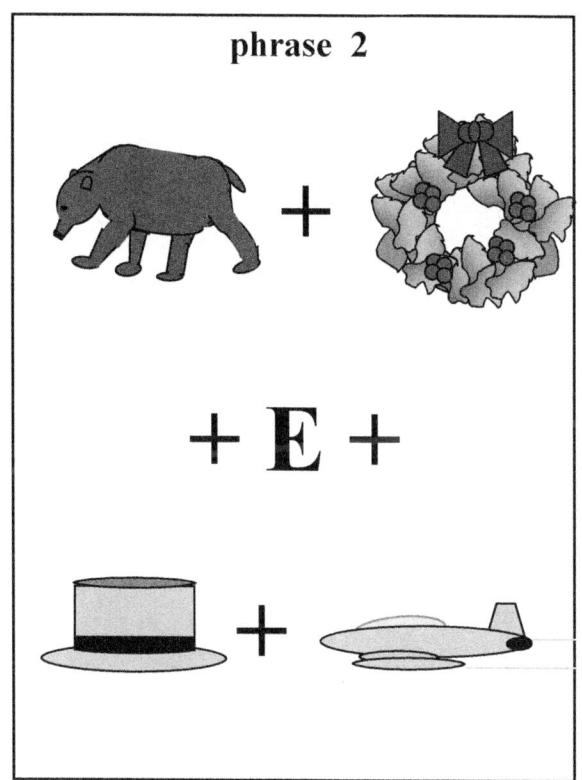

phrase 3

phrase 4

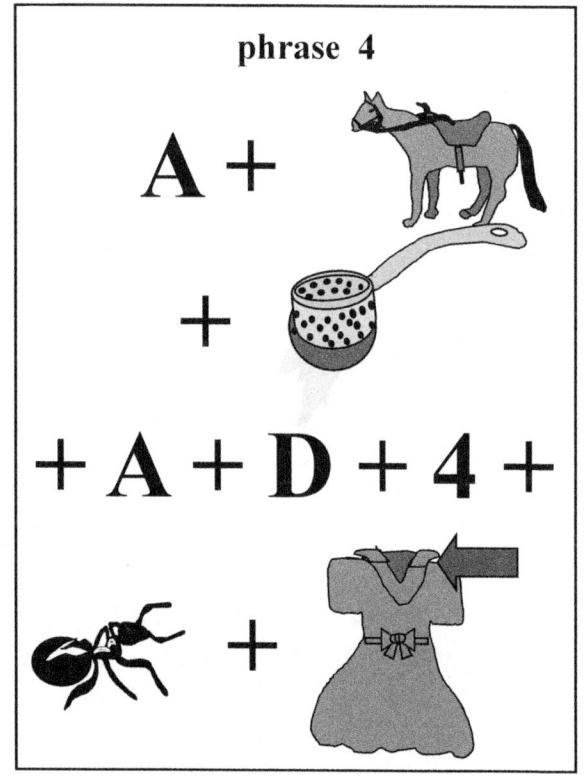

ANSWERS :

1. A dear john letter. 2. Bury the hatchet. 3. No man is an island. 4. A horse of a different color

REBUS PHRASES

Directions: Decode the rebus phrases, left to right, as you would a sentence.
Sample phrase: 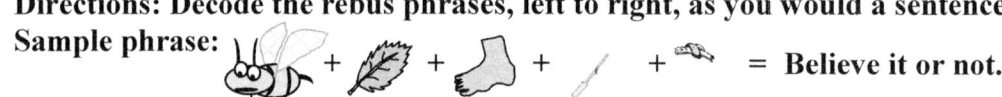 = Believe it or not.

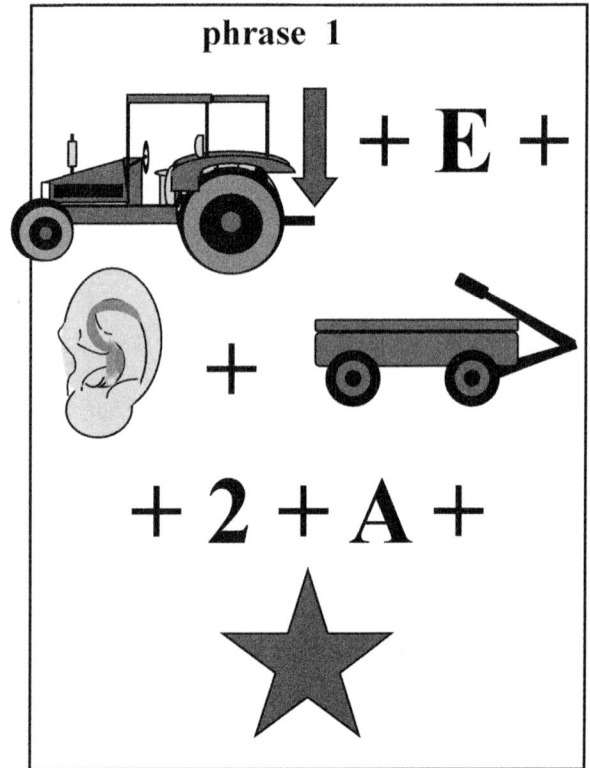

phrase 1

+ **E** +

+

+ **2** + **A** +

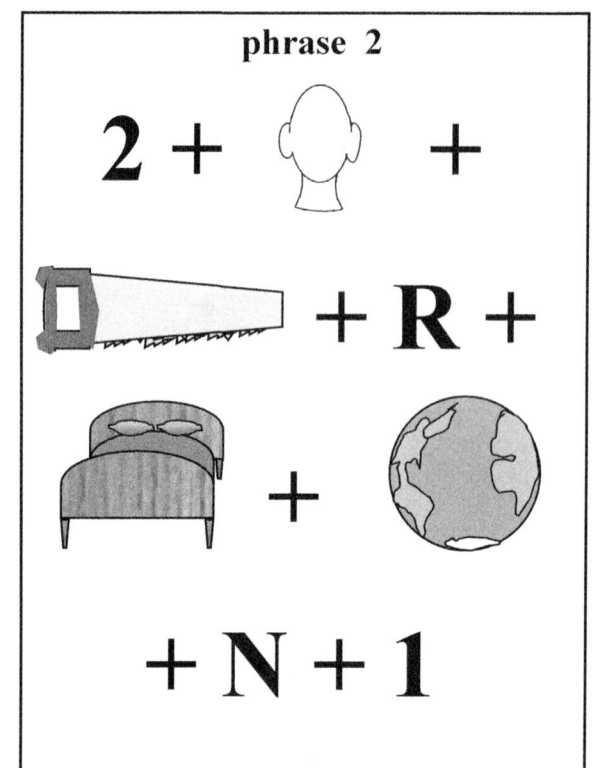

phrase 2

2 + +

+ **R** +

+

+ **N** + **1**

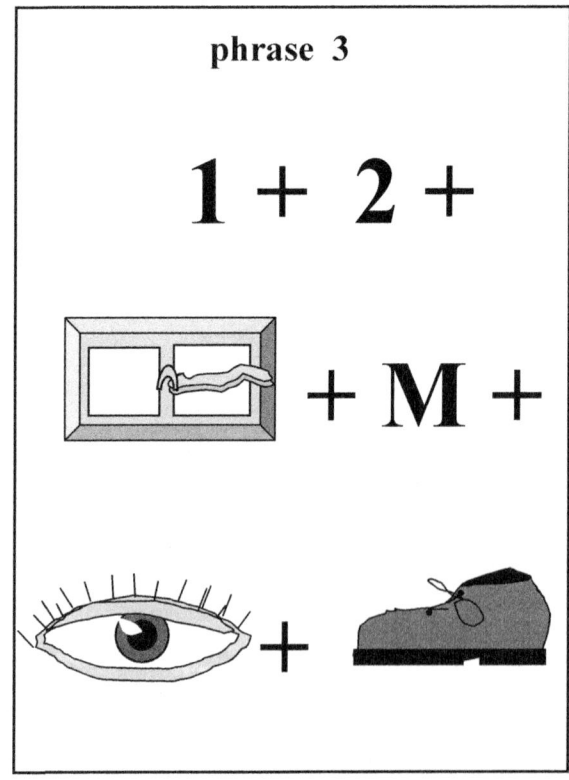

phrase 3

1 + **2** +

+ **M** +

+

phrase 4

+ **E** +

+ + **E**

+ **3** +

162

ANSWERS :

1. Hitch your wagon to a star. 2. Two heads are better than one. 3. One, two, buckle my shoe 4. Goldilocks and the three bears

REBUS PHRASES

Directions: Decode the rebus phrases, left to right, as you would a sentence.
Sample phrase: 🪰 + 🌿 + 👣 + ✏ + 💨 = Believe it or not.

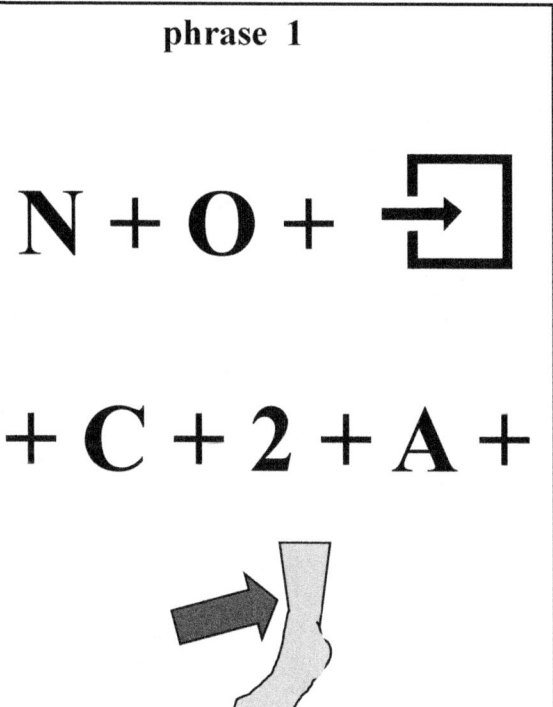

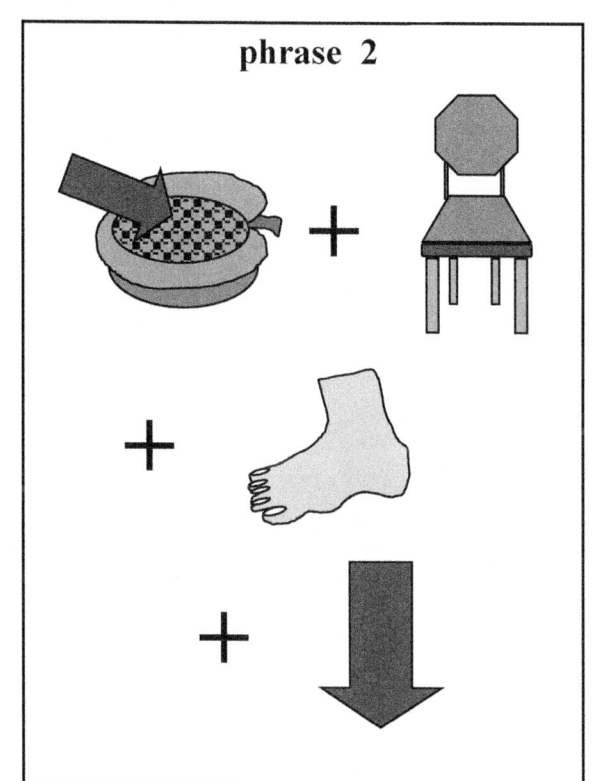

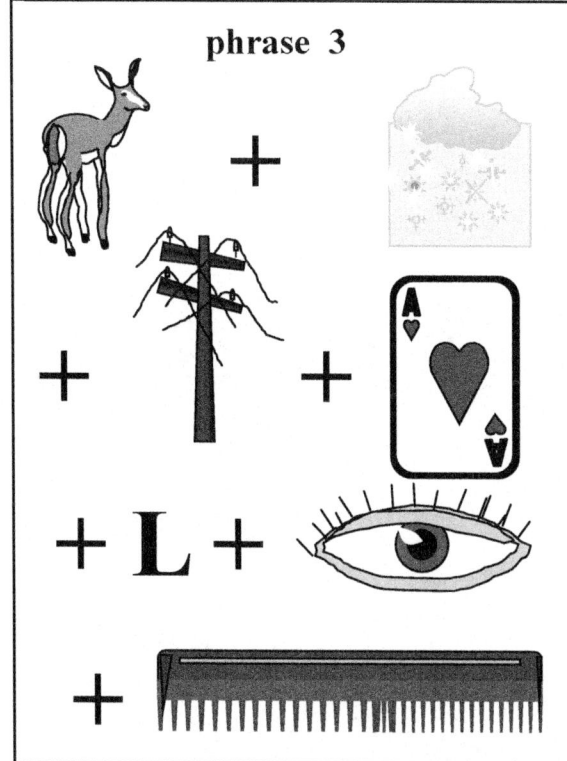

ANSWERS :

1. A no-win situation. 2. Put your foot down. 3. There's no place like home. 4. When the cat's away, the mice will play.

REBUS PHRASES

Directions: Decode the rebus phrases, left to right, as you would a sentence.
Sample phrase: 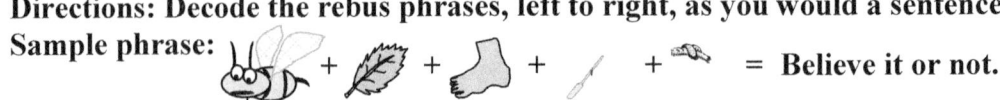 = Believe it or not.

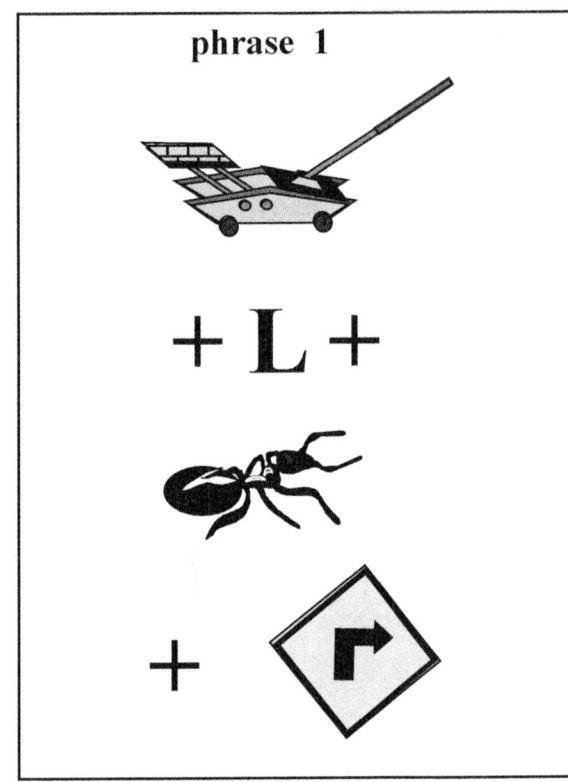

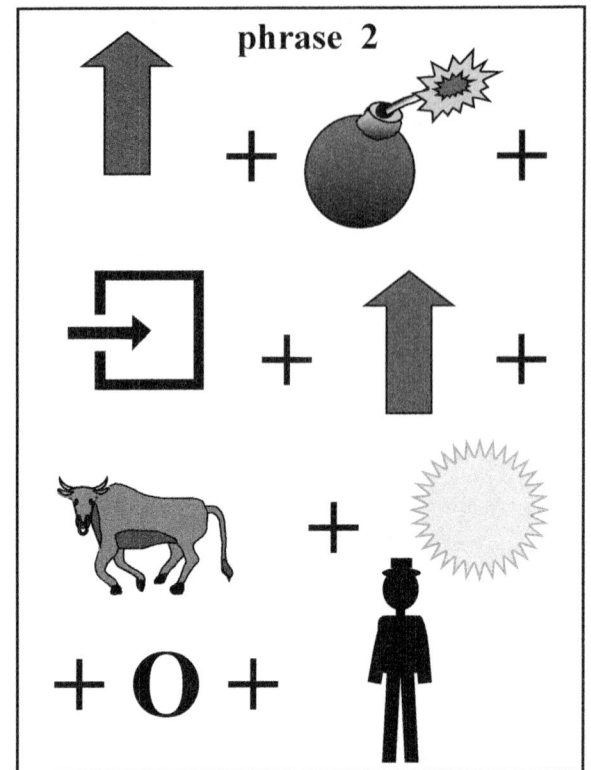

164

REBUS PHRASES

Directions: Decode the rebus phrases, left to right, as you would a sentence.
Sample phrase: 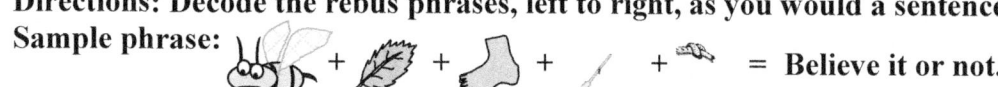 = Believe it or not.

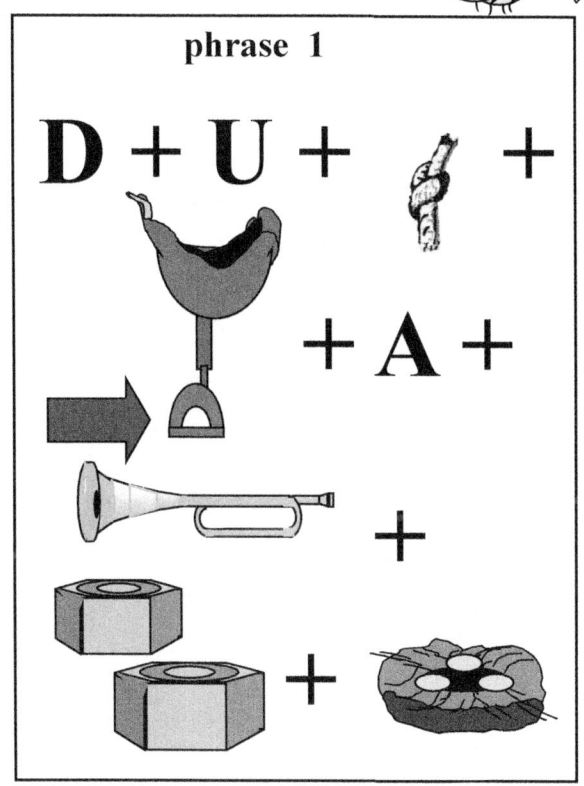

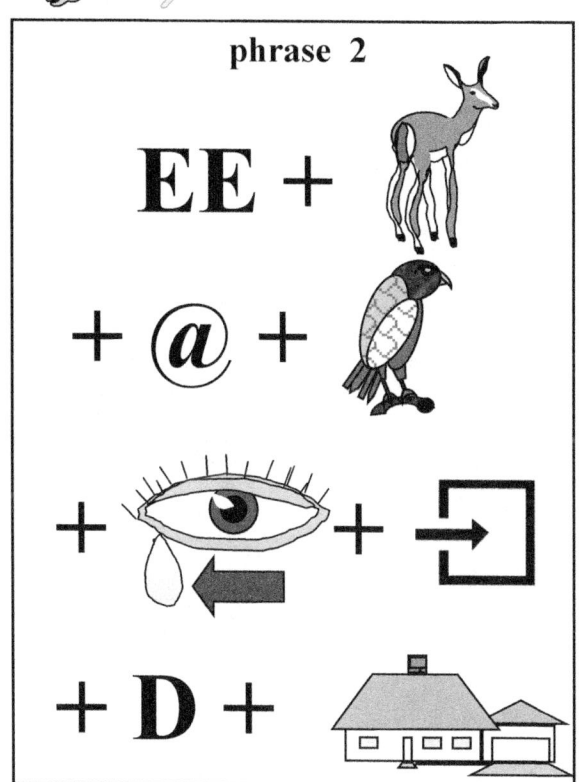

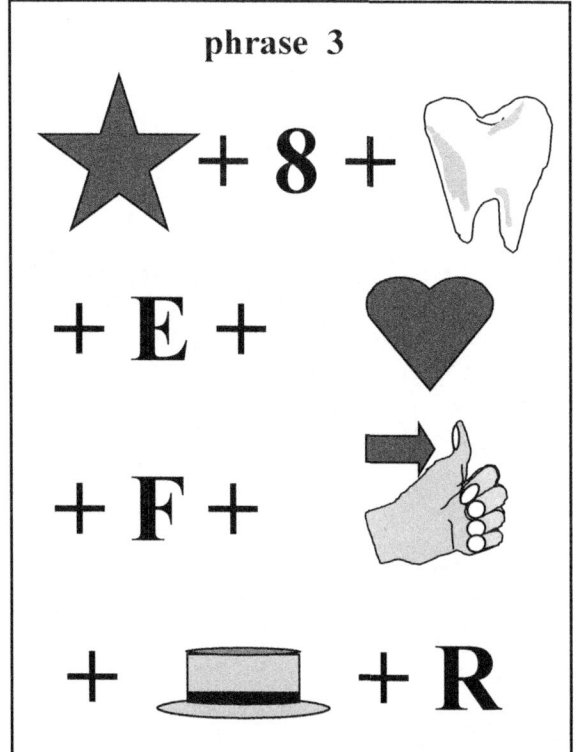

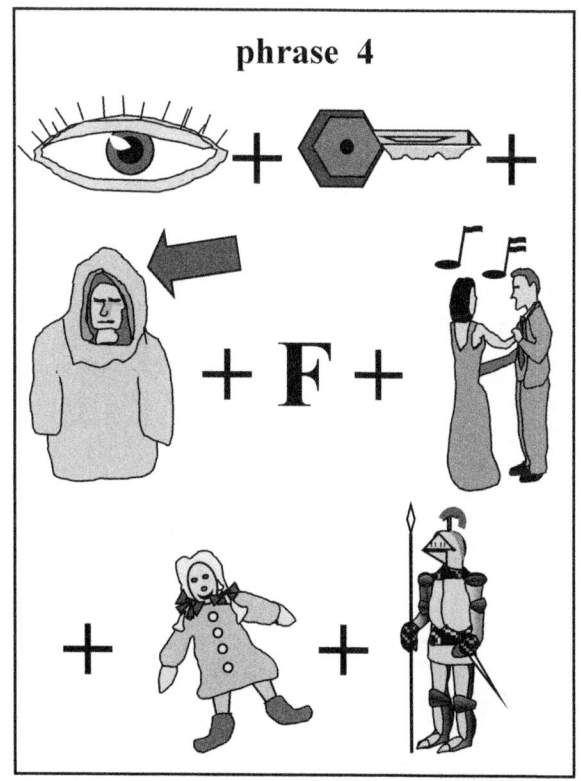

REBUS PHRASES

Directions: Decode the rebus phrases, left to right, as you would a sentence.

Sample phrase: 🐝 + 🍃 + 👣 + ✏️ + 🔔 = Believe it or not.

phrase 1

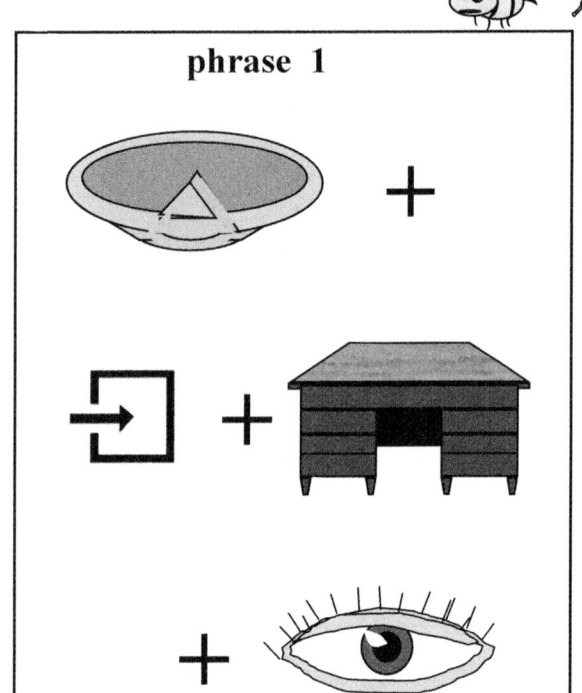

phrase 2

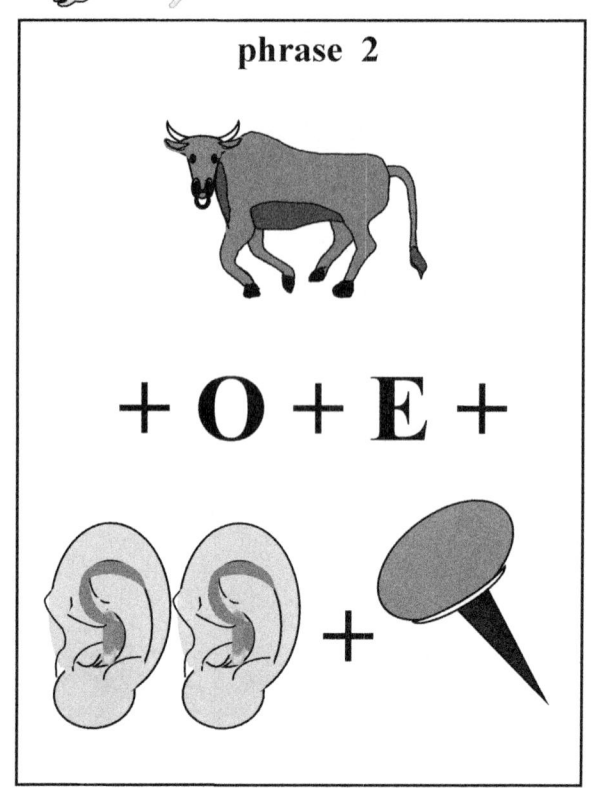

+ **O** + **E** +

phrase 3

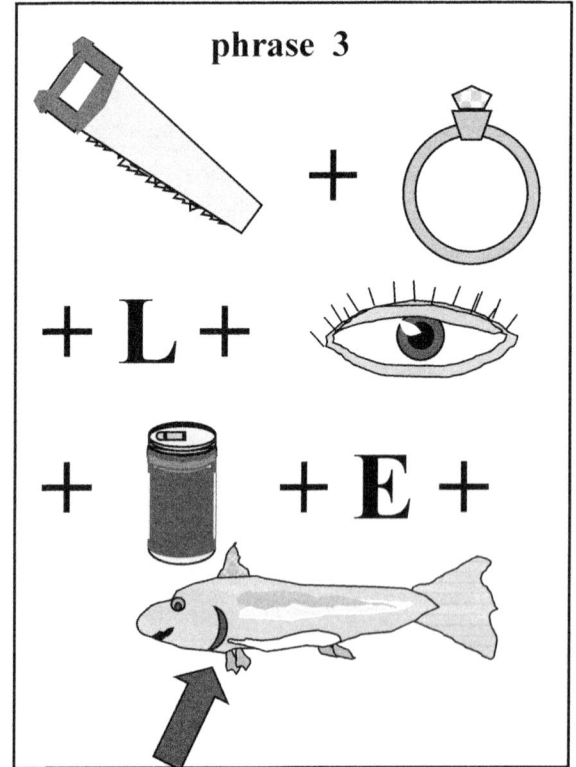

+ **L** +

+ + **E** +

phrase 4

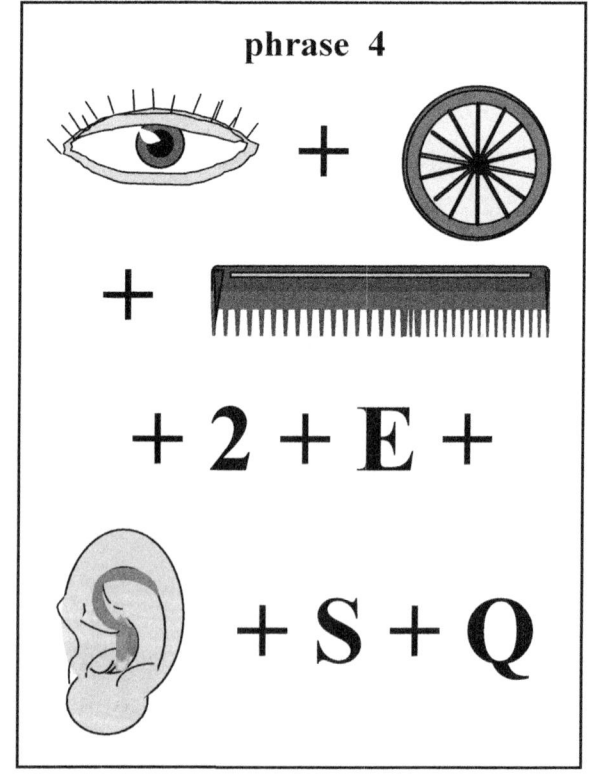

+ **2** + **E** +

+ **S** + **Q**

166

ANSWERS :

1. Pie in the sky 2. Blow your stack 3. Soaring like
an eagle 4. I will come to your rescue.

REBUS PHRASES

Directions: Decode the rebus phrases, left to right, as you would a sentence.
Sample phrase: 🐝 + 🍃 + 🦶 + 🪡 + = Believe it or not.

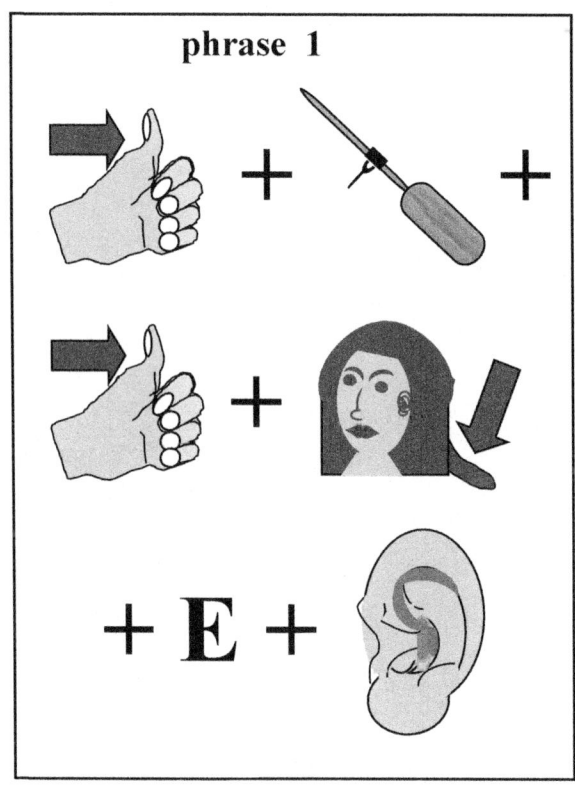

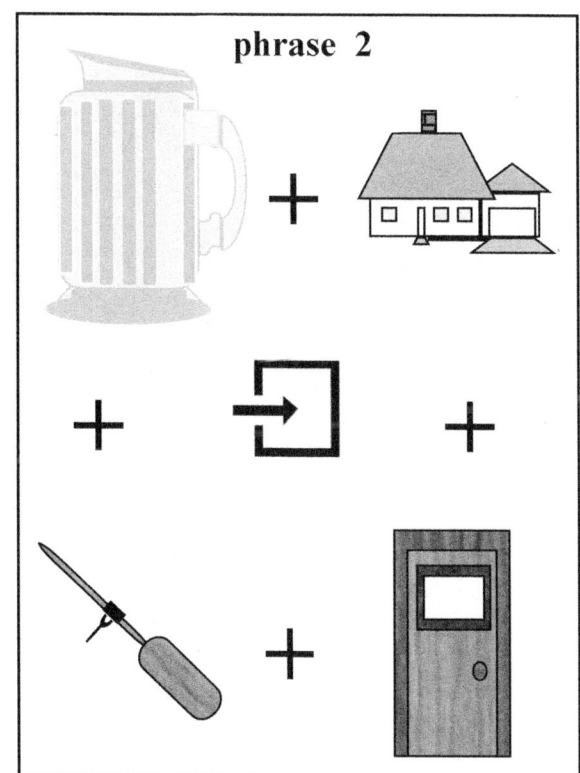

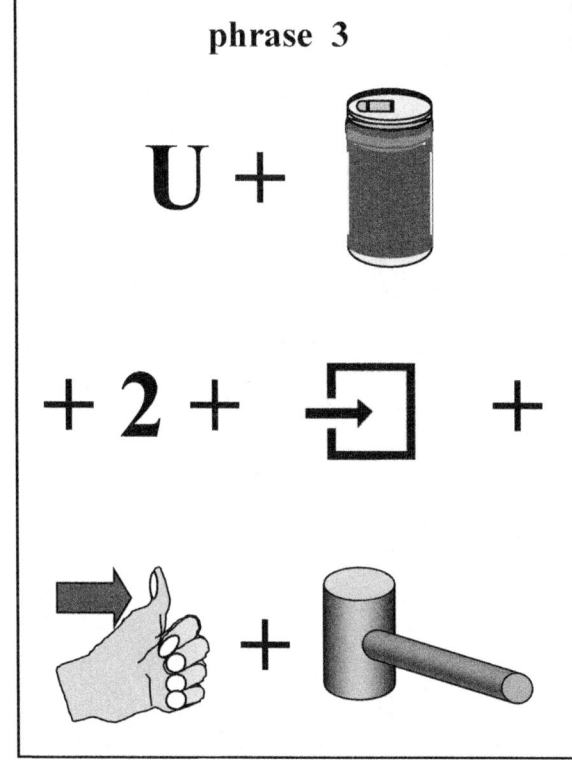

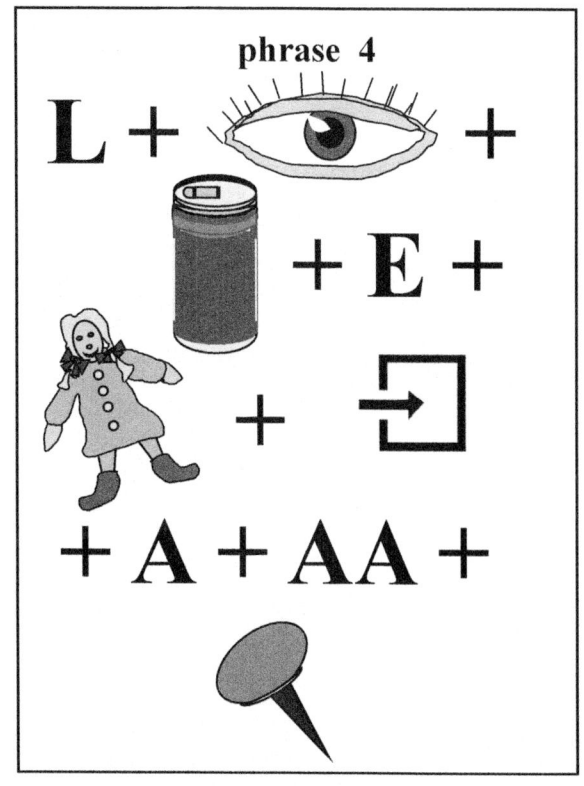

167

1. The more the merrier. 2. Put your house in order.
3. You can't win them all. 4. Like a needle in a hay
stack.

REBUS PHRASES

Directions: Decode the rebus phrases, left to right, as you would a sentence.

Sample phrase: 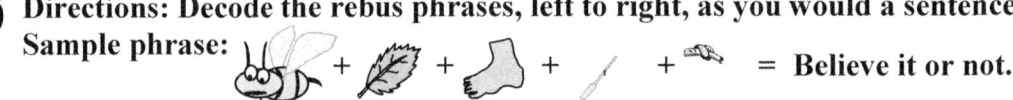 = **Believe it or not.**

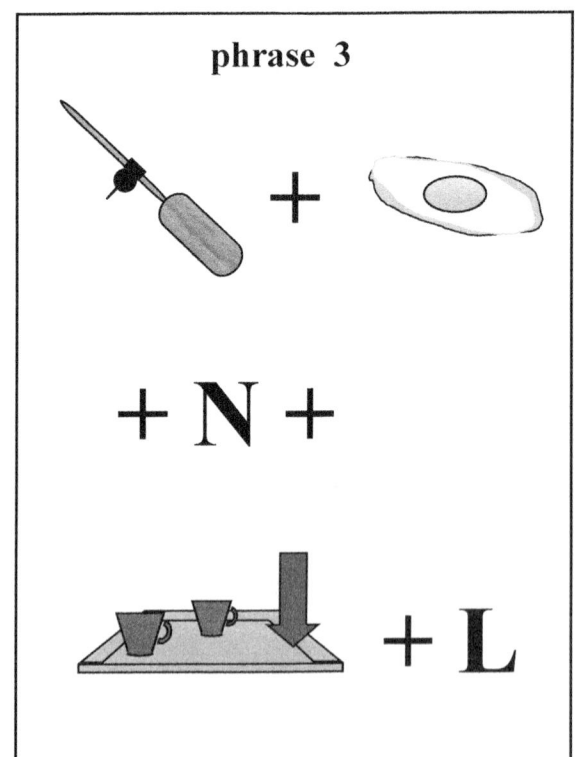

ANSWERS :
championship tennis match
1. Do not put all your eggs in one basket. 2. You
cannot keep a good man down. 3. Oregon Trail 4. A

REBUS PHRASES

Directions: Decode the rebus phrases, left to right, as you would a sentence.
Sample phrase: 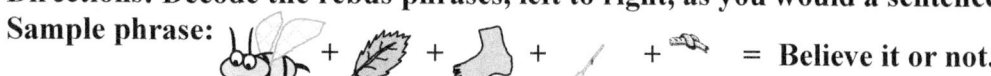 = Believe it or not.

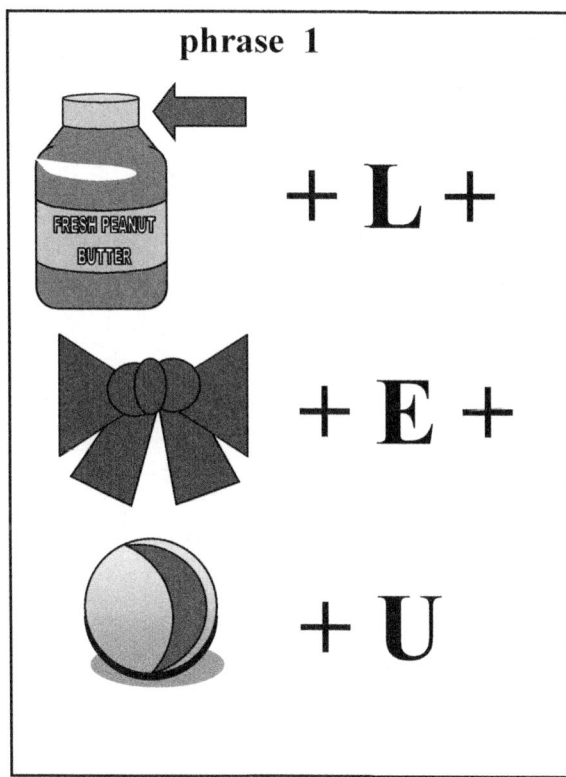

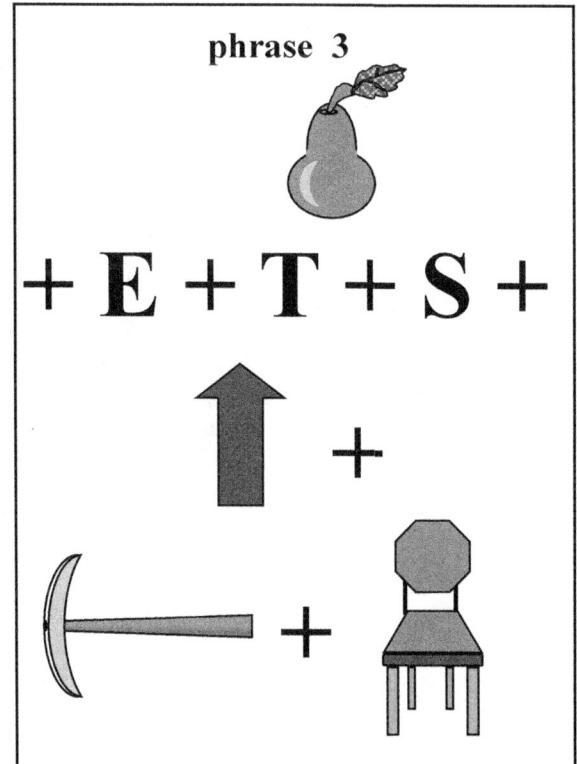

REBUS PHRASES

Directions: Decode the rebus phrases, left to right, as you would a sentence.
Sample phrase: 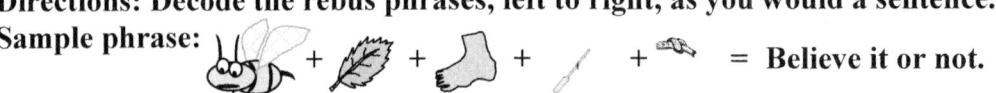 = Believe it or not.

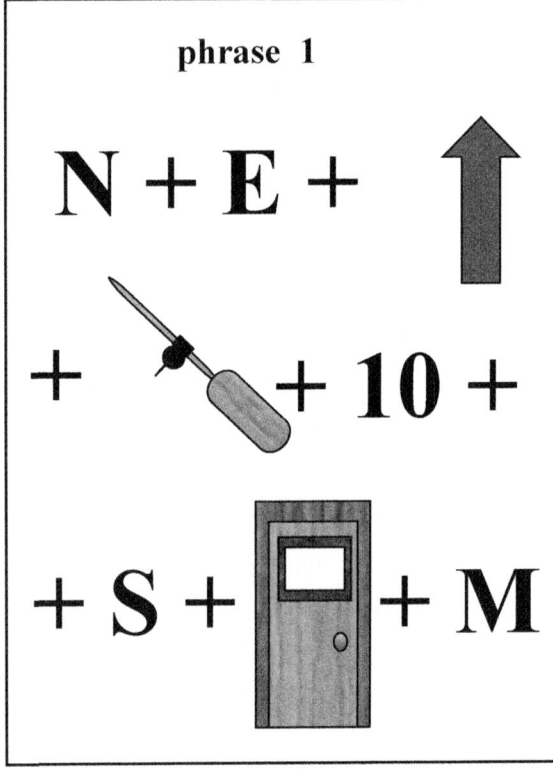

phrase 1

$$N + E + \uparrow$$
$$+ \quad + 10 +$$
$$+ S + \quad + M$$

phrase 2

$$1 +$$
$$+ 4 +$$

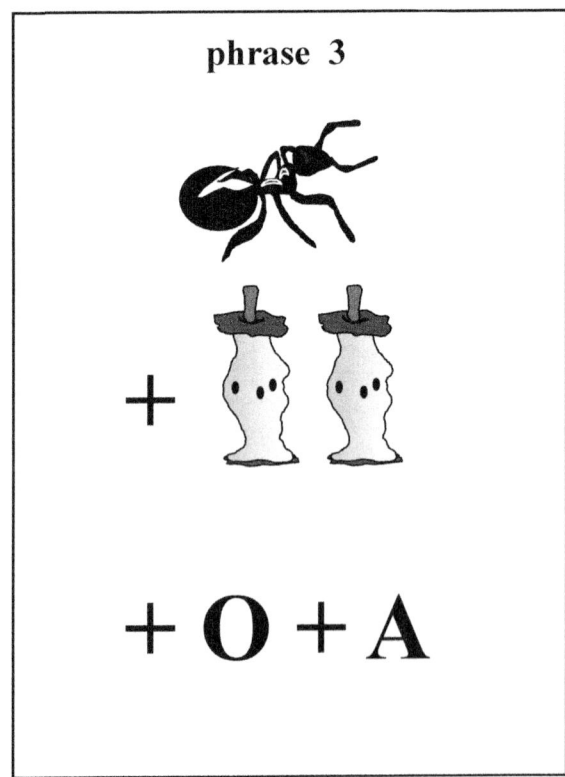

phrase 3

phrase 4

$$D + U +$$
$$+ A +$$
$$+ E +$$
$$+ N +$$

ANSWERS :

1. Any port in a storm. 2. Once and for all. 3. Anchors away. 4. Do not take any wooden nickels.

REBUS PHRASES

Directions: Decode the rebus phrases, left to right, as you would a sentence.
Sample phrase: 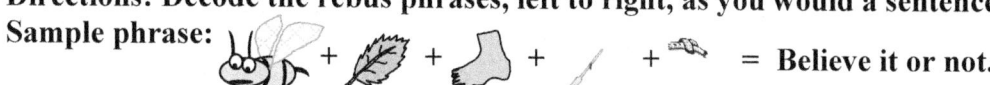 = Believe it or not.

---

phrase 1

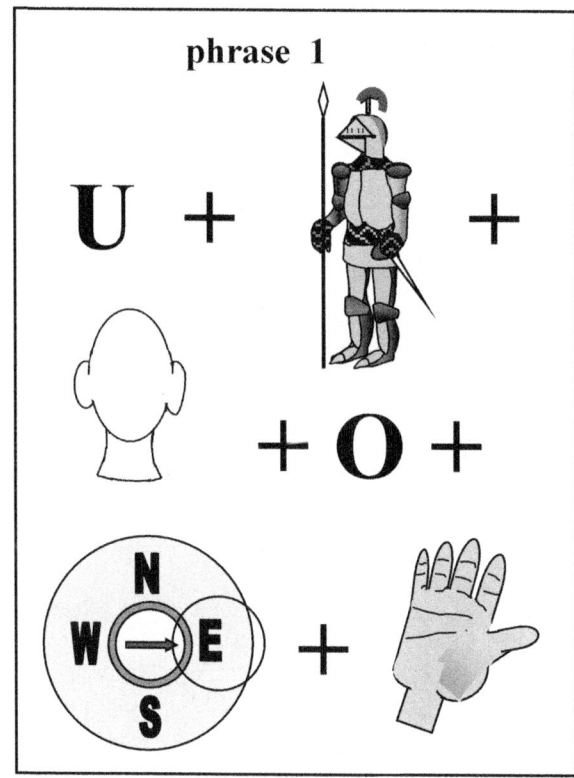

U + +

 + O +

---

phrase 2

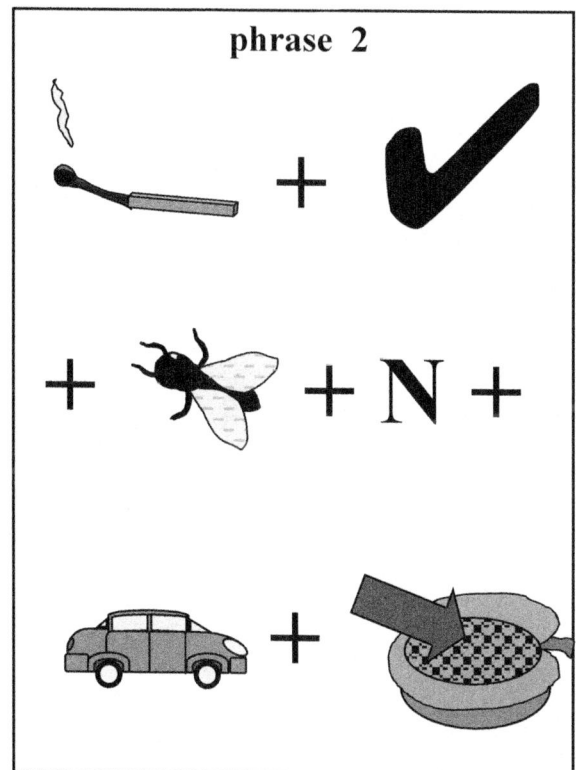

 + + N +

---

phrase 3

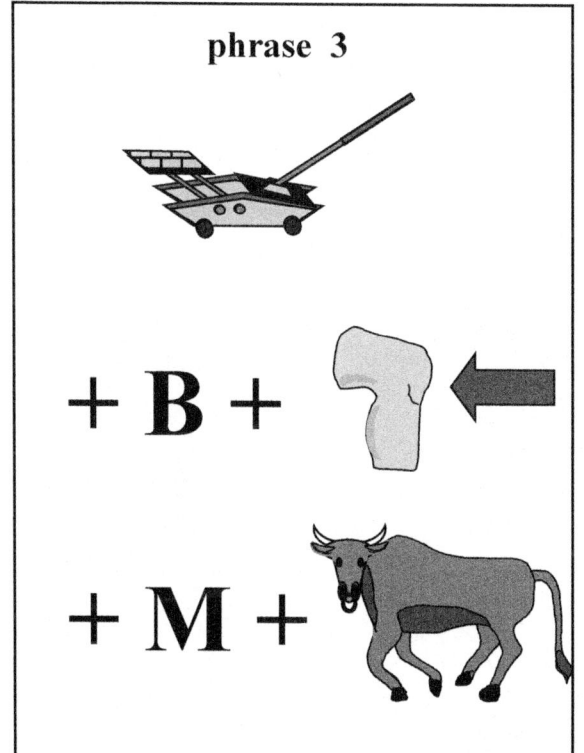

+ B +

+ M +

---

phrase 4

1 + C +

 +

+ U +

ANSWERS :

1. United we stand. 2. Magic flying carpet 3. Jack be nimble. 4. Once in a blue moon.

REBUS PHRASES

Directions: Decode the rebus phrases, left to right, as you would a sentence.
Sample phrase: 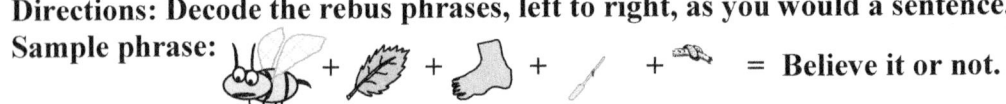 = Believe it or not.

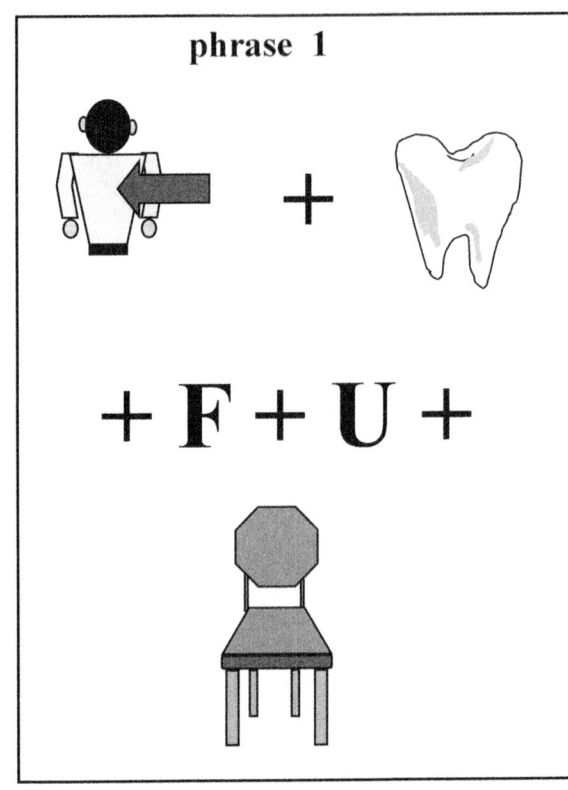

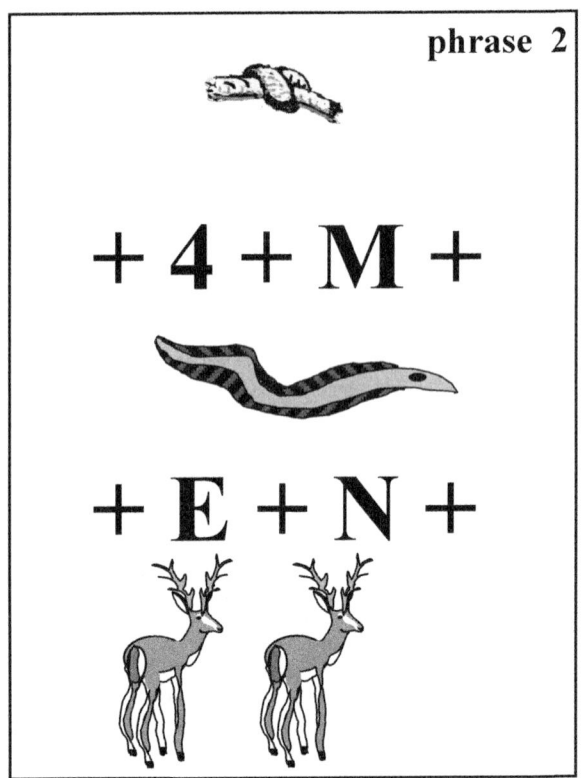

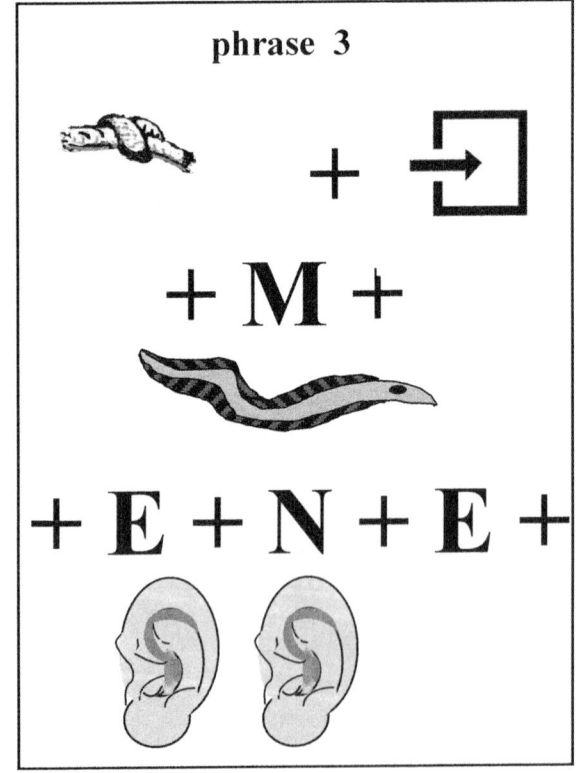

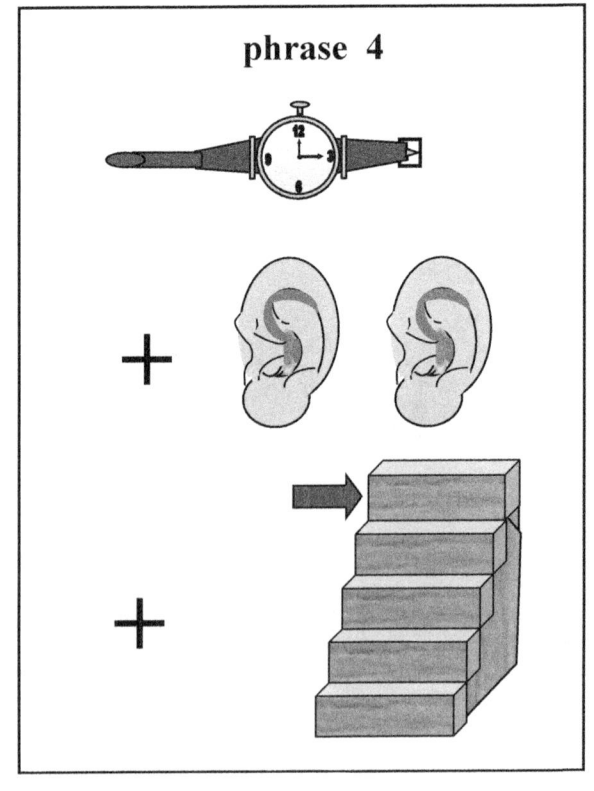

ANSWERS :

1. Back to the Future 2. Not for a million bucks 3. Not in a million years. 4. Watch your step

REBUS PHRASES

Directions: Decode the rebus phrases, left to right, as you would a sentence.
Sample phrase: 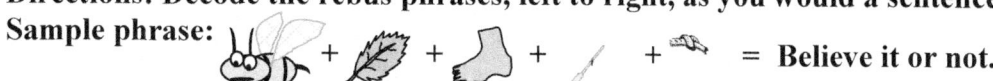 = Believe it or not.

---

phrase 1

R + (man) +

(car) +

O + INK

+ L

---

phrase 2

YY + S +

(sun)

+ (owl)

---

phrase 3

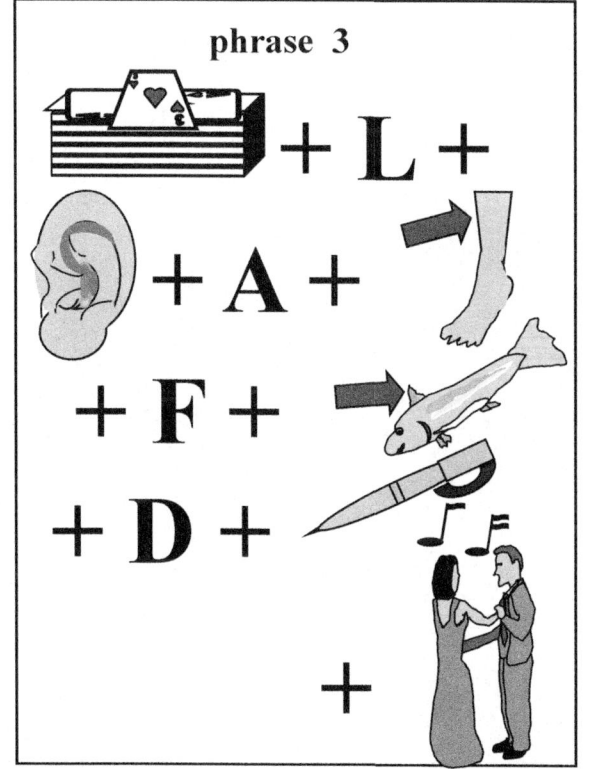

(card) + L +

(ear) + A +

+ F +

+ D +

+

---

phrase 4

1 + (horse)

+ O + (pens)

+ L + A

ANSWERS :

1. Rip Van Winkle 2. Wise as an owl 3. Declaration of Independence 4. One horse open sleigh

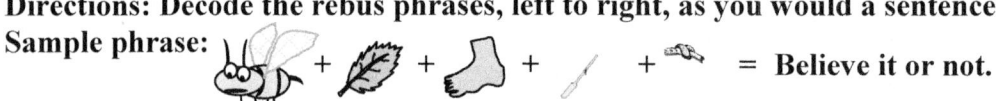

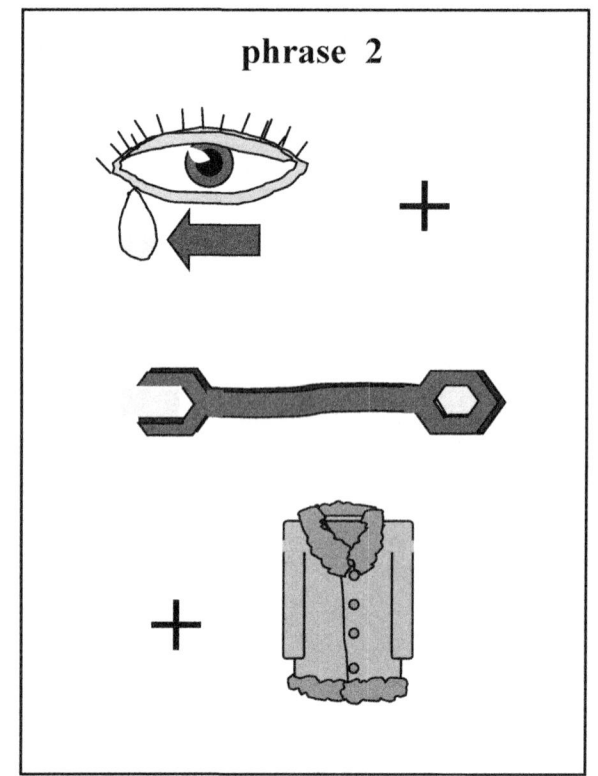

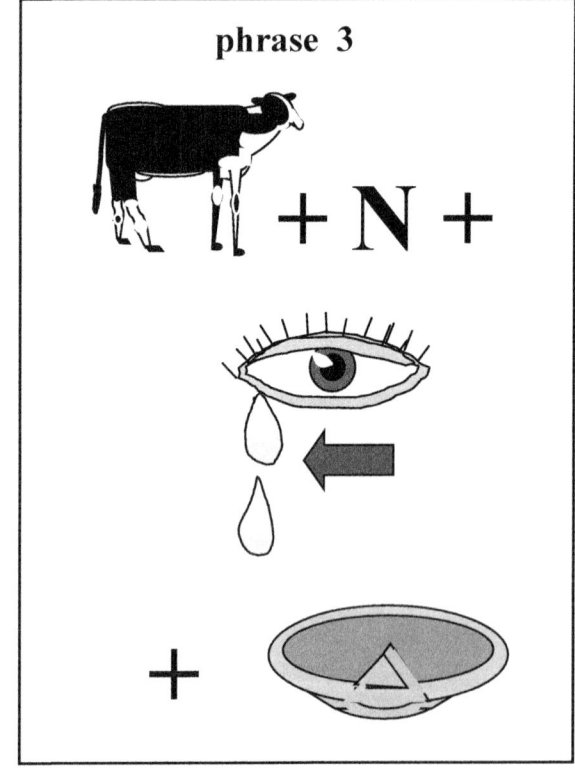

174

ANSWERS :

REBUS PHRASES

Directions: Decode the rebus phrases, left to right, as you would a sentence.

Sample phrase:  = Believe it or not.

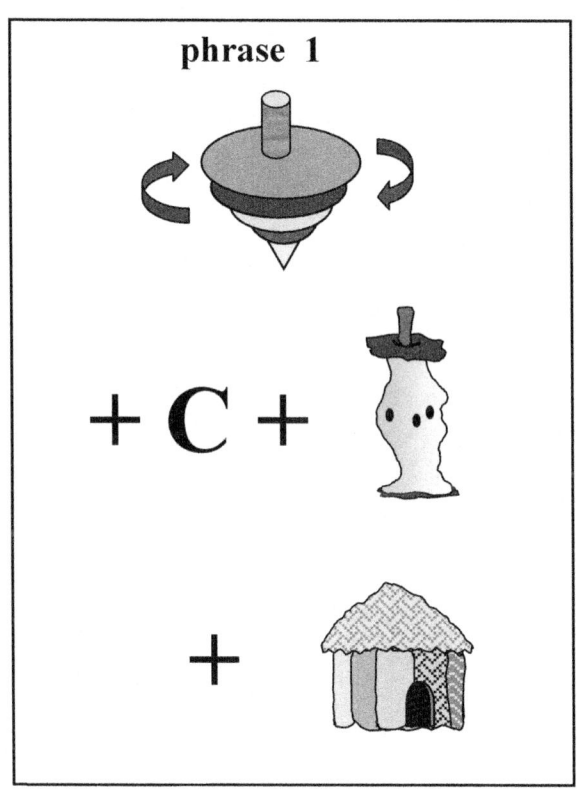

phrase 1

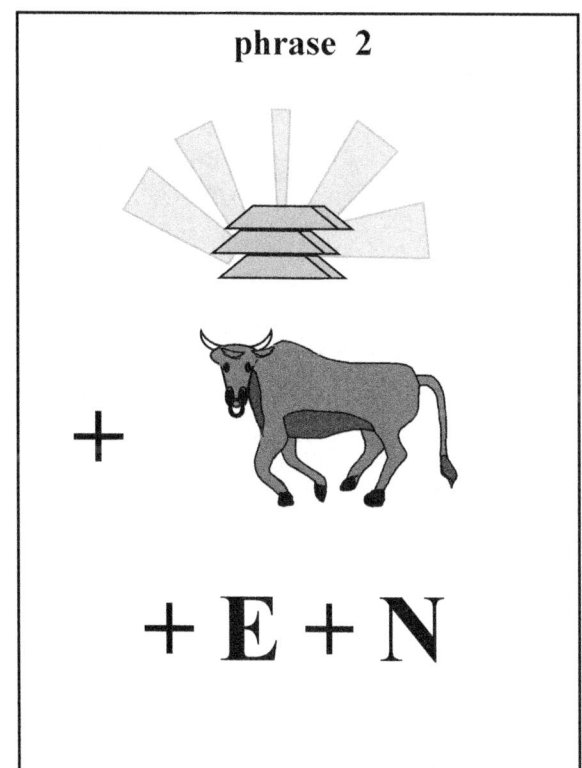

phrase 2

phrase 3

phrase 4

ANSWERS :

1. Top secret 2. Gold bullion 3. Night watchman 4. Tick tack toe

REBUS PHRASES

Directions: Decode the rebus phrases, left to right, as you would a sentence.

Sample phrase: 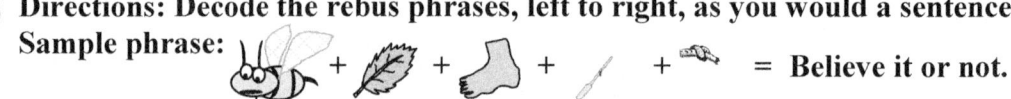 = Believe it or not.

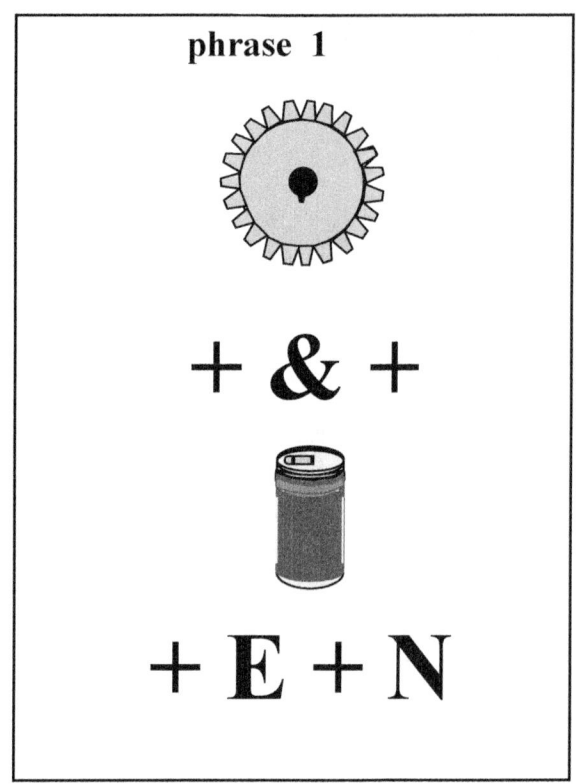

phrase 1

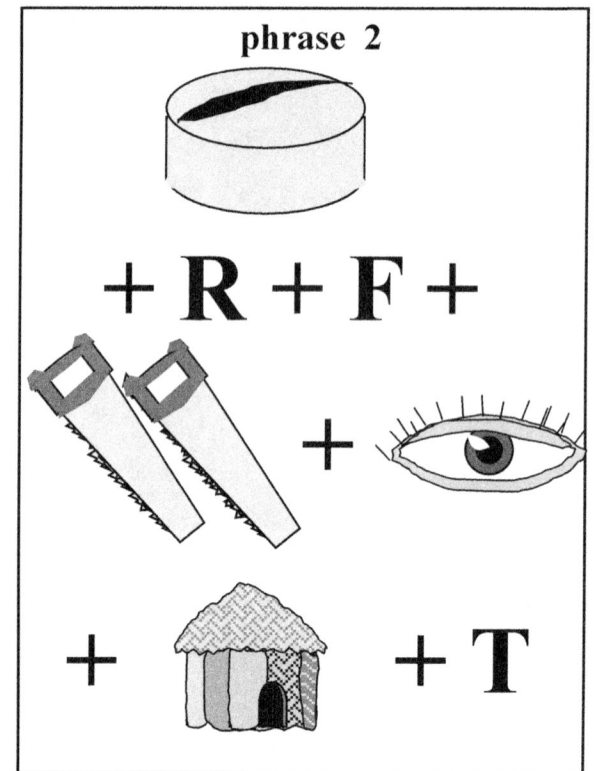

phrase 2

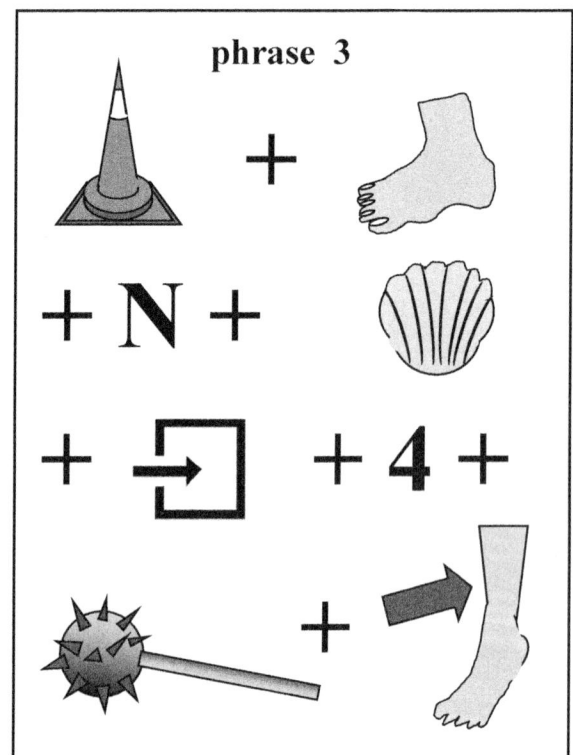

phrase 3

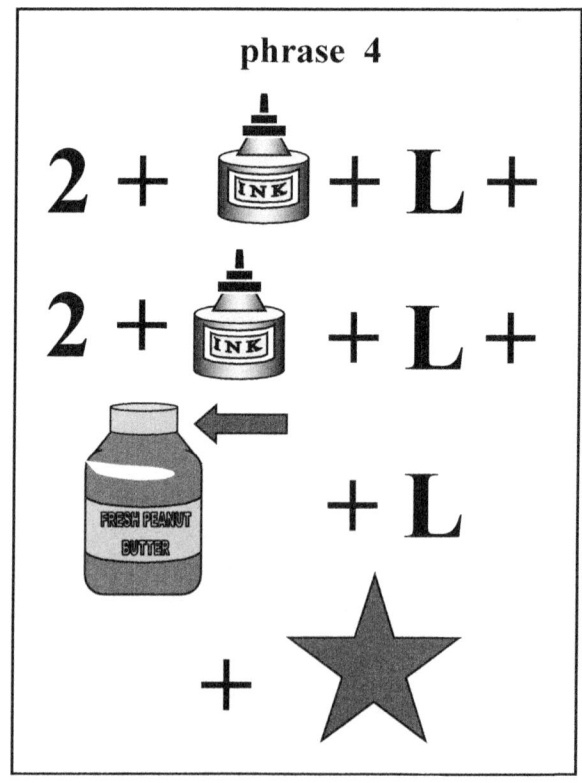

phrase 4

REBUS PHRASES

Directions: Decode the rebus phrases, left to right, as you would a sentence.
Sample phrase:  = Believe it or not.

phrase 1

+ **E** +

+ **OO** + **U**

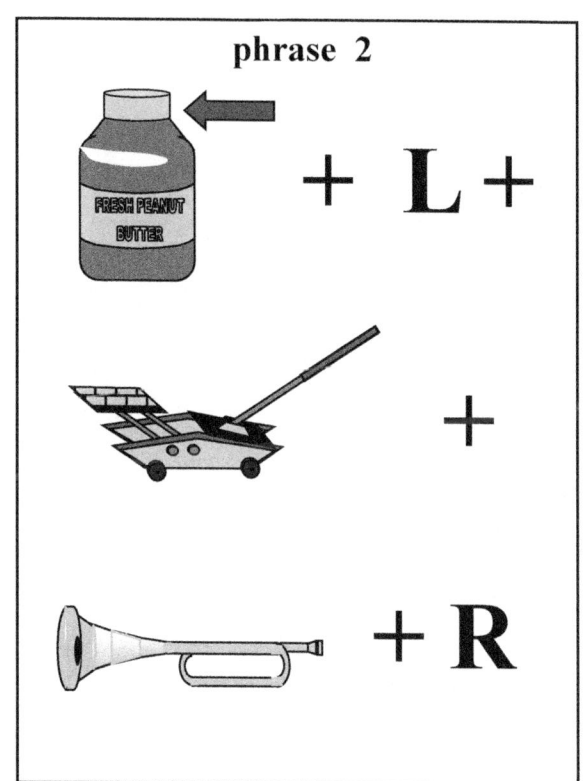

phrase 2

+ **L** +

+

+ **R**

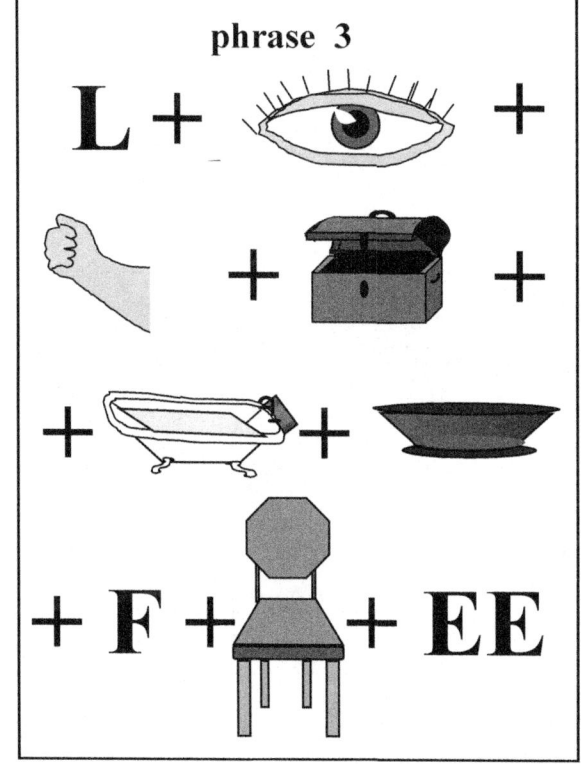

phrase 3

L +

+

+

+

+ **F** +

+ **EE**

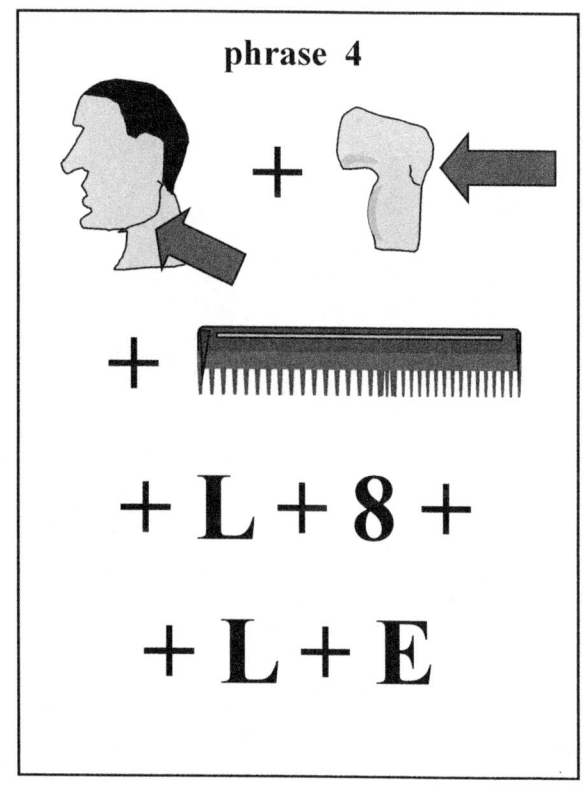

phrase 4

+

+

+ **L** + **8** +

+ **L** + **E**

REBUS PHRASES

Directions: Decode the rebus phrases, left to right, as you would a sentence.

Sample phrase: 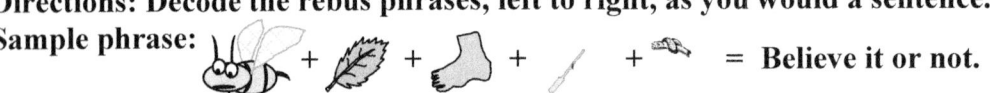 = Believe it or not.

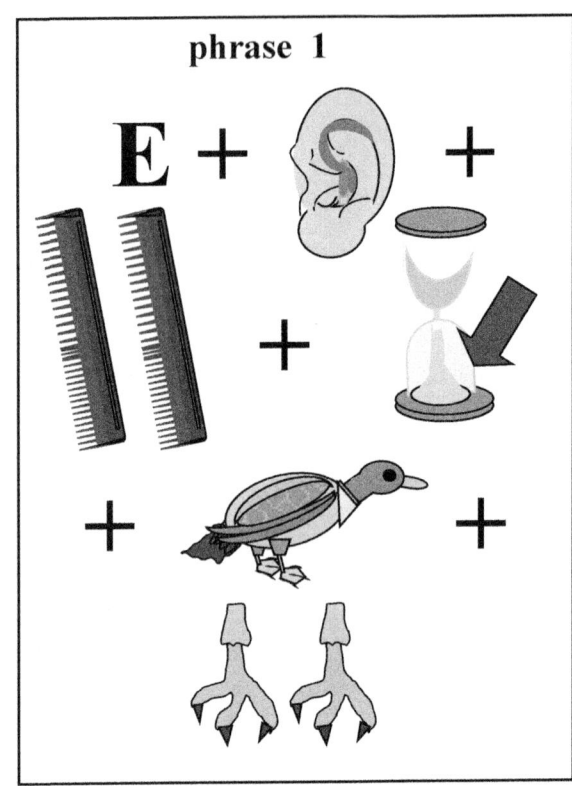

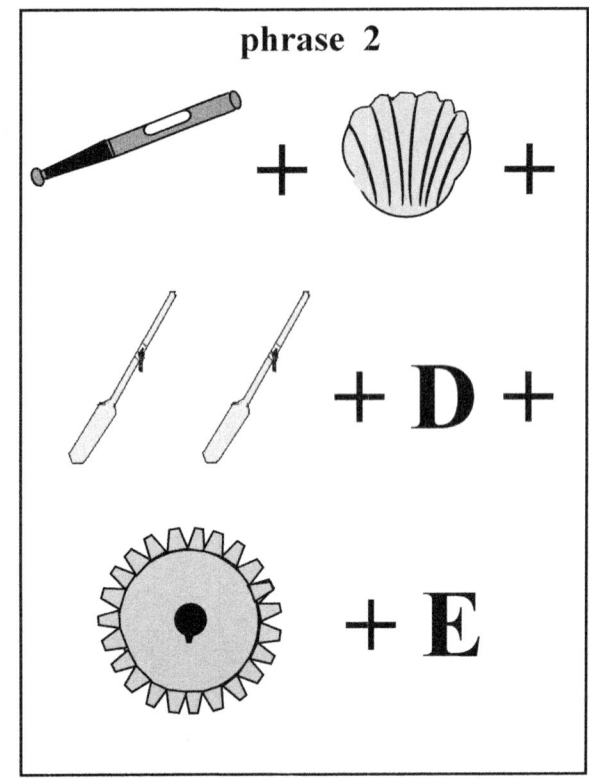

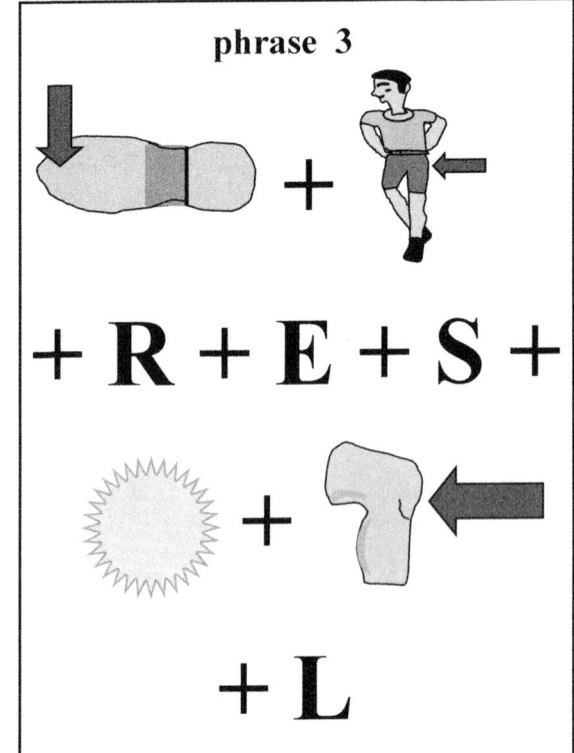

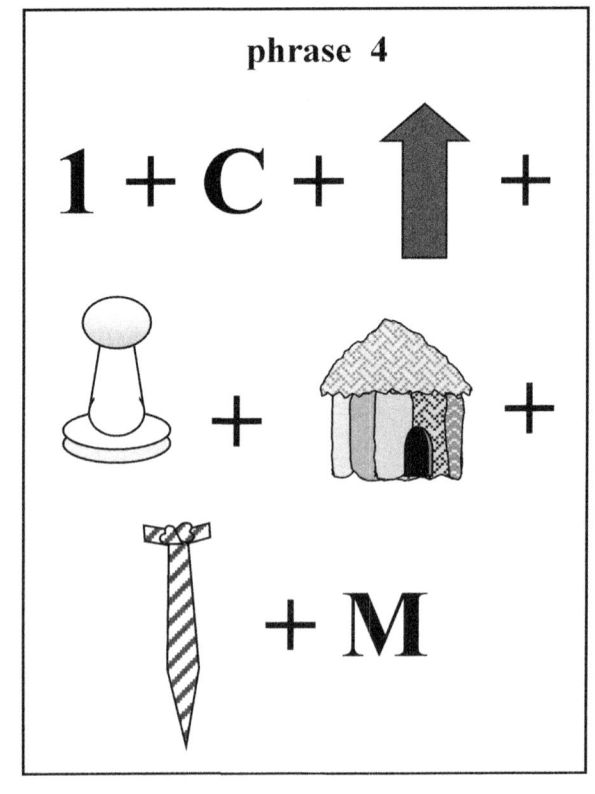

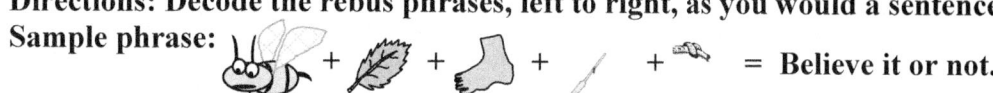
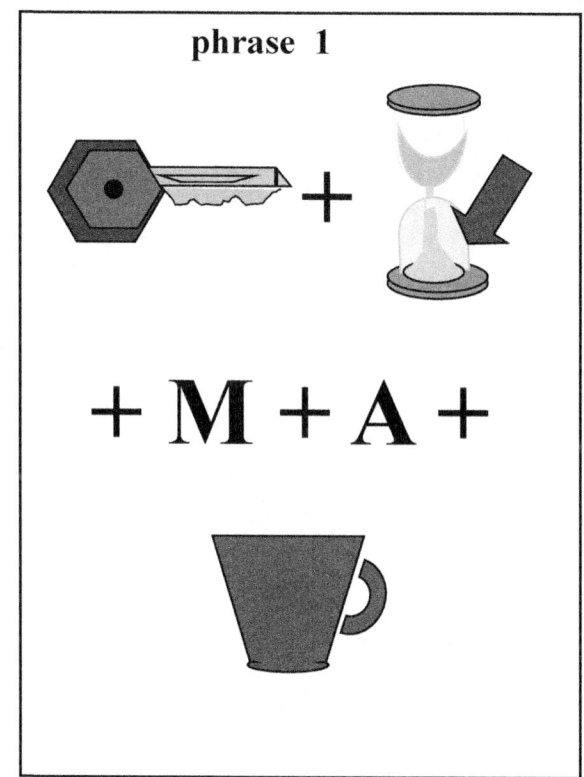

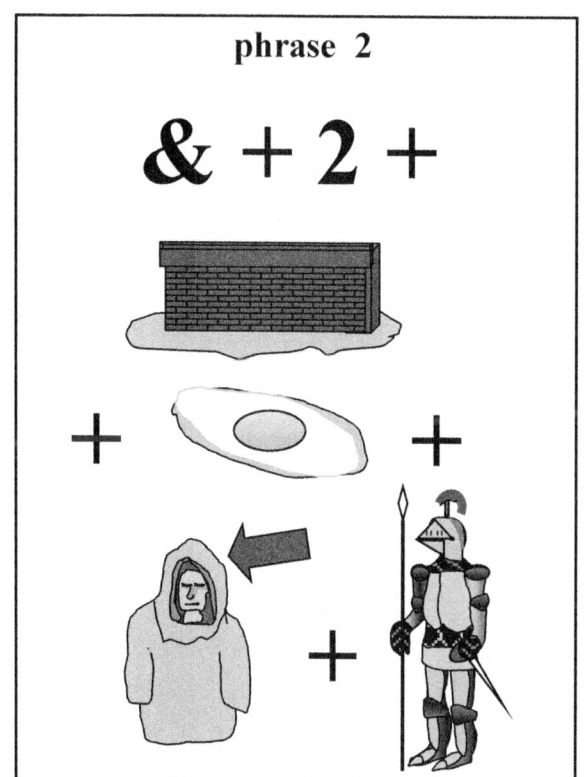

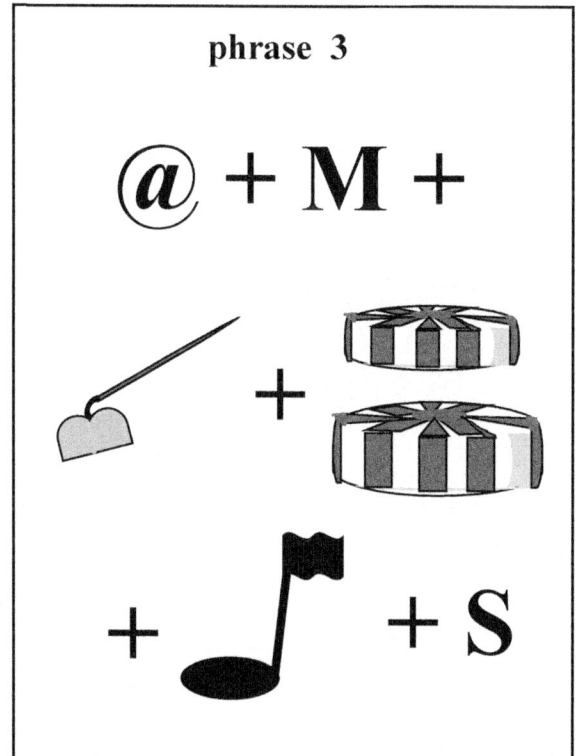

ANSWERS :

1. Kiss and make up. 2. And to all a good night. 3.
At a moment's notice 4. Quick as a wink.

REBUS PHRASES

Directions: Decode the rebus phrases, left to right, as you would a sentence.
Sample phrase: 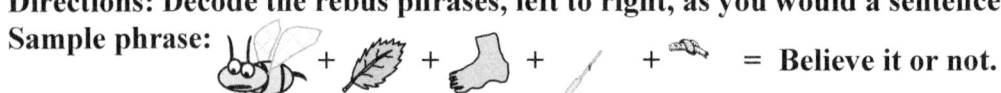 = Believe it or not.

phrase 1

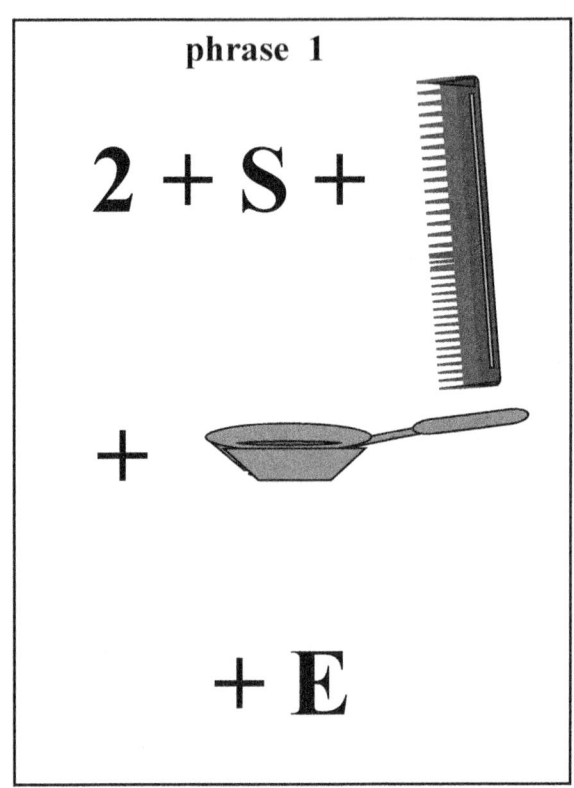

$2 + S +$ (comb)

$+$ (pan)

$+ E$

phrase 2

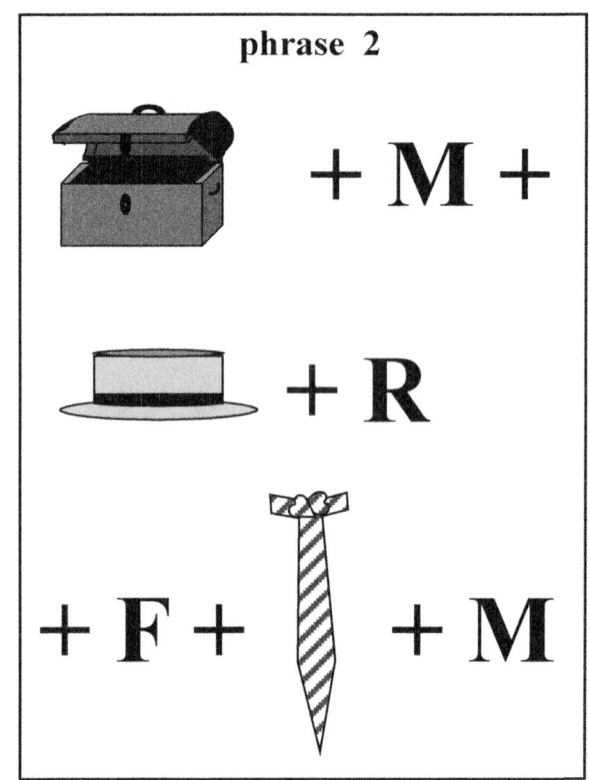

(chest) $+ M +$

(hat) $+ R$

$+ F +$ (tie) $+ M$

phrase 3

$T + L +$

(duck) $+$

(cows) $+$

(comb) $+$ (hoe) $+ M$

phrase 4

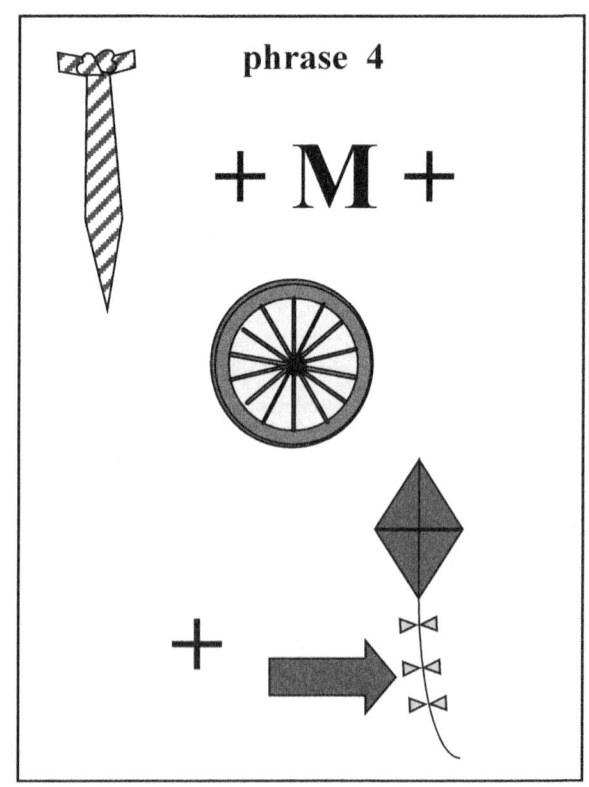

(tie) $+ M +$

(wheel)

$+$ (arrow) (kite)

REBUS PHRASES
Directions: Decode the rebus phrases, left to right, as you would a sentence.
Sample phrase: 🐝 + 🍃 + 👣 + 🔪 + 🌿 = Believe it or not.

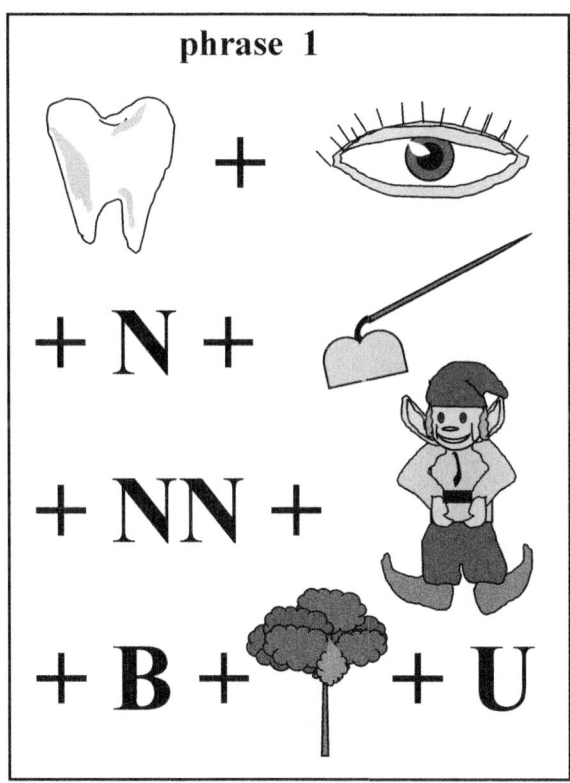

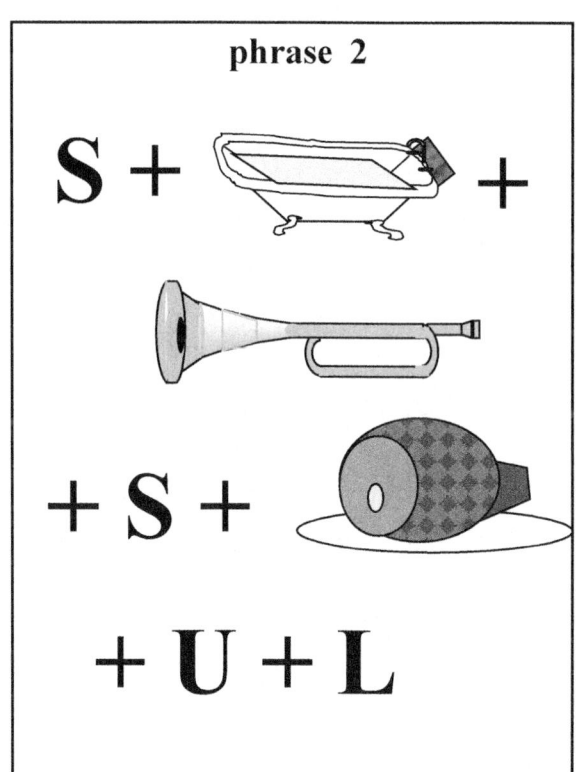

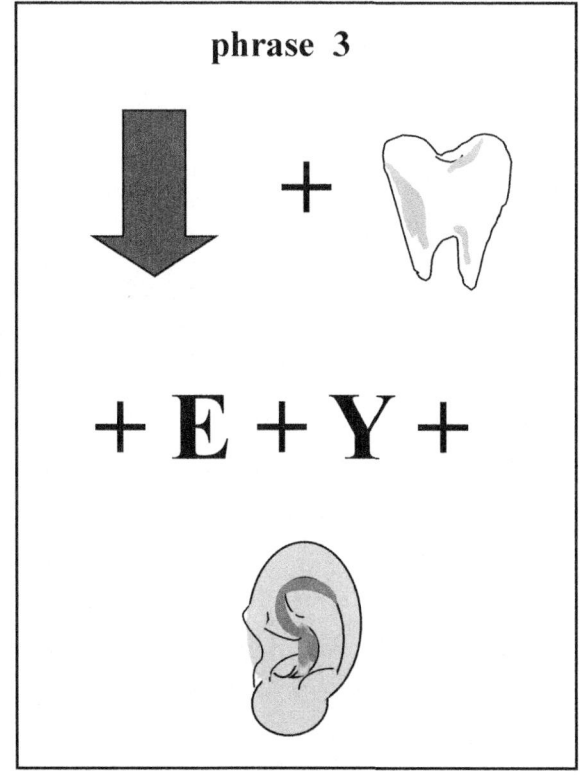

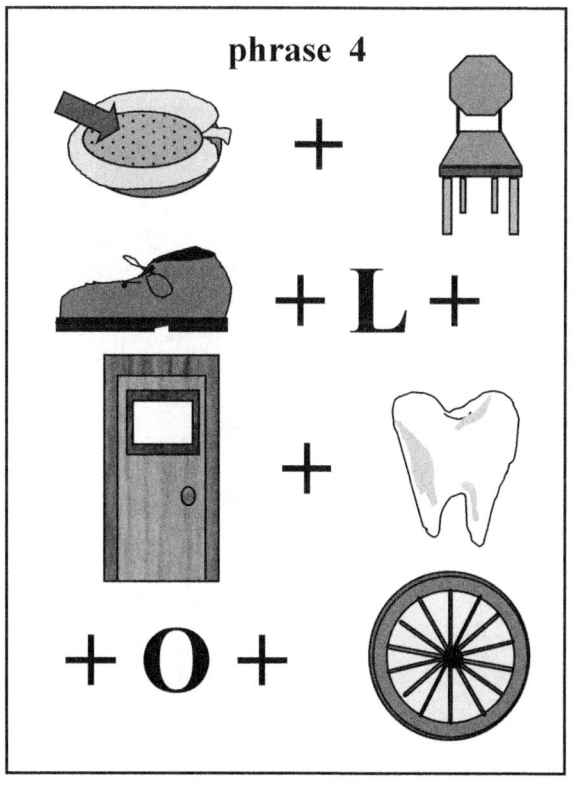

181

ANSWERS :

1. To thine own self be true. 2. As stubborn as a mule 3. Down to the wire 4. Put your shoulder to the wheel

REBUS PHRASES

Directions: Decode the rebus phrases, left to right, as you would a sentence.
Sample phrase:  + 🍃 + 🦶 + / + 🪶 = Believe it or not.

---

phrase 1

$$R + A + B + N +$$

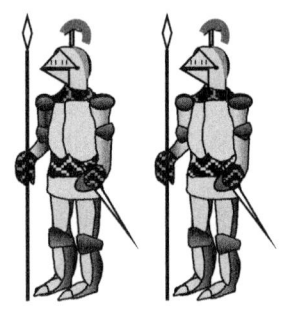

---

phrase 2

🦉 $+ X + \& +$

🌍 $+$ 🥚

$+$ ⚙ $+ 8$

---

phrase 3

$M +$

$+ E +$

$+$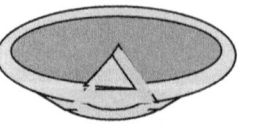

---

phrase 4

🦉 $+ S +$ ⊐

$+ 1 +$ 🦌

$+ L +$ ✋

REBUS PHRASES

Directions: Decode the rebus phrases, left to right, as you would a sentence.
Sample phrase: 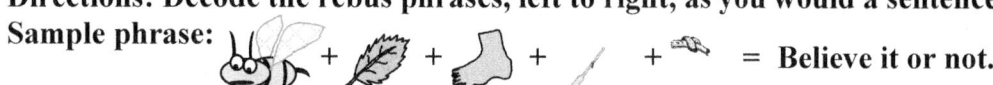 = Believe it or not.

phrase 1

$Q + Y +$

$+ S + M +$

phrase 2

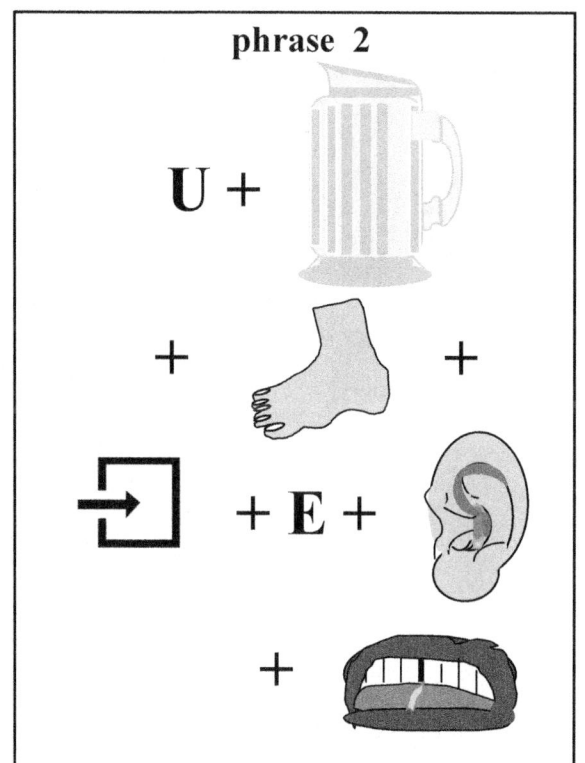

$U +$

$+ E +$

phrase 3

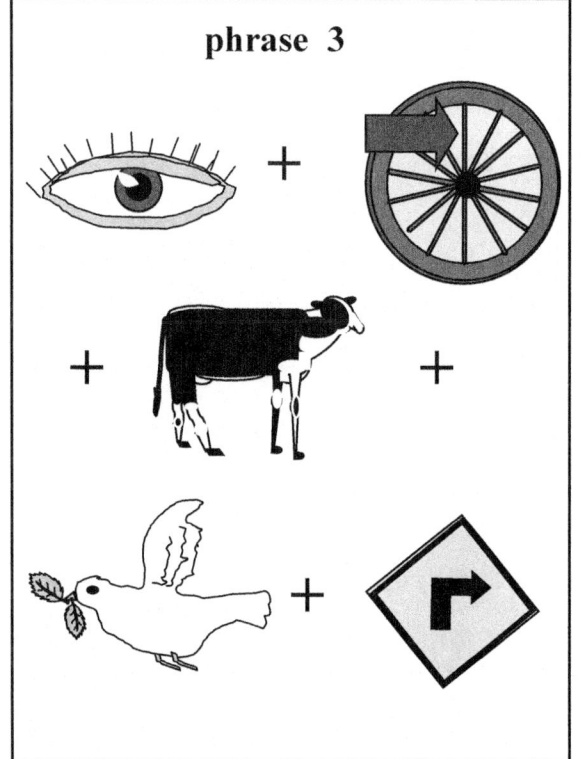

phrase 4

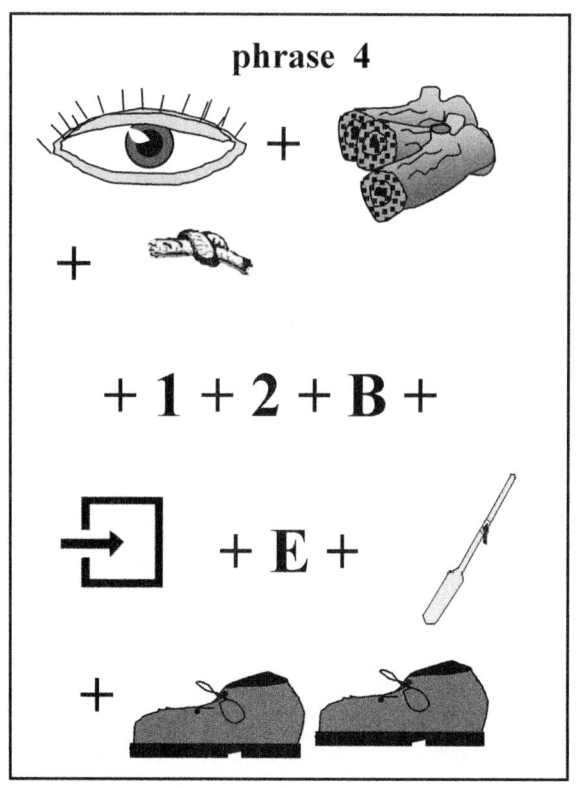

$+ 1 + 2 + B +$

$+ E +$

ANSWERS :

1. Quiet as a mouse 2. You put your foot in your mouth. 3. I spoke out of turn. 4. I would not want to be in your shoes.

REBUS PHRASES

Directions: Decode the rebus phrases, left to right, as you would a sentence.

Sample phrase: 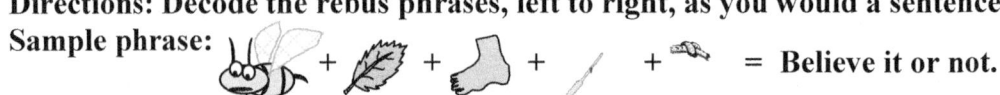 = Believe it or not.

phrase 1

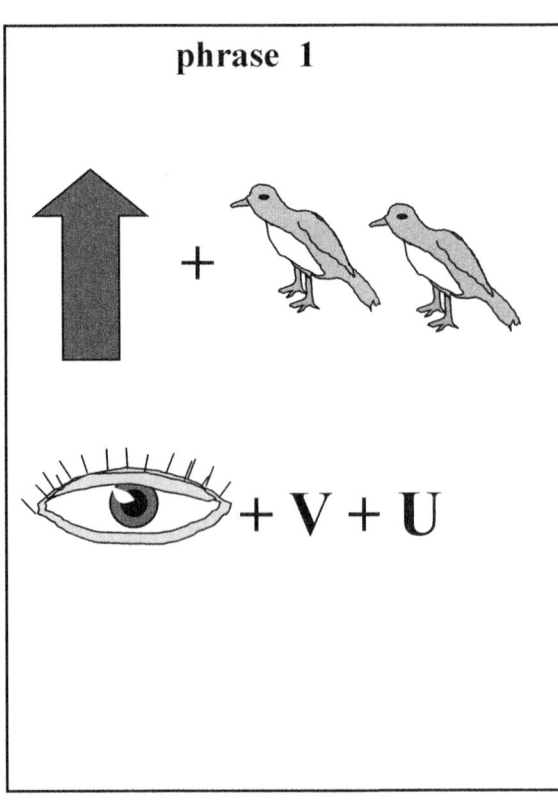

phrase 2

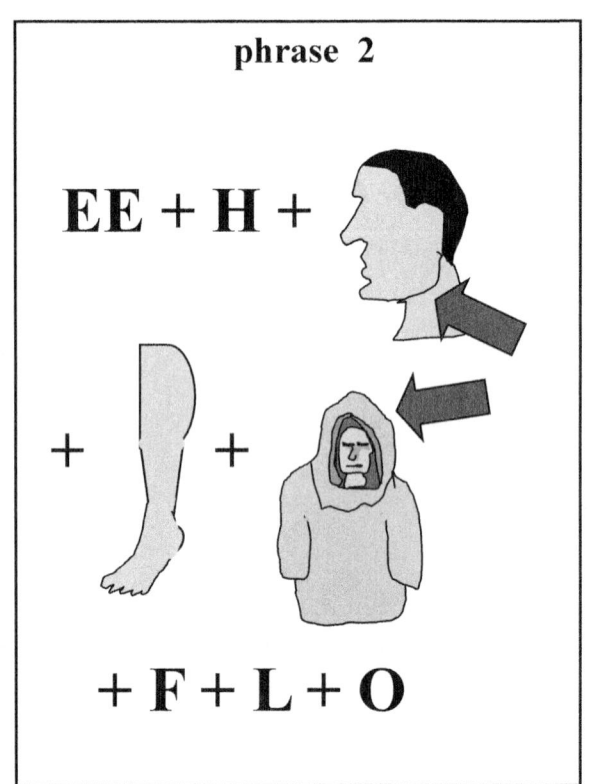

phrase 3

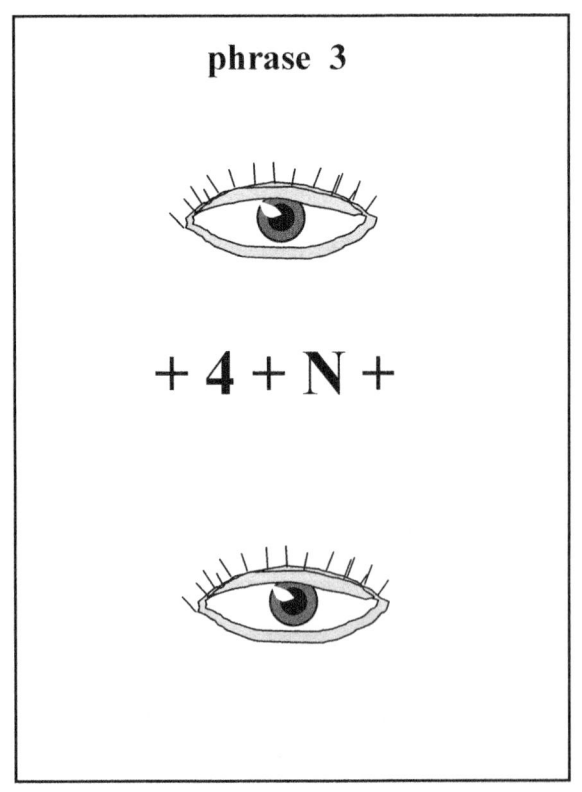

phrase 4

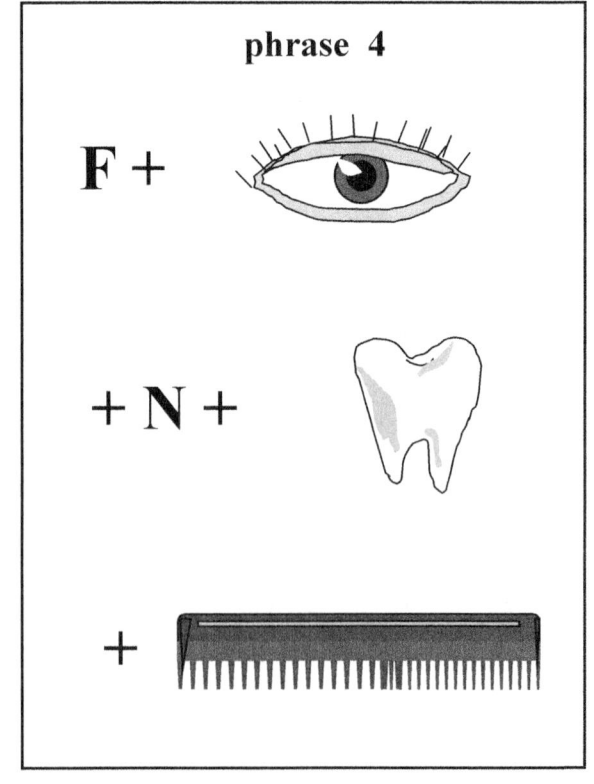

ANSWERS :

1. A bird's-eye view 2. He's a jolly good fellow. 3.
Eye for an eye 4. A fine-tooth comb

REBUS PHRASES

Directions: Decode the rebus phrases, left to right, as you would a sentence.

Sample phrase:  = Believe it or not.

phrase 1

☐ + O + 4 +

E +

+

phrase 2

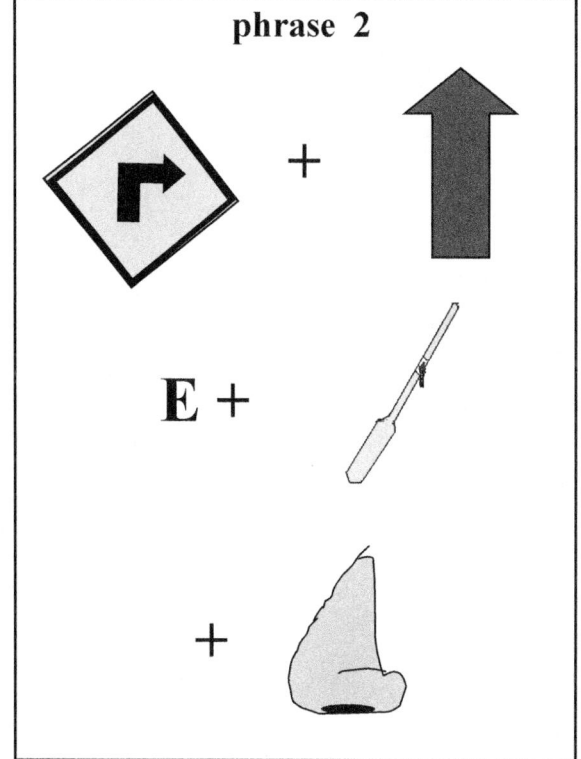

E +

+

phrase 3

UU + E +

+

phrase 4

+ L + & +

+

+ L

ANSWERS :

REBUS PHRASES

Directions: Decode the rebus phrases, left to right, as you would a sentence.
Sample phrase: 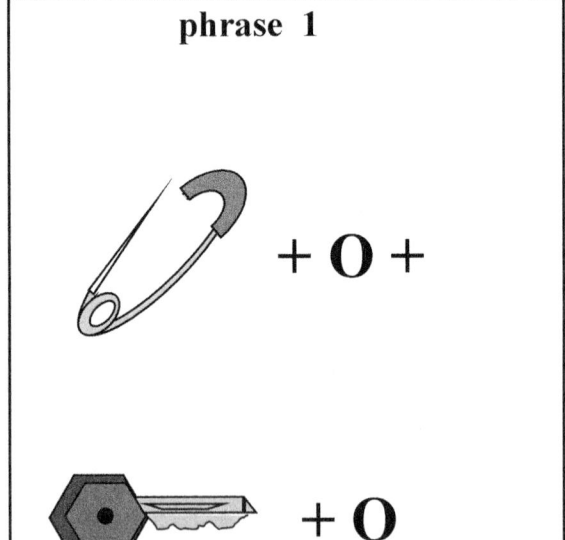 ... = Believe it or not.

---

phrase 1

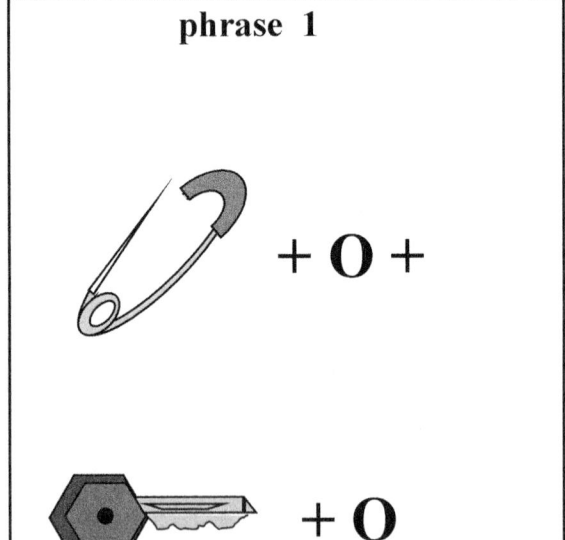

+ O +

+ O

---

phrase 2

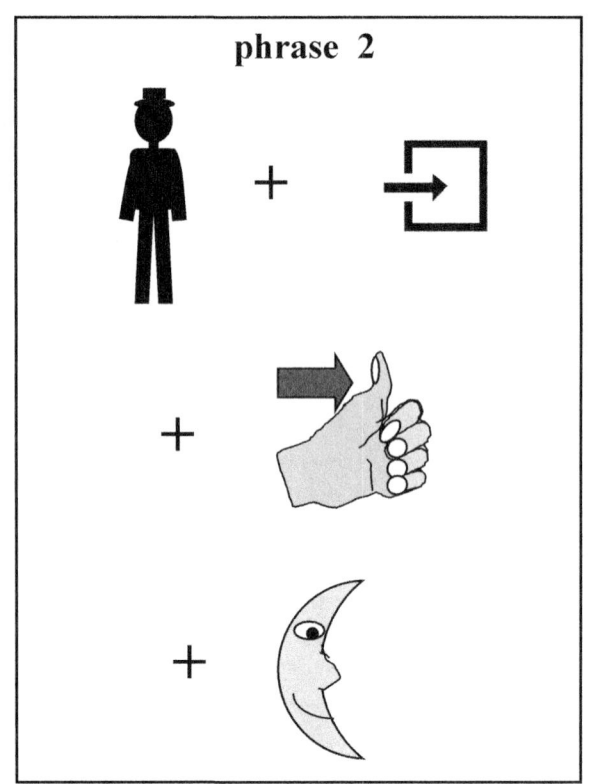

+

+

+

---

phrase 3

+ L +

+

---

phrase 4

3 + YY +

ANSWERS :

REBUS PHRASES

Directions: Decode the rebus phrases, left to right, as you would a sentence.

Sample phrase:  = Believe it or not.

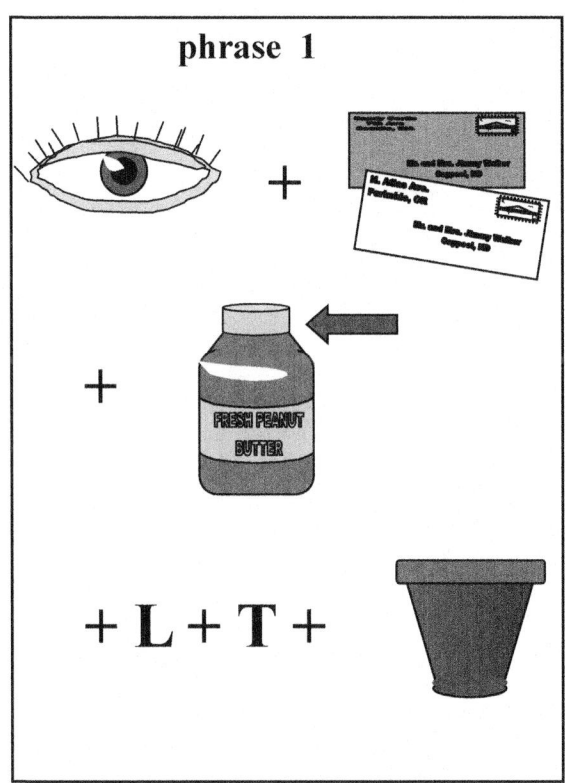

phrase 1

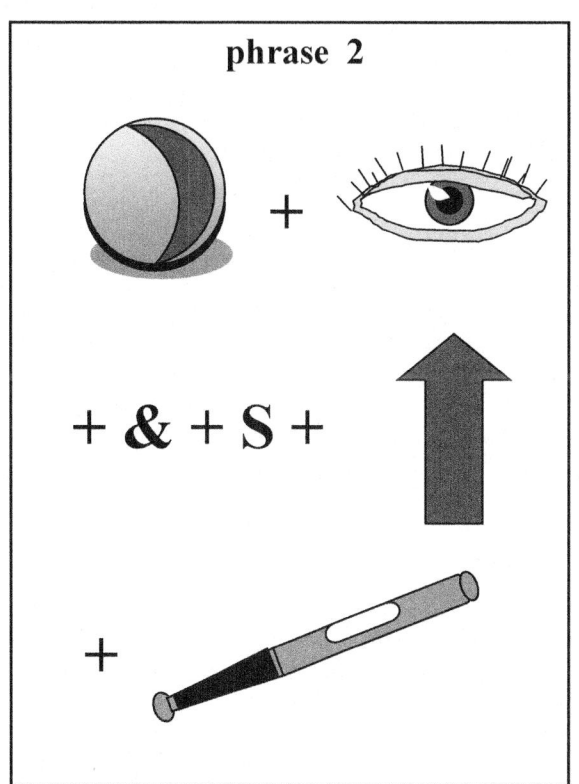

phrase 2

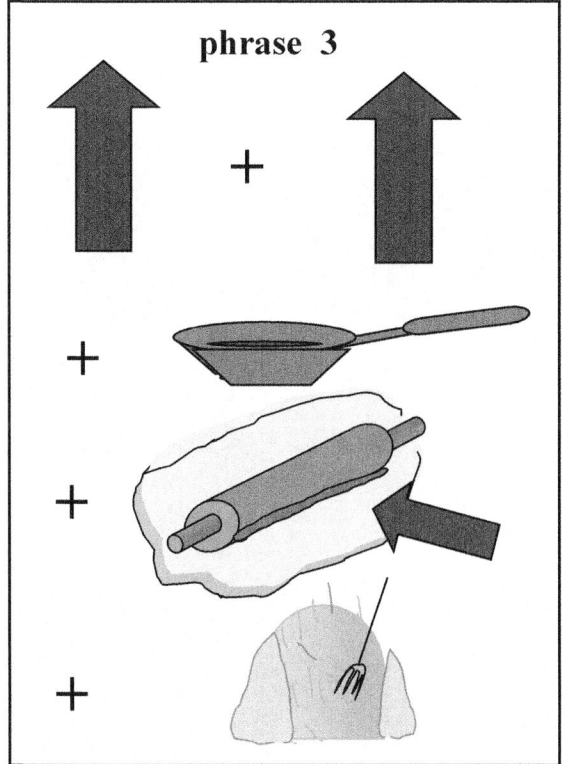

phrase 3

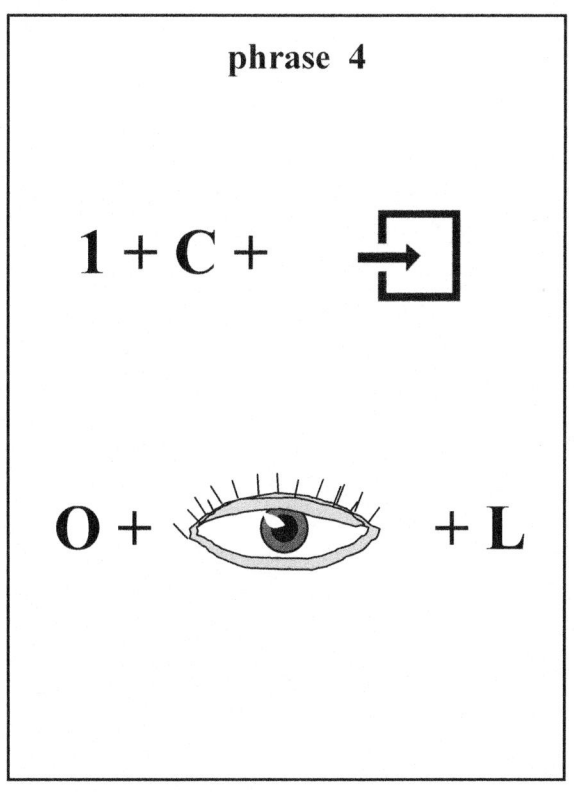

phrase 4

187

REBUS PHRASES

Directions: Decode the rebus phrases, left to right, as you would a sentence.
Sample phrase: 🐝 + 🍃 + 🦶 + ✒ + 🥜 = Believe it or not.

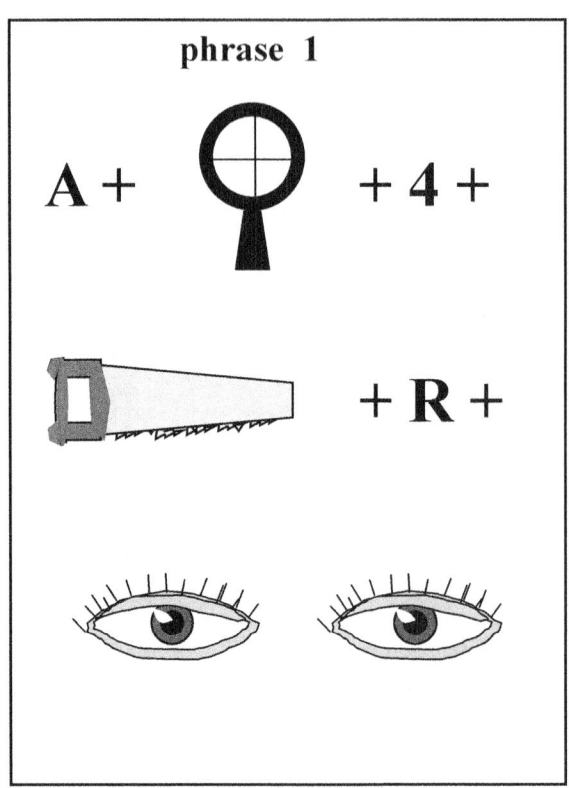

phrase 1

A + ⊕ + 4 +

🪚 + R +

👁 👁

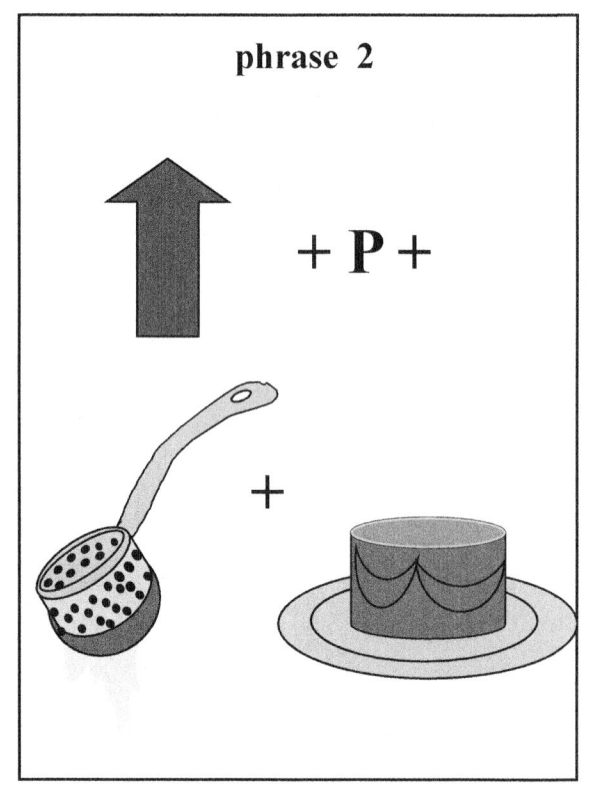

phrase 2

⬆ + P +

🥄 + 🎩

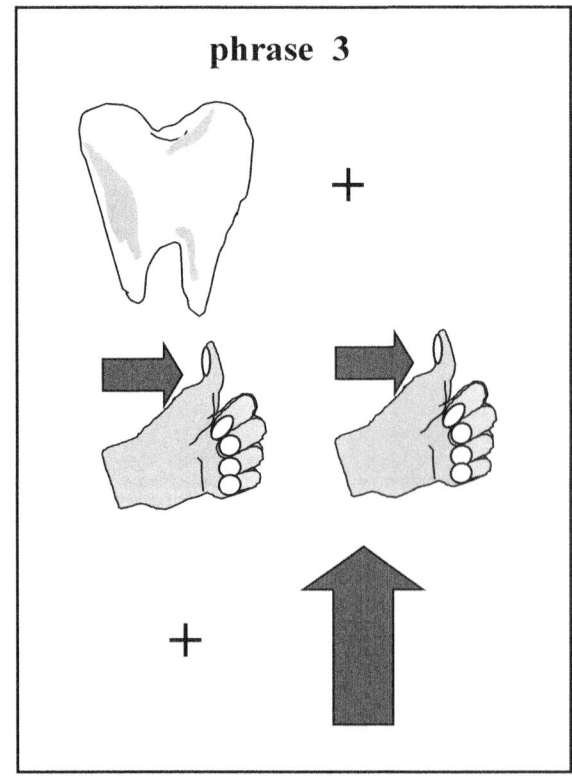

phrase 3

🦷 +

👍 👍

⬆ +

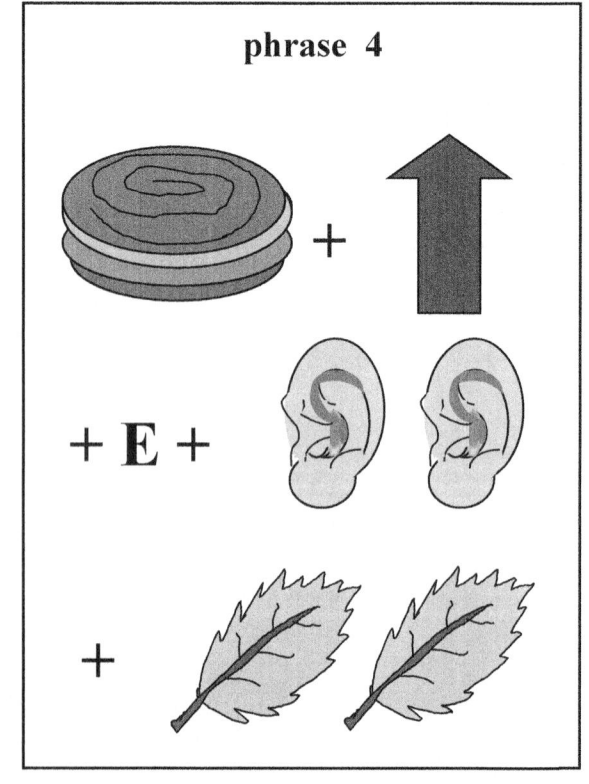

phrase 4

🌀 + ⬆

+ E + 👂 👂

+ 🍃 🍃

ANSWERS :

1. A sight for soar eyes 2. A piece of cake 3. "Two thumbs up 4. Roll up your sleeves.

Printed in Great Britain
by Amazon

43701359R00110